AMERICAN INDIAN WOMEN

WOMEN'S HISTORY AND CULTURE
(VOL. 4)

GARLAND REFERENCE LIBRARY
OF SOCIAL SCIENCE
(VOL. 515)

WOMEN'S HISTORY AND CULTURE

1. *Feminism and Women's Issues: An Annotated Bibliography and Research Guide*
   G. Llewellyn Watson

2. *The Indian Captivity Narrative: A Woman's View*
   Frances Roe Kestler

3. *Mothers and Mothering: An Annotated Feminist Bibliography*
   Penelope Dixon

4. *American Indian Women: A Guide to Research*
   Gretchen M. Bataille and Kathleen M. Sands

AMERICAN INDIAN WOMEN
A Guide to Research

Gretchen M. Bataille
Kathleen M. Sands

Editorial Assistant:
Catherine Udall

GARLAND PUBLISHING, INC. • NEW YORK & LONDON
1991

Library of Congress Cataloging-in-Publication Data

Bataille, Gretchen M., 1944–
    American Indian Women : a guide to research / Gretchen M.
Bataille, Kathleen M. Sands ; editorial assistant, Catherine Udall.
        p. cm. — (Women's history and culture ; vol. 4) (Garland
reference library of social science ; vol. 515)
    Includes index.
    ISBN 0-8240-4799-0 (alk. paper)
    1. Indians of North America—Women—Bibliography. I. Sands,
Kathleen M. II. Title. III. Series: Women's history and culture ;
4. IV: Series: Garland reference library of social science ; v.
515.
Z1209.2.N67B36   1991
[E98.W8]
016.920.72'08997—dc20   91–2961
                                                              CIP

Printed on acid-free, 250-year-life paper
Manufactured in the United States of America

CONTENTS

PREFACE

When we began work on this book, it was our intention to correct what we believed to be the severe neglect of Indian women in scholarly research and writing. Work on this volume began as a direct outgrowth of the bibliography we prepared for our study of American Indian women's personal narratives, *American Indian Women: Telling Their Lives* (Lincoln: University of Nebraska, 1984), a genre of expression by Indian women which had, indeed, been neglected.

What had begun as a project centered on autobiographies, biographies, creative literature and literary criticism, grew to include works from a wide variety of disciplines from anthropology to education, the arts, law, and a number of other categories. As the volume of material on North American Indian women began to mount, we realized that while it is undeniable that more scholarly and popular attention has been paid to American Indian men, there is no dearth of scholarly writing on North American Indian women. The over 1500 annotated citations presented in this text are not, however, an indication of the quality of the scholarly and popular depiction of Indian women in North America over the last five centuries. The hundreds of essays, histories, ethnographies, biographies, and novels we have annotated give clear evidence that much of the material collected and written about tribal women, particularly representations of them up to the 1960s, perpetuates romanticized images of Native women as "princesses," or conversely, presents derogatory images of them as "squaws."

There are, however, a great many works cited in this book that reveal the individuality and reality of Indian women's experiences, accomplishments, and beliefs. The feminist movement in the academy, particularly the growing attention to women's culture in the social sciences, and the recent increase in scholarship by Indian women have made significant contributions to the accurate portrayal of women in Native American cultures, one that we anticipate will continue and be refined in the coming years.

This bibliography is offered as a resource for the ongoing research and writing on Indian women. It is our hope that it will contribute to a greater understanding of Indian women and that it will facilitate the production of intensive, imaginative, and accurate research and writing on American Indian women in the future.

ACKNOWLEDGMENTS

Compiling a bibliography of this magnitude requires the work and support of many people. For the development and application of the efficient and effective computer program and for the many hours of work she contributed to this project, we owe a great debt of gratitude to Catherine Udall; without her aid this would have been an overwhelming task. Arlon Benson, a graduate student in the Department of English at Arizona State University, was an important contributor to the final product, searching for obscure library resources and assisting with final editing. We appreciate the following people for their assistance: Roxana L. Martin for preparing the index, Daniel T. Brink for his expert computer advice, and student workers Erik Rapp, Chris Hogan, and Gary Kinser, who aided in copying and clerical work and made numerous trips to the Hayden Library.

To the Arizona State University College of Liberal Arts and Sciences, our thanks for grant support for photocopying and research staff funding. To the competent and helpful library staff members of the Hayden Library at Arizona State University and the Millar Library at Portland State University, particularly those in the inter-library loan service, our appreciation for their cheerful services.

It is the Indian women of North America to whom we owe the greatest debt; it is these women who have lived, spoken and written with such resonance, who are, finally, responsible for this volume.

G.B. and K.S.

INTRODUCTION

The portrayal of American Indian women in North America over the last four centuries offers an uneven body of documentary evidence about the lives of Native women as individuals and members of their tribal groups. During the colonial period, European explorers, trappers, missionaries, and settlers, in their need to justify the manipulation, mistreatment, and murder of indigenous people they encountered in the New World, portrayed Indian people as inherently inferior. In the case of Indian women, the development of two powerful but contradictory stereotypes served the process of justification equally well.

Narratives of the life of Pocahontas, the legendary "Indian princess" who saved a white man from death and was taken to Europe as a model of refinement, established the image of the female "noble savage" eager to please white conquerors. Reports of Sacajewea's contribution to the Lewis and Clark expedition bolstered this stereotype. Conversely, reports of the degraded state of Indian "squaws" as virtual slaves to Indian men, beasts of burden, and vicious torturers of prisoners created an equally distorted image of Native women as less than human. Thus there is little written from the sixteenth to the twentieth century about those Native women who resisted colonialism, those who were honored and beloved within their own cultures. Because matrilineal, matriarchal societies were both mysterious and threatening to the Euro-American patriarchal system, most early documentation of Indian women's experience is misinformed and ethnocentric, more attuned to the colonists' norms for female behavior than to the actuality of indigenous cultures or any interpretation of them Indian women might have articulated. Muted by the absence of any realistic representation of their lives either by themselves or their conquerors, Native women of North America were consistently, in the rare cases where they were given any attention at all, depicted in either romantic or degraded roles.

Most of the early material written about Indian women is, in fact, anecdotal--diary entries by "squaw men" in the fur trade, conversion reports by zealous missionaries, brief observations by military men. Indian women, incomprehensible to their observers and accorded no opportunity to voice their own stories, remained elusive until well into the nineteenth century when social reformers took up the cause of Indian rights and selectively used women such as Sarah Winnemucca to articulate their outrage at the abuses of Native Peoples. In a land founded on freedom and equal opportunity, public policies toward Indians were clearly discriminatory and worse, and in an atmosphere of conflict over and abolition of slavery in the South and the forced removal of tribes from the Southeast to the Indian Territories, the maltreatment of tribal peoples was becoming difficult for some Americans to justify with simple-minded stereotypes.

The voices of Indian women and their advocates were ignored in the halls of Congress and by a general populace more interested in the settlement of the West than the welfare of Indian peoples. It is not until the twentieth century and the coming-of-age of anthropology as an academic discipline, and particularly the work of women anthropologists in the American Southwest, that documentation of the day-to-day lives and the ceremonial and leadership roles of Indian women received intense study. Even then, the emphasis was on women's roles in the domestic sphere or as subjects of life cycle research, although this focus eventually led to a reassessment of matriarchy as a tribal system as a result of interest in gender roles in traditional societies. With the advent of personality-in-culture studies and health and fertility studies, many narratives were collected from Native women, collaborative texts that documented full life histories or episodic narratives, usually with an emphasis on traditional life or skills, or specific case histories. Some were psychoanalytic studies with emphasis on "deviant behavior," and others recorded the lives of selected Native women artists like Maria Martinez and Pablita Velarde, while others presented full autobiographies with attention to literary style. Although still controlled by white collector/editors, these narratives gave voice to women in representing, if not interpreting, their lives.

Little of the work done by scholars before mid-century centers on the dynamics of change and the reassertion of women's power in modern tribal systems; anthropologists were too busy preserving data on "vanishing" traditional Indian life to concern themselves with the dynamics of change and the roles of women in reservation and urban Indian societies. It is not until the 1960s when consciousness raising among North American Indian women parallels the women's movement in the dominant society that documentation of Indian women's activities in the political arena, as in the case of the ⸏mand by Canadian Native women for non-discrimination in legal status, gains attention in print. In this decade a substantial body of material on Indian women by Indian women in anthropology, history, creative writing, politics, art, education, and health services finally gives voice to genuinely Native viewpoints in the representation of the lives of Indian women, viewpoints that authoritatively challenge the degrading stereotypes established and sustained over four hundred years.

That much of the material cited in this volume is ethnocentric and that some is even ignorant or malicious in its depiction of North American Indian women does not mean that the material published about Native women before the revisionist, feminist, theoretical and creative writing of the post-1960 period is not an enormously important historical and ethnographic record that provides enduring tribal specific data and data useful for comparative studies and the study of the history of the depiction of Indian women itself. Much of the material cited here is fair-minded and of high quality; in some cases it is the only material on women in tribes no longer in existence; often it offers intense, intimate and lyrical portrayal of Indian women's lives. The extensive number of citations in the annotated bibliography which follows is a tribute to the interest in North American Indian women by popular writers and scholars over four centuries, to the rising quality of the scholarship on tribal women, to the broadening attention to all aspects of Native women's lives, and to the growing number of accomplishments and the endurance of Indian women.

A number of criteria were used in compiling and annotating this bibliography. In order to make the bibliography genuinely useful, we chose to cite primarily published works on North American Indian women which are accessible through major research university libraries and inter-library loan services. Some obscure references are indeed cited, often because we found the material particularly interesting in terms of the insights offered by diverse perspectives. Although it is the most comprehensive annotated bibliography of items on Native women thus far published, it is by no means exhaustive. We eliminated many references to works we could not locate for annotation because they were no longer housed in research institutions or were too obscure to track down. We have also excluded such items as unpublished conference records, dissertations, theses, pamphlets, and the like. Nor does this volume include book reviews which are easily found through other reference tools. Works with only passing mention of Indian women were also excluded on the basis that they would not provide adequate material to those doing research specifically on tribal women.

Popular fiction depicting Indian women, usually in very stereotypical ways, has not been included unless it has significantly influenced views of Indian women or contributed specifically to the legends of such figures as Sacajewea or Pocahontas. Nor have we cited the numerous references to Indian women in travel journals by European visitors to the United States and Canada, although we have included articles in English which offer critical study of such travel literature. We also chose not to include works aimed at children or juvenile audiences because these works are accessible through other bibliographies cited in our volume and many do not contribute reliable or useful material for scholarly research. We also eliminated works published in languages other than English; although there is a growing body of material on Indian women being written in or translated into both tribal and other languages, most non-English items we traced were accessible in English.

We chose not to extend the bibliography to include material on Indian women in Mexico or to include material on Indian women in Central and South America primarily because of the restriction of length, but also because this volume is aimed at English language readers and most of the writing on Indian women in Latin America is in Spanish or Portuguese.

Had we included all of the above, this would be a multi-volume work requiring complicated apparatus to use and would have defeated our intention to provide a major resource tool for locating the most significant scholarly and literary work by and about Indian women in the United States and Canada. Because the Native women of the United States and Canada have been colonized largely by Northern Europeans and governed by similar policies, the obvious parallels in their histories and experiences led us to concentrate our effort on gathering references on U.S. and Canadian Native women. There is substantially more material on U.S. women than on Canadian due in part to greater volume and accessibility of materials published in the U.S., but also due to a much higher population density and a more intensive research program on Native peoples in the U.S. Reference works cited in the first section of this volume contain additional material on Canadian tribes and Native women.

In order to make using this volume more efficient, we have divided it into several categories and provided an index for locating items by period, tribe, name, and subject. The index provides quick reference to items for scholars with particular topics in mind. A glance at the index reveals a dominance of certain tribes in the research and writing about Indian women; while the Iroquois, Ojibwa, Navajo, and Pueblo cultures have received a great deal of attention, little has been published on the Southeastern tribes, particularly in the past one hundred years. The index also makes clear that urban Indian women and Native women in the areas of economics and politics, especially those who govern tribes today, have been given far less attention than women in more traditional settings and roles, suggesting a preference among scholars for the tribes and areas in which tribal women act in traditional ways and are more visibly identifiable as bearers of traditional cultures.

Eight separate sections based on related categories are provided to allow readers to "browse" through topic areas. The number of citations in the various categories gives evidence to the areas of concentration in research and writing about Indian women. Not surprising is the fact that "Ethnography, Cultural History and Social Roles" and "Autobiography, Biography and Interviews" contain the greatest number of citations since these are the areas in which scholarship on Indian women has been concentrated. In "Bibliographies and Reference Works" we have included many items not specifically on Indian women but that provide background, context, or comparative material for research and writing about Indian women.

We also recommend the many tribal bibliographies, regional, and local historical bibliographies on tribes and holdings of tribes on their own cultures, for example: *The Ojibwas: A Critical Bibliography* by Helen Hornback Tanner (Bloomington: University of Indiana Press, 1976); *Bibliography of the Sioux* by Jack Marken and Herbert T. Hoover (Metuchen, NJ: Scarecrow Press, 1980); *The Indians of Maine: A Bibliographical Guide* by Roger B. Ray (Portland, ME: Maine Historical Society, 1972); and many others. In "Health, Education, and Employment" we have not included the many articles on childhood disease, fetal alcohol syndrome, or pregnancy-related drug use unless the material seemed particularly compelling. Readers might wish to consult such bibliographies as *Native American Youth and Alcohol: An Annotated Bibliography* (Westport, CT: Greenwood Press, 1989) by Michael L. Lobb and Thomas D. Watts for sources on alcoholism, suicide, and mental health. In "Visual and Performing Arts" we selected from a vast number of studies on American Indian arts those sources which focus on women rather than craft or product. Basketmakers such as Dat-So-La-Lee and potters such as Maria Martinez have provided subject matter for scholarly articles, studies of "crafts," and children's books not listed here. Readers interested in pursuing a specific artisan should look at specialized bibliographies such as *Native American Basketry: An Annotated Bibliography* by Frank W. Porter II (Westport

CT: Greenwood Press, 1988). In "Literature and Literary Criticism" and "Autobiography, Biography, and Interviews" we have noted tribal affiliations of authors or subjects of biographies.

The last section, "Film and Video," includes films, film strips, and videotapes we believed might be useful to teachers, tribal groups, and other organizations interested in Native women. A few of the items in this section are fictional; most are documentary. Some are made by Indian production companies; many are not. They address all aspects of Indian women's lives from traditional activities and ceremonies to their involvement in contemporary tribal governments. For further information on availability of these films and videos, see *Native Americans on Film and Video*, volumes I and II (New York: Museum of the American Indian, 1981 and 1988) by Elizabeth Weatherford. Entries are included only once, so readers are encouraged to use the index. Often entries were appropriate for more than one section, and we made arbitrary decisions about placement. The annotations included in this volume are largely descriptive, aimed at giving the user enough information to determine whether the book, article, or film, is applicable to her or his research.

Critical or interpretative comments are few and confined to judgments concerning the accuracy of portrayal, evidence of sentimentality, overtly Christian viewpoint, ethnocentric bias, or new age appropriation of Indian women's cultures; they are meant to save the user time by indicating those sources not usable for serious research. In some cases comments are made on a particularly valuable resource for researchers, such as Rayna Green's introduction to her book *Native American Women: A Contextual Bibliography* (Bloomington: University of Indiana Press, 1983) which gives an excellent overview of the scholarship and popular writing on Indian women from the colonial to the contemporary period.

Compiling this bibliography has made it very clear to us that while there is a great body of material available on Indian women, there is much work yet to be done. Research and publication on the continuity of Indian women's traditions from pre-colonial times to contemporary urban society, through the dynamics of culture change, and through the changes in scholarly approaches is still needed to provide an accurate and balanced view of Indian women's experiences on this continent. The old stereotypes still thrive in the American imagination, still do harm to Indian women. The shift from "vanishing" to "enduring" as descriptive terms is a start, but perhaps the real accomplishment will only come when Indian women are represented simply as women who are tribal.

It is our hope that the bibliography we have compiled and annotated will contribute to the quality of scholarship on American Indian women and that it will help Indians, both men and women, to know more about themselves and encourage them to write more about their experiences so that specialists and casual readers alike will be able to abandon the biases and stereotypes of the past and gain reliable historical, cultural, scientific, artistic, literary, and personal knowledge of the first women of North America.

Bibliographies and Reference Works

BIBLIOGRAPHIES AND REFERENCE WORKS

1. *American Indian Reference Book.* Portage, MI: eARTH, 1976.

   Reference book which lists tribes, population, cultural events, museums, and media sources of information on American Indians.

2. *Book Collection on Microfilm Relating to the North American Indian.* Glen Rock, NJ: Microfilming Corporation of America, 1973.

   This is an index of book material on Indians available on microfilm listed by title and author. Covers a wide variety of topics, tribes, and periods, but is not subject indexed.

3. *Dictionary of Indian Tribes of the Americas.* 4 vols. Newport Beach, CA: American Indian Publishers, 1980.

   Illustrated with maps and indexed, this reference guide gives brief cultural histories of the tribes of North, Central, and South America. Provides an introduction to tribes and to regionally grouped tribes.

4. *Native American Women: A Selected Topics Bibliography of ERIC Documents.* University Park, NM: New Mexico State University, 1977. EDRS, ED 152 472.

   A fifty-item bibliography listing resource materials, research findings, and developments related to Native American women.

5. *Report of the Royal Commission on the Status of Women In Canada*. Ottawa: Royal Commission on the Status of Women, 1970.

    A section on Native women focuses specifically on Eskimo and Indian women north of the 55th parallel. Education and housing issues are highlighted, and recommendations include that universities, private industry, and the government take an active role in improving conditions for Native women. Most of the report ignores the specific conditions of Native women.

6. Abler, Thomas S. and Sally M. Weaver. *A Canadian Indian Bibliography, 1960-1970*. Toronto: University of Toronto Press, 1974.

    Over 3000 annotated entries on all topics related to Canadian Indians except physical anthropology. Includes a case-law digest on Indian litigation and an extensive section organized by tribal headings.

7. Associated Country Women of the World and Country Women's Council, U.S.A. *Indian Women Plan for the Seventies*. Report of the Associated Country Women on the World's National Seminar of American Indian Women, August 8, 1970, Fort Collins, CO. EDRS, ED 103 176.

    This report covers the proceedings of the above meeting, which included reports from 43 tribes from 23 states on such topics as education, employment preparation, community environmental development, alcoholism, and drug use.

8. Bataille, Gretchen M. *American Indian Literature: A Selected Bibliography for Schools*. Pomona: NAIES, 1981.

    Bibliography of materials for students from elementary through high school with resources for teachers.

9. Bataille, Gretchen M. "Bibliography on Native American Women." *Concerns: The Newsletter of the Modern Language Association Women's Caucus* 10, 2 (1980): 16-27.

A brief bibliography focusing primarily on literature, but also including several autobiographies and references to Indian women's lives.

10. Beidler, Peter G. *The American Indian in Short Fiction.* Metuchen, NJ: Scarecrow, 1979.

Annotated bibliography with plot summaries of 900 short stories about Indians appearing in both magazines and books since 1890. Includes stories by Indian and non-Indian authors and by and about Indian women.

11. Bradley, Ian L. and Patricia Bradley. *A Bibliography of Canadian Native Arts: Indian and Eskimo Arts, Crafts, Dance and Music.* Victoria, BC: GLC Publishers, 1977.

Nearly 1500 entries on a wide variety of arts and folk crafts includes theses and manuscript materials as well as books and periodicals. Indexed by Indian and Eskimo craft classifications such as soapstone carving, basketmaking, blankets, beadwork, ceramics. Also indexed by artists.

12. Brennan, Jane L. *The Forgotten American--American Indians Remembered: A Selected Bibliography for Use in Social Work Education.* New York: Council on Social Work, 1972.

Aimed at improving institutional education and practices toward American Indians, this annotated bibliography includes selected entries on government-Indian relations, missionary and military relationships with Indians, biographies, fiction, books by Indian authors, and Indian newspapers.

13. Brumble, H. David III. *An Annotated Bibliography of American Indian and Eskimo Lives.* Lincoln: University of Nebraska Press, 1981.

This is a bibliography of first-person narratives and does not include biographies. It does include as-told-to narratives. The compiler cites all works by narrator's name and tribal identification; collector-editor name is included after the narrator's identification. Annotations are substantive and contain critical and interpretative comments on style and methodology. A comprehensive work with insightful commentary.

14. Brumble, H. David III. "A Supplement to *An Annotated Bibliography of American Indian and Eskimo Autobiographies*." *Western American Literature* 17, 3 (1982): 243-60.

Twenty-eight annotated citations update the original bibliography published in 1981. A brief introduction refers to recent work related to Indian personal narrative; citation numbers mesh with original bibliography.

15. Clements, William M. and Frances Malpezzi. *Native American Folklore: 1879-1979: An Annotated Bibliography*. Chicago: Swallow Press, 1984.

Focuses on verbal arts--myths, legends, tales, proverbs, riddles, ballads and songs, narratives, chants, orations, ceremonies, dance, games, music--of tribes north of Mexico. Organized by tribe with author, title and subject indices, the work includes over 5500 citations. Subject index includes extensive citations under "women."

16. Colonese, Tom and Louise Owens. *American Indian Novelists: An Annotated Critical Bibliography*. New York: Garland, 1985.

Includes biographies and bibliographies for Paula Gunn Allen, Janet Campbell Hale, Mourning Dove, Leslie Marmon Silko, and Virginia Driving Hawk Sneve.

17. Cushman, Marc, ed. *Bibliography of American Ethnology*. Rye, NY: Todd, 1976.

This is a basic research tool for ethnographic research and includes many citations on American Indian women.

18. Daniel, Robert. *American Women in the 20th Century: The Festival of Life*. San Diego: Harcourt Brace Jovanovich, 1986.

Systematic analysis of the changes in women's lives since 1900 in politics, labor, law and other categories of the public arena. The author sees the American women's population as culturally pluralistic and focuses on several racial and ethnic groups, among them American Indian women, to explore how their values and lives diverge from those of Anglo-American women, and the plural nature of American feminism. A good general reference work.

19. Dennis, Henry C., ed. *The American Indian, 1492-1970*. Dobbs Ferry, NY: Oceana Publications, 1971.

This general reference book on the history of American Indians includes two sections of brief biographies of prominent Indian figures which include sixteen Indian women from the historical past and the contemporary period.

20. Dockstader, Frederick J. *Great North American Indians: Profiles in Life and Leadership*. New York: Van Nostrand Reinhold, 1977.

A collection of biographies on notable Indian men and women who are no longer living, including some photographs. Indexed by tribe and chronology as well as alphabetically, it contains over 500 entries.

21. Dockstader, Frederick J. *The American Indian in Graduate Study: A Bibliography of Theses and Dissertations*. New York: Museum of the American Indian, 1957.

Includes over 3500 dissertations and theses in the fields of anthropology, history, sociology, education, music, art, and literature from over 200 schools, all indexed by the author.

22. Donovan, Lynn. "Women's History: A Listing of West Coast Archival and Manuscript Sources." *California Historical Quarterly* 55 (Spring and Summer 1976): 74-83; 170-85.

Lists archives with holdings on women's history includes some sources on Indian women including bibliographies, manuscripts, letters, newspapers, oral history transcripts, interviews, government records. Institutions include libraries, historical societies, museums, universities, research centers.

23.   Emery, Marg and Ann Laquer, eds. *Indian Truth: Special Issue on Native Women*, 239 (May-June 1981): 4-12.

Four essays on Indian women address such issues as challenging historical stereotypes, goals of Indian women's organizations, and Indian women active in public life. Good initial resource on Indian women.

24.   Field, Thomas W. *An Essay Towards an Indian Bibliography. Being a Catalogue of Books Relating to the History, Antiquities, Languages, Customs, Religion, Wars, Literature and Origin of the American Indians*. New York: Scribner, Armstrong and Company, 1875. Rpt. Detroit: Gale Research Co., 1967.

Catalogue of the author's personal library with descriptive annotations. No subject headings. Includes materials on North and South America dating from Columbian contact, including texts in several European languages and Latin. Useful for colonial views on Native cultures and customs.

25.   Freeman, John F. *A Guide to Manuscripts Relating to the American Indian in the Library of the American Philosophical Society*. Philadelphia: American Philosophical Society, 1966.

This two-volume annotated reference guide has no index category on women, but does have very detailed tribal categories, a guide to manuscript collections, and subject index.

26.   Green, Rayna. *Native American Women: A Bibliography*. Wichita Falls, TX: Ohoyo Resource Center, 1981.

A lengthy bibliography divided into several sections; includes books for children and films.

27.   Green, Rayna. *Native American Women: A Contextual Bibliography*. Bloomington: Indiana University Press, 1983.

A comprehensive bibliography covering political, social, cultural and biological issues. Contains over 600 entries with brief annotation, subject and date indices.

28. Gridley, Marion. *The Vanishing Race: Selections from Edward S. Curtis's The North American Indian.* Seattle: University of Washington Press, 1987.

   This single volume condenses the twenty volumes of Curtis's photographs and texts published from 1907-1930. Of particular interest are sections on social customs, ceremonies, and mythology. Sections are keyed to the original volumes for more information. Good resource for visual images of Indians.

29. Haas, Marilyn L. *Indians of North America; Methods and Sources for Library Research.* Hamden, CT: Shoe String Press, 1983.

   Although little information specifically about resources on women is included, Haas provides a wide range of general resources useful to scholars beginning research in general topics related to Indian experience.

30. Harding, Anne D. and Patricia Bolling. *Bibliography of Articles and Papers on North American Indian Art.* New York: Kraus Reprint Co., 1969.

   This is an index of many categories of Indian arts--pottery, basketry, woodworking, clothing, jewelry--much of which is produced by women. Also indexed by tribe. Does not include popular periodical literature.

31. Harrison, Cynthia E., ed. *Women in American History: A Bibliography.* Santa Barbara, CA: Clio Press, 1979.

   Under the category "Women and Ethnicity" a section on Native Americans includes nearly 100 annotated entries on Indian women including biographies and autobiographies, cultural histories, ethnographies, identity studies, urban studies, fine arts, health, and law categories.

32.   Henry, Jeanette, ed. *Index to Literature on the American Indian.*
      5 vols. San Francisco: Indian Historian Press, 1970-1975.

      Organized by sections on subject, tribe, and Native American
      publications. The editors describe the volumes as a "fair
      sampling" of book and periodical publications on North and
      South American Indians. Does not include a subject reference to
      women.

33.   Hill, Edward E. *Guide to Records in the National Archives of the
      United States Relating to American Indians.* Washington, DC:
      National Archives and Records Service, General Services
      Administration, 1981.

      This is a guide to federal records on American Indian tribes.
      Index includes references on several Indian women who had
      direct dealings with the U.S. government, such as Sarah
      Winnemucca.

34.   Hinding, Andrea, Ames Sheldon Bower, and Clark Chambers.
      Women's History Sources. 2 vols. New York: R. R. Bowker
      Company, 1979.

      Result of a survey of 11,000 archives and collections of
      sources pertaining to women's history. Special attention is paid
      to minority women's sources.

35.   Hirschfelder, Arlene B. *Annotated Bibliography of the Literature
      on American Indians Published in State Historical Publications.*
      Millwood, NY: Kraus International Publications, 1982.

      This annotated reference work covers material from New
      England and the Middle Atlantic states and has three index
      categories: subject, author, and tribe.

36.   Hirschfelder, Arlene B., Mary Gloyne Byler, and Michael A.
      Dorris. *Guide to Research on North American Indians.*
      Chicago: American Library Association, 1983.

Basic guide with sections on general sources, history, economics, and social aspects, religion, art, and literature. Useful subject index which includes a reference heading on women.

37. Hirschfelder, Arlene. *American Indian and Eskimo Authors: A Comprehensive Bibliography.* New York: Association on American Indian Affairs, 1970.

While this is not actually a comprehensive bibliography, it is a very useful annotated resource on literary works by Indian and Eskimo writers including over 40 citations on women writers.

38. Hirschfelder, Arlene. *American Indian Authors: A Representative Bibliography.* New York: Association on American Indian Affairs, 1970.

This is a broadly ranging bibliography with brief annotations and is aimed at acquainting the public with the extensive body of works by Indian authors. Listed by author but also with tribal index. Includes citations on autobiography, anthropology, arts, language, myth, literature, history.

39. Hodge, F. W., ed. *Handbook of American Indians North of Mexico.* Washington, DC: Smithsonian Institution. Bureau of American Ethnology Bulletin 30, 1907.

Basic index of names and subjects based on research by Bureau of American Ethnology. Includes all tribes, confederacies, sub-tribes, tribal divisions and settlements identified by the Bureau, including history and locations at various periods. Entry on Indian women addresses misconceptions about Native women as drudges and discusses the complexity of factors determining women's status in various tribes, noting that considerable power and control over her body and domestic spheres of activity are generally characteristic of Indian experience.

40. Hood, Jane Renner. "A Reader's Guide to Women in *Nebraska History Magazine*, 1918-1977." *Nebraska History* 59 (Spring 1978): 70-83.

Bibliography organized into several categories, one of which is Native American Women.

41.   Icolari, Dan and Barry Klein, eds. *Reference Encyclopedia of the American Indian*. 2 vols. Rye, NY: Todd, 1973-74.

This two volume work includes a 2500-entry bibliography on various aspects of Indian cultures and is a who's who of living American Indians including many biographies of women who are active in areas of public service.

42.   Jacobs, Sue-Ellen. *Women in Perspective: A Guide for Cross-Cultural Studies*. Urbana: University of Illinois Press, 1974.

This general study includes material on American Indian women as well as a bibliography.

43.   Jacobson, Angeline. *Contemporary Native American Literature: A Selected and Partially Annotated Bibliography*. Metuchen, NJ: Scarecrow Press, 1977.

An extensive and partially annotated bibliography, this reference work is divided into categories of poetry, traditional narratives, personal narratives, fiction, humor, interviews, and collections. Has an author index which includes nearly 100 women.

44.   James, Edward T., ed. *Notable American Women*. 4 vols. Cambridge, MA: Harvard University Press, 1971, 1982.

A biographical dictionary with fairly detailed entries. The first volumes cover from 1607-1950. Volume four goes up to 1980. This work includes references to Sarah Winnemucca, Pocahontas, Gertrude Bonnin, Susan LaFlesche, Catherine Tekakwitha, Nancy Ward, Roberta Campbell Lawson, Marie Dorion, Mary Brant, Sacajawea, and others. Each entry is followed by a selected bibliography.

45. Jensen, Joan M. and Darlis A. Miller, eds. *New Mexico Women: Intercultural Perspectives.* Albuquerque: University of New Mexico Press, 1986.

    This collection of essays includes three focused on women from Pueblo tribes ranging from analysis through archaeological findings of women's pre-history roles to an examination of the effect of traditional arts on contemporary pottery.

46. Joyce, T. Athol and N. W. Thomas, eds. *Women of All Nations; A Record of Their Characteristics, Habits, Manners, Customs and Influence.* Vol. II. London: Cassell and Company, Limited, 1908.

    A major section of the second volume of this early work focuses on Indian women of North America. This is an early and often misguided view of Indian women with many superficial generalizations. There are several photographs of Native women which provide insight into traditional dress and artifacts. Useful for tracing attitudes toward tribal women.

47. Kelso, Dianne R. and Carolyn Attneave. *Bibliography of North American Indian Mental Health.* Westport, CT: Greenwood Press, 1981.

    This bibliography of over 1300 items includes nearly 100 entries dealing with Indian women's mental health issues. Many of the articles deal with the general social or psychological states of both males and females.

48. Klein, Barry. *Reference Encyclopedia of the American Indian.* 5th ed. New York: Todd Publications, 1990.

    Good one-volume basic research tool, profiles prominent living Indians in areas ranging from tribal government to museum, academic and business professionals, including many tribal women.

49. Koehler, Lyle. "Native Women of the Americas: A Bibliography." *Frontiers: Journal of Women Studies* 6 (Fall 1981): 73-101.

A brief introduction providing additional bibliographical sources is followed by a bibliography which includes ethnographic materials as well as artistic and literary citations. Koehler's bibliography includes Hispanic references.

50.   Light, Beth and Veronica Strong-Boag. *True Daughters of the North; Canadian Women's History: An Annotated Bibliography.* Toronto: OISE Press, 1980.

Although the majority of the entries in this bibliography are about Anglo women, there are references to Indian and Metis women in Canada.

51.   Lindsay, Beverly, ed. *Comparative Perspectives of Third World Women: The Impact of Race, Sex and Class.* New York: Praeger, 1980.

Includes three overview essays on the status of Third World women and numerous essays on women in Africa, Asia, the Caribbean, and the Americas, including one on the history and contemporary experience of American Indian women.

52.   Littlefield, Daniel, Jr. and James Parins. *A Bibliography of Native American Writers 1772-1924.* Metuchen, NJ: Scarecrow Press, 1981.

The compilers of this extensive bibliography list over 4000 works by early Indian writers not included in most other bibliographies. A significant number of entries are by or about Indian women.

53.   Littlefield, Daniel, Jr. and James Parins. *A Bibliography of Native American Authors 1772-1924: A Supplement.* Metuchen, NJ: Scarecrow Press, 1985.

Additional entries to the extensive bibliography compiled on early Indian writers including many works by and about Indian women.

54. Lobb, Michael L. and Thomas D. Watts. *Native American Youth and Alcohol: An Annotated Bibliography*. Westport, CT: Greenwood Press, 1989.

   Indian women are victims of alcoholism as well as the contributors to the effects of alcoholism on families and children. This bibliography includes annotated entries on literature which examines alcohol use among American Indian youth.

55. Mail, Patricia D. and David R. McDonald. *Tulapai To Tokay: A Bibliography of Alcohol Use and Abuse Among Native Americans of North America*. New Haven: HRAF Press, 1988.

   Though this extensive reference volume has no subject index on Indian women, many of the annotated entries address the issue of alcohol and women and may be found via the "sex differences" index heading.

56. Mainiero, Lina, ed. *American Women Writers*. 4 vols. New York: Frederick Ungar, 1982.

   A dictionary of women writers, this multi-volume work claims to include all women writers of literary reputation, including writers of diaries, letters, and autobiographies, but is marked by the absence of all Indian women writers except Leslie Marmon Silko, who is erroneously identified as the first Indian woman to publish a novel, and Sarah Winnemucca who is recognized for her authentic Indian viewpoint in an era of Indian suppression. Non-Indian women who wrote about Indians, such as Helen Hunt Jackson, author of *Ramona*, are included.

57. Marken, Jack W. *The Indians and Eskimos of North America: A Bibliography of Books in Print Through 1972*. Vermillion: University of South Dakota, 1973.

   Compiler attempts to list all books by and about American and Canadian Indians and Eskimos. Entries are divided into sections on bibliographies, handbooks, autobiographies, myths and legends, reprints in archaeology and ethnology, and other books. Books for children are designated by grade and level, and paperback editions are indicated. A very brief subject index is included. Limited number of works on or by Indian women.

58. Martin, M. K. and B. Voorhies. *Female of the Species*. New York: Columbia University Press, 1975.

    In discussing the roles of women in gathering, horticultural, pastoral, agricultural and industrial societies, this study draws on examples from Hopi, Papago, Mojave, Omaha, Pima and other tribes and addresses biological as well as sociological and personality traits linked to gender.

59. Matthiasson, Carolyn J., ed. *Many Sisters: Women in Cross-Cultural Perspective*. New York: Free Press, 1974.

    Essays written by female anthropologists on the lives of women in several societies throughout the world. The chapters are divided to focus on three types of societies, those which Matthiasson calls manipulative, complementary, or ascendent. Eskimo women are described in a chapter by Jean Briggs as "makers of men," and the Onondaga are discussed by Cara E. Richards as participants in a society in which it is an advantage to be a woman.

60. Medicine, Bea. "The Role of Women in Native American Societies: A Bibliography." *Indian Historian* 8 (Summer 1975): 50-53.

    Medicine includes 100 citations of books and articles on American Indian women.

61. Murdock, George Peter and Timothy J. O'Leary. *Ethnographic Bibliography of North America*. 4th ed. New Haven: Human Relations Area Files Press, 1975.

    A five-volume basic research tool on North American Indians organized by region and tribe. Citations up to 1972. Includes regional maps and brief introductions, over 40,000 entries.

62. Oshana, Maryann. *Women of Color; A Filmography of Minority and Third World Women*. New York: Garland, 1985.

Includes information and plot summaries of over 100 feature films which include Indian women as characters whether played by non-Indians or Indians.

63. Peyer, Bernd C. "A Bibliography of Native American Prose Prior to the 20th Century." *Wassaja* 13, 3 (1980): 23-25.

In this brief essay Peyer discusses letters written by 17th century Indians; sermons, diaries, letters and autobiographies written in the 18th century; and the introduction of ethnohistorical writing and fiction in the late 19th century. Includes a selected bibliography.

64. Porter, Frank W. III. *Native American Basketry: An Annotated Bibliography*. Westport, CT: Greenwood Press, 1988.

An annotated bibliography dealing with American Indian basketry, divided according to region. Most significant Indian women who are basketmakers are included.

65. Prucha, Francis Paul. *A Bibliographical Guide to the History of Indian-White Relations in the United States*. Chicago: University of Chicago Press, 1977.

Comprehensive sourcebook: National Archives, federal documents, manuscripts and published materials on several subjects. Includes several sources of information on the Women's National Indian Association.

66. Quinn, Naomi. "Anthopological Studies on Women's Status." *Annual Review of Anthropology*. 6 (1977): 181-225.

This periodical was begun in 1959 under the title *Biennial Review of Anthropology*, and since 1972 it has been published annually. This article, like many others in a wide range of anthropological categories, includes an extensive bibliography.

Extensive subject index in each volume, including a heading on women.

67.   Rock, Roger O. *The Native American In American Literature: A Selectively Annotated Bibliography*. Westport, CT: Greenwood Press, 1985.

Over 900 citations, 517 annotated, are included in this reference work aimed at facilitating initial research on American Indians as they are depicted in American literary works, films and critical studies. Included are works by Indian authors, but no tribal identification is included, nor are works on women identified separately.

68.   Rohrlich-Leavitt, Ruby, ed. *Women Cross-Culturally: Change and Challenge*. The Hague: Mouton Publishers, 1975.

This collection of essays on women in many societies has very little on American Indian women; however, the selections provide material for interesting comparative studies.

69.   Rosaldo, M. Z. and L. Lamphere, eds. *Women, Culture and Society*. Palo Alto: Stanford University Press, 1974.

This collection of essays is a landmark in the feminist approach to the study of women's roles in cultures. While no essay focuses exclusively on Indian women, two use examples-- from Navajo and Iroquois--and others refer to tribal forms of kinship, domestic practices, self-concepts, ceremonies, etc. Useful for comparison of women's roles cross-culturally.

70.   Roscoe, Will. "Bibliography of Berdache and Alternative Gender Roles Among North American Indians." *Journal of Homosexuality* 14, 3-4 (1987): 81-171.

Roscoe includes materials which focus on alternative sex and gender roles for men and women among North American tribes. The bibliography is coded so that the reader can find tribal designations as well as specific material about either men or women. Includes a glossary of Native terms for alternative gender roles.

71. Ruoff, A. LaVonne Brown and Karl Kroeber. *American Indian Literatures in the United States: An Annotated Bibliography.* New York: Association for the Study of American Indian Literatures, 1983.

Comprehensive bibliography of primary and secondary sources related to American Indian literatures, both traditional and contemporary.

72. Sicherman, Barbara, ed. *Notable American Women.* Vol. 4. Cambridge, MA: Harvard/Belknap, 1980.

Includes Muriel Wright and Ella Deloria.

73. Smith, Dwight L. *The History of Canada: An Annotated Bibliography.* Santa Barbara: ABC-Clio Information Services, 1983.

An annotated bibliography of periodical literature on subjects ranging from the prehistoric period to the present. Section on "Native Peoples" includes categories on pre-Columbian history, Inuits, and Indian tribes. Containing about 200 entries primarily on cultural history and ethnography, many referenced articles are pertinent to women's identity, roles, arts, and personal narratives.

74. Smith, Dwight L. *Indians of the U.S. and Canada: A Bibliography.* Santa Barbara: ABC-Clio Press, 1974.

This two-volume research guide includes tribal histories by region with annotated entries, subject and author indices. Major categories of entries are Pre-Columbian, 1492-1900, and twentieth century. Emphasis on ethnography and cultural history. Subject index includes many entries on women.

75. Stensland, Anna Lee. *Literature by and About the American Indian: An Annotated Bibliography.* Urbana, IL: National Council of Teachers of English, 1979.

Substantive annotations on citations in areas of oral literature, fiction, biography and autobiography, history, traditional culture, modern Indian life, music, arts. Has both author and title index, selected author biographies (seven on women), and an introduction discussing the teaching of literature by Indian authors.

76. Sturtevant, William C. *Handbook of North American Indians*. Washington, DC: The Smithsonian Institution, 1978.

This is a 20-volume series which gives a comprehensive view of Indian cultures by region and tribes giving geography, archaeology and cultural history.

77. Terrell, John Upton. *American Indian Almanac*. New York: World Publishing Co., 1971.

Organized by region, this volume gives brief cultural histories of North American tribes and such data as population, means of livelihood, important historical events, and geographical features.

78. Waldman, Harry, *et al. Dictionary of Indians of North America*. St. Clair Shores, MI: Scholarly Press, 1978.

Biographical dictionary which includes brief and incomplete sketches of several Indian women; the majority of the entries are on males who were tribal leaders.

79. Weatherford, Elizabeth, ed. *Native Americans on Film and Video*. New York: Museum of the American Indian, 1981.

Weatherford has annotated 400 documentary films and videotapes, most produced between 1970 and 1981. Several films on women are listed.

80. Weatherford, Elizabeth and Emelia Seubert, eds. *Native Americans on Film and Video*. Vol. II. New York: Museum of the American Indian, 1988.

Annotated catalog describes approximately 200 productions, mostly documentary films, made since 1980.

81. Zophy, Angela Howard, ed. *Handbook of American Women's History*. New York: Garland, 1990.

This volume of over 700 pages includes sections on Native women, Native women's literature, Gertrude Bonnin, Sarah Winnemucca Hopkins, berdache, and naming systems, plus brief references to American Indian women in art and history.

Ethnography, Cultural History, and Social Roles

ETHNOGRAPHY, CULTURAL HISTORY, AND SOCIAL ROLES

82. "First Person." *Canadian Woman Studies* 10, 2 & 3 (Summer/Fall 1989): 167-68.

    This article written by an anonymous Indian lesbian explains the difficulties she had growing up, coping with her sexuality, and with Native attitudes.

83. "Hopi Womanpower." *Human Behavior* 3 (November 1974): 49-50.

    In this brief discussion of the matrilineal, matrilocal society of the Hopi, women's duties and the education of children are explained.

84. "Indian Mothers and Indian Girls." *Indian's Friend* 2, 10 (June 1890): 1, 3.

    Navajo mothers are described as the stronghold of paganism and superstition in a summary of a report to the commissioner of Indian Affairs. Their conservatism is blamed on early marriages and isolation from the example of Christian women. The government is urged to appoint middle-aged Christian women as field matrons to educate Indian women to give up "savagery." This is seen as particularly important in view of the influence Indian mothers have on their daughters. The author praises the "civilizing" effects of boarding school education on Indian girls since it teaches them "womanly industries" such as knitting, canning and crocheting which will result in "an upward movement" in Indian households.

85. *Many Smokes* 15, 2 (Fall 1981): 4-28.

   Special issue on Indian women which includes articles on transcending stereotypes of Indian women, Seneca education of women, the power of the "Great Mother" and the contributions of Indian women. Articles have a new age slant.

86. "Navajo Women." *Indian's Friend* 6, 12 (August 1894): 8.

   The ownership of property by women in Navajo culture is not seen as an advantage or status sign because women also perform most of the labor. Education and Christianity are offered as solutions to what the writer sees as Navajo women's degraded state.

87. "The Navajo Woman." *Indian's Friend* 3, 10 (1891): 4.

   A brief account of the role of Navajo women and the need to continue to Christianize them, a main theme of articles in *The Indian's Friend*.

88. *Western Canadian Journal of Anthropology.* "Special Issue: Cross Sex Relations: Native Peoples." 6, 3 (1976).

   Nine essays in this volume address topics on Indian women in Canadian, Arctic, and U.S. tribes, covering issues of roles and identity; violence and exploitation; conservation in agriculture and economic areas; political power; activism and public life; and status changes through traditional, historical, and contemporary eras.

89. "When Sexism Was Born." *USA Today* 109 (February 11, 1981): 11.

   Based on a "task inventory" of the Hidatsa Indians of the Great Plains, the author argues that Indian women were traditionally much more important to their tribe's economies than has been recognized by scholars and notes that their cultures became more sexist with the development of agriculture.

90. Ackerman, Lillian A. "The Effect of Missionary Ideals on Family Structure and Women's Roles in Plateau Indian Culture." *Idaho Yesterdays* 31, 1-2 (Spring/Summer 1987): 64-73.

Missionaries imposed their ideas of family structures and relationships on Indian extended families and in the process caused Indian families to be dysfunctional. Missionary attitudes toward pregnancy, polygamy, legitimacy and divorce all disrupted traditional women's roles.

91. Ackerman, Lillian. "Marital Instability and Juvenile Delinquency among the Nez Perces." *American Anthropologist* n.s., 73 (1971): 595-603.

Discussion of the decline of traditional modes of instructing and disciplining children and the rise of delinquent behavior resulting from poorly defined roles within the modern family and marital instability. Revision of male and female role behavior is posited as a solution.

92. Ackerman, Lillian A. "Sexual Equality on the Colville Indian Reservation in Traditional and Contemporary Contexts." In *Women in Pacific Northwest History: An Anthology.* Karen J. Blair, ed. Seattle: University of Washington Press, 1988, 152-69.

The author argues that modern economic conditions are not incompatible with sexual equality, citing the continuity of balance in sex roles from traditional to contemporary times in the spheres of economics, politics, domestic labor, and religion. The Colville reservation from which she gathers her data includes eleven Plateau tribes. Power, authority, and autonomy are also areas where she finds continuing sexual equality.

93. Albers, Patricia and Beatrice Medicine, eds. *The Hidden Half: Studies of Plains Indian Women.* Washington, DC: University Press of America, 1983.

Collection of essays on Plains tribal women covering such topics as slaves, male/female roles, work division, women's production of ceremonial objects, women's political roles, changing status of Plains women, the warrior woman, and female roles in traditional Lakota culture.

94. Allen, Paula Gunn. "Beloved Women: Lesbians in American Indian Culture." *Conditions* 7 (1981): 67-87.

American Indian women who are lesbian have historically been ignored by ethnographers in their accounts of Native cultures, primarily because of the Christian viewpoint of most scholars. Various kinds of bonding, however, were and are a part of Native cultures where the concept of family is much broader and female relationships much more central to identity and power. Further, bonding of women was traditionally seen as destined and nurtured by spirit beings, thus giving sanction to lesbian relationships.

95. Allen, Paula Gunn. *The Sacred Hoop: Recovering the Feminine in American Indian Traditions*. Boston: Beacon Press, 1986.

Allen analyzes the gynocentric character of pre-contact Pueblo culture and the erosion of women's power through imposition of European patriarchal systems. She discusses the role of the woman writer within the context of contemporary Indian women's culture and in light of her own family experiences.

96. Allen, Paula Gunn. "Tribal Cultures." *Revision: The Journal of Consciousness and Change* 19, 1 (Summer-Fall 1986): 26-31.

In a broadly ranging presentation on Indian cultures, Allen discusses the importance of oral tradition in Indian cultures and notes that women carry the line of continuance in many tribes and are central figures in myth.

97. Amylee. "Womantime, Womanplace." *Many Smokes* 15, 2 (Fall 1981): 14-15.

The author, a new age teacher, looks to traditional practices regarding the isolation of Indian women during menstruation as a positive model for women valuing the menstrual periods as times for reflection and meditation.

98. Anderson, Karen. "As Gentle as Little Lambs: Images of Huron and Montagnais-Naskapi Women in the Writings of 17th Century Jesuits." *The Canadian Journal of Sociology and Anthropology* 25, 4 (1988): 560-76.

Jesuit Relations, the annual reports sent to France and Rome from New France in the 17th century, provides an interesting look at the redefinition of Huron and Montagnais-Naskapi Indian women and their relationships with Indian men.

99. Anderson, Karen. "Commodity Exchange and Subordination: Montagnais-Naskapi and Huron Women, 1600-1650." *Signs* 11, 1 (Autumn 1985): 48-62.

Anderson analyzes the effect of French contact on women's status among two hunter-gatherer tribes on the shores of the St. Lawrence River. She sees Jesuit missionaries as eroding women's equal status and explains that newly converted Christian males intensified the pressure on women to become subordinate in Montagnais-Naskapi culture, but that the authority of Huron women over the means of production and labor systems prevented male domination or a significant intrusion of French political or religious values.

100. Anderson, Kim. "Native Women and Literacy." *Canadian Woman Studies* 10, 2 & 3 (Summer/Fall 1989): 79-80.

As many as one in two Native women are illiterate, and Ontario has twenty-five Native literacy programs to address this problem.

101. Anderson, Robert. "The Northern Cheyenne War Mothers." *Anthropological Quarterly* 29, 3 (1956): 82-90.

A ceremonial solidarity which began in the 1950s with mothers of men in the armed services, the War Mothers group among the Northern Cheyenne is responsible for service men's send-offs and welcomes, give-away ceremonies, and victory dances. These activities and the organization of war mothers are seen as a means of meeting the threats of separation and death caused during war.

102. Armitage, Susan and Elizabeth Jameson, eds. *The Woman's West.* Norman: University of Oklahoma Press, 1987.

Three chapters on Canadian and U. S. Indian women; all challenge stereotypes and question traditional interpretation of Indian women's roles in the opening of the frontier.

103. Axtell, James, ed. *The Indian Peoples of Eastern America: A Documentary History of the Sexes.* New York: Oxford University Press, 1981.

Axtell provides excerpts from journals and reports from the 1600s to early in the twentieth century. The material focuses on birth, growing up, marriage, social interaction, and death among tribes on the east coast in accounts mostly written by Europeans. Axtell provides informative introductions to each entry.

104. Babcock, Barbara and Nancy J. Parezo. *Daughters of the Desert.* Albuquerque: University of New Mexico Press, 1988.

This catalogue, which accompanies an exhibit on women who contributed seminal work in ethnography and archaeology of Southwest Indian tribes, includes information on work with Indian women and gives biographical and career data and includes bibliographies on each figure.

105. Babcock, Barbara and Nancy Parezo. "The Leading Edge: Women Anthropologists in the Native American Southwest, 1880-1945." *El Palacio* 92, 1 (Summer/Fall 1986): 41-49.

This discussion of women anthropologists' work among tribes in the American Southwest includes women who were among the first in the discipline to look seriously at the roles and lives of Indian women.

106. Badley, Jo-Ann, Anthea Bussey, Tracey Read, and Audrie Walker, eds. *Yukon Women*. Whitehorse, Yukon: Yukon Status of Women Council, 1975.

     Provides information about the legal rights of Yukon women and health care programs which are available. The history of Yukon women provides insights into contemporary life and biographical sketches of several women personalize the generalizations about Yukon life. This work on Yukon women contains "Yukon History and Women, 1850-1950," by Audrie Walker, which discusses the social, economic and legal status of both Native and white women in the Yukon over a hundred-year period.

107. Bailey, Flora L. "Navajo Women and the Sudatory." *American Anthropologist* n.s. 43 (January-March 1941): 484-85.

     Contrary to studies indicating that Navajo women do not participate in sweat bathing, or only rarely in the case of post menstrual women, the author's field interviews indicate that women of all ages may and frequently do participate in social sweat bathing whenever desired, but not with men. Account of a sweat bath with three women is given.

108. Baird, Irene. "The Eskimo Woman: Her Changing World." *Beaver* 289 (Spring 1959): 48-55.

     Because culture change has come extremely rapidly in Eskimo cultures, women are being called upon to make severe changes to accommodate contemporary living patterns, particularly wage work on a seasonal or permanent basis. Benefits in food supply, medical care and education must be balanced with erosion of the traditional role as the central figure in the family and the stability of cyclical activities of tribal life.

109. Balikci, Asen. "Female Infanticide on the Arctic Coast." *Man* 2, 4 (1967): 615-25.

     Statistics corroborate the practice of female infanticide among several Eskimo groups. Balikci theorizes there are three categories of infanticide: social causes, ecological pressure, and female infanticide because women are simply less useful to the tribe.

110. Balikci, Asen. *Vunta Kutchin Social Change: A Study of the People of Old Crow, Yukon Territory.* Ottawa: Department of Northern Affairs and National Resources, Northern Co-ordination and Research Centre, 1963.

In this study of the Old Crow people, women's roles are discussed within the context of overall social organization. The study is based on observation of the Old Crow during the 1960s.

111. Ball, Eve and Lynad Sanchez. "Legendary Apache Women." *Frontier Times* 54, 6 (October-November 1980): 8-12.

Lozen, sister of the Apache leader Victorio, is described as "an evocative and mystical figure in Apache folklore" because of her healing and prophecy powers. The author also discusses Anandiah and Tah-des-ta who accompanied their husbands in battle. Both Lozen and Tah-des-ta acted as emissaries for Geronimo.

112. Bannan, Helen M. "'True Womanhood' and Indian Assimilation." In *Essays on Minority Cultures: Selected Proceedings of the Third Annual Conference on Minority Studies*, Vol. II. La Crosse, WI: Institute for Minority Studies, 1976, 187-94.

The Women's National Indian Association led a late-nineteenth century reform movement based on the "cult of true womanhood" and the belief that they could remedy both the wrongs and ignorance bestowed upon American Indians. Missionaries, teachers, and government employees all sought to "elevate" Indians from their "savage" state.

113. Bannan, Helen M. *'True Womanhood' on the Reservation: Field Matrons in the United States Indian Service.* Tucson, AZ: Southwest Institute for Research on Women, University of Arizona, 1984.

From 1891 through the 1930s the BIA sent matrons to reservations to inculcate in American Indian women the ideal of "True Womanhood." Gradually these matrons were replaced by public health nurses and extension agents.

114. Baskin, Cyndy. "Women in Iroquois Society." *Canadian Woman Studies/Les Cahiers de la Femme* 4, 2 (Winter 1982): 42-46.

A discussion of the position of women in traditional Iroquois society.

115. Basso, Keith. *The Cibecue Apache*. New York: Holt, Rinehart and Winston, 1970.

Chapter five is about the girl's puberty ceremony and includes personal accounts. It discusses the relationship of the ceremony to the figure of Changing Woman who gives longevity and the physical capabilities of perpetual youth.

116. Basso, Keith. "The Gift of Changing Woman." *BAE Bulletin* 196. Washington, DC: Smithsonian Institution, 1966, 119-73.

For this discussion of Apache girls' puberty rites, information was gathered at Cibecue, Arizona. The ceremony gives power to the community through the girl who re-enacts the role of the first woman in Apache mythology.

117. Battiste, Marie Anne. "Mikmag Women: Their Special Dialogue." *Canadian Woman Studies* 10, 2 & 3 (Summer/Fall 1989): 61-63.

Mikmag women's lives are balanced with the lives of men and they are socialized to provide for the education of their children. Their continuance of traditional values exists through language and customs.

118. Beauchamp, W. M. "Iroquois Women." *Journal of American Folklore* 13 (April-June 1900): 81-91.

Discusses the position of women among the Iroquois, their roles, responsibilities, and prestige. This essay reflects common roles of Indian women held at the turn of the century.

119. Beck, Peggy V. and Anna Lee Walters. *The Sacred Ways of Knowledge: Sources of Life*. Tsaile, AZ: Navajo Community College, 1977.

Information about sacred ways gathered through interviews, speeches, prayers, songs, and conversations. Includes chapters on girls' puberty ceremonies, peyote, and studies of selected tribes. Chapter nine describes girls' puberty ceremonies and menstruation practices in Papago, Cheyenne, Winnebago, Washo, Puyallup, Havasupai, Apache, Luiseno, and Cupeno tribes. Includes mythic stories of origins of menstruation from several tribes.

120. Begay, Shirley M. *Kinaalda, and Navajo Puberty Ceremony*. Rough Rock, AZ: Title IV-B Materials Development Project, Navajo Curriculum Center, Rough Rock Demonstration School, 1983.

This is the first account of a Navajo who has participated in the Kinaalda ceremony as an initiate and as a member of the sponsoring family. Interviews with elders supplement Begay's account. The book includes the origin story in both English and Navajo as well as a bilingual description of the ceremonial events.

121. Bishop, Charles A. and Shepard Krech, III. "Matriorganization: The Basis of Aboriginal Subarctic Social Organization." *Arctic Anthropology* 17, 2 (1980): 34-45.

Matriorganization ensured Algonkin and Athapaskan survival prior to European contact because exo-marrying males were knowledgeable about two hunting territories and conflict over scarce resources was diminished by distributing males outside the area of the natal village.

122. Blackwood, Evelyn. "Sexuality and Gender in Certain American Indian Tribes: The Case of Cross-Gender Females." *Signs: The Journal of Women in Culture and Society* 10, 1 (1984): 27-42.

The existence in some American Indian tribes of women who assume male roles permanently and marry women challenges Western assumptions about gender roles. Analysis of Kaska, Klamath, Mohave, Maricopa and Cocopa examples of female berdache institutions suggest egalitarian relations of the sexes served as basis for cross-gender possibility. Data on Plains culture, while limited, points to medicine and warrior women who were not counterparts to male berdache or considered cross-gendered. Cross-gender behavior declined drastically in response to rejection and suppression of it by the dominant Western culture.

123. Blanchard, Kendall. "Changing Sex Roles and Protestantism among the Navajo Women in Ramah." *Journal for the Scientific Study of Religion* 14 (March 1975): 43-50.

Author postulates that economic and social changes have had more negative impact on traditional life styles of Navajo females than males. Women affiliating with the missions are less traditional than other Navajo women who have suffered a "loss of prestige and security within the family."

124. Bloomfield, Leonard, ed. *Menomini Texts*. Publications of the American Ethnological Society 12. New York: G. E. Strechert & Co., 1928.

This bilingual study of the Menomini includes information gathered from Josephine Sotterlee and Louise Dutchman (Maskwawanahkwatok). Botanical information and brief accounts of the economic and social roles of women are included. In a longer section, Dutchman tells about her childhood and how she got the name of Red Cloud Woman.

125. Boggs, Stephen T. "Culture Change and the Personality of Ojibwa Children." *American Anthropologist* 60, 1 (February 1958): 47-58.

Boggs discusses the effect of marital instability and blurring of parental gender roles in the formation of personality. Particular attention is paid to contrasting traditional and modern child care practices focusing on breakdown of extended family and maternal neglect of children.

126. Briggs, Jean L. "Eskimo Women: Makers of Men." In *Many Sisters: Women in Cross-Cultural Perspective*. Carolyn J. Matthiasson, ed. New York: Free Press, 1974, 261-304.

Briggs lived among the Utku and Qipi in the Arctic and observed the interaction between men and women in these traditional societies. Although Eskimo societies are not free from conflict, Briggs concludes that there is little institutionalized conflict between men and women.

127. Briggs, Jean L. "Kapluna Daughter: Living with Eskimos." *Transaction* 7 (June 1970): 12-24.

Experiences of a white woman "adopted" by an Eskimo family and treated as their "daughter" are discussed as anthropological role playing.

128. Briggs, Jean. "Kapluna Daughter." In *Women in the Field*. Peggy Golde, ed. Chicago: Aldine, 1970, 17-44.

Discussion of Briggs' research with Eskimos in Chantrey Inlet. She was adopted as a daughter of the family and she describes the Utkusiksalingmiut life she encountered as a kapluna (white) within this culture. By being adopted, she learned the role of an Utkusiksalingmiut daughter.

129. Briggs, Jean L. *Never in Anger: Portrait of an Eskimo Family*. Cambridge: Harvard University Press, 1970.

Briggs spent seventeen months with the Utku people northwest of Hudson Bay living as an adopted daughter. Her study of emotional patterning in the community reveals much about Utku interaction between women and men in social settings and in the family.

130. Bronson, Ruth Muskrat. *Indians Are People Too*. New York: Friendship Press, 1944.

Discussion of reservation life, values, family, education and Indian leadership in the first half of the twentieth century by a Cherokee woman.

131. Brown, Jennifer S. *Strangers in Blood*. Vancouver: University of British Columbia Press, 1980.

In the chapter "North West Company Men and Native Women," Brown contrasts the North West Company's policies and practices toward Indian women with those of the French fur traders and with the Hudson's Bay Company from the 1700s to the early 1800s, noting the company instituted fairly strict protection policies in order to halt trafficking in Native women and to establish stable family units in trapping outposts throughout Canada.

132. Brown, Jennifer S. "Woman as Centre and Symbol in the Emergence of Metis Communities." *Canadian Journal of Native Studies* 3 (1983): 39-46.

This study suggests that Metis life was characterized by matriorganization with daughters more likely to remain in and marry in the West and contribute to the Metis population growth during the nineteenth century. More detailed family histories are called for to trace the changing nature of relationships of Metis women to traders through generations from the seventeenth through nineteenth centuries.

133. Brown, Judith K. "A Cross-Cultural Study of Female Initiation Rites." *American Anthropologist* 65, 4 (August 1963): 837-53.

In this study of fifty-five areas of the world, one hundred societies, thirteen in North America, are examined. Discusses the decline of traditional modes of disciplining children and the rise of delinquent behavior resulting from poorly defined roles within the modern family and marital instability. Revision of male and female role behavior is posited as a solution.

134. Brown, Judith K. "Iroquois Women: An Ethnohistoric Note." In
     Toward an Anthropology of Women. Rayna R. Reiter, ed. New
     York: Monthly Review Press, 1975, 235-51.

     This essay, based on examination of the food production and
     distribution activities of Iroquois women, argues that their
     powerful position in tribal political institutions is the result of
     their control of the economic organization of the tribe and
     ultimately of the wealth of the tribe.

135. Buchanan, Kimberly Moore. *Apache Women Warriors*. El Paso:
     Texas Western Press, 1986.

     Accounts of Apache wives and women who have chosen
     alternative gender roles and who earned status as warriors.
     Lozen, "The Woman Warrior," joined Geronimo's band, as did
     Dahteste, a Chiricahua Apache woman married to an Apache
     warrior. Lozen was the only known unmarried Apache woman
     warrior. The book ends with a summary of other women
     warriors.

136. Buell, Crawford R. "The Navajo 'Long Walk': Recollections by
     Navajos." In *The Changing Ways of Southwest Indians: A
     Historic Perspective*. Albert H. Schroeder, ed. Glorieta, NM:
     Rio Grande Press, Inc., 1973, 171-88.

     A brief history of the capture of Navajos and their forced
     march and incarceration at Bosque Redondo is illustrated from
     translated statements of male and female survivors and
     descendants, among them several who were children at the time
     of the events and recall hardship, starvation, and disease.

137. Buffalohead, Priscilla K. "Farmers, Warriors, Traders; A Fresh
     Look at Ojibway Women." *Minnesota History* 48, 6 (Summer
     1983): 236-44.

     Indian cultures are traditionally less concerned with equality of
     the sexes and more with the inherent rights and dignity of the
     individual within the community. Ojibway women are discussed

as examples of the dimensions of women's status and the egalitarian nature of traditional tribal societies.

138. Burgesse, J. Allan. "The Woman and the Child Among the Lac-St.-Jean Montagnais." *Primitive Man* 17, 1 & 2 (January-April 1944): 1-18.

    Burgesse worked for the Hudson's Bay Company from 1930 to 1940. This article develops his impressions of the women of Lac-St.-Jean, Quebec, whom he viewed as dominant or equal to the men. He describes the children in terms of education--physical, mental, vocational, religious, and moral. His views of Indians are generally positive.

139. Butler, Anne M. "Military Myopia: Prostitution on the Frontier." *Prologue* 13, 4 (Winter 1981): 233-254.

    Documentary evidence proves that officers kept Indian women as mistresses, thus challenging the commonly held idea that only enlisted men consorted with Indian women.

140. Butterfield, Nancy. "Transcending the Stereotypes." *Many Smokes* 15, 2 (Fall 1981): 6-7.

    The Hollywood image of Indian women as drudges is countered by factual data on the rights and responsibilities and status of Indian women in traditional societies. Traditional roles are seen as the source of contemporary Indian women's roles today.

141. Byler, William. "Removing Children: The Destruction of American Indian Families." *Civil Rights Digest* 9, 4 (Summer 1977): 18-28.

    Indian children are placed in foster or adoptive homes at from five to one thousand times the rate of white children, and inadequate placement standards contribute to the already destructive pattern. Lack of the legal process makes Indian parents, particularly single mothers, vulnerable to this pattern

that creates identity confusion in children and grief on the part
of parents.

142. Campbell, Marjorie Wilkins. "Her Ladyship, My Squaw." *The
     Beaver* 285 (September 1954): 14-17.

     Discusses the role Native women played in the seventeenth and
     eighteenth century Canadian fur trade, using evidence from male
     fur traders.

143. Carr, Lucien. "On the Social and Political Position of Women
     among the Huron Iroquois Tribes." In *16th Annual Report of
     the Peabody Museum of American Archaeology and
     Ethnography.* Cambridge: Harvard University Press, 1884,
     207-32.

     This is an interesting but dated view of Indian women. Many
     later sources rely on this interpretation of women's roles.

144. Carr, Malcolm, Katherine Spencer, and Dorianne Wooley.
     "Navaho Clans and Marriage at Pueblo Alto." *American
     Anthropologist* n.s. 41, 2 (April-June 1939): 245-57.

     Study of Navajo clans in northwestern New Mexico with focus
     on marriage prohibitions and preferences. Data show the rule of
     clan exogamy is followed and clan marriage affiliations depend on
     kinship and family relationships. Tendency is for siblings to marry
     other groups of siblings and for second wives to be chosen from
     the same clan as the first wife.

145. Cartwright, Willena D. "A Washo Girl's Puberty Ceremony."
     Proceedings of the International Congress of Americanists 30
     (1952): 136-42.

     Cartwright relates a description of a Washo puberty ceremony
     told to her by a woman who taught school in a small Washo
     community in 1929, and who refers to the ritual as a "fire dance."
     Comparisons with puberty ceremonies of California coastal tribes
     and other Nevada tribes are included in the analysis of the
     ceremony.

146. Castellano, Marlene Brant. "Women in Huron and Ojibwa Societies." *Canadian Woman Studies* 10, 2 & 3 (Summer/Fall 1989): 45-48.

Historical account of the roles Huron and Ojibwa women played in their traditional societies and explanation of how their roles have influenced contemporary Indian women.

147. Christensen, Rosemary A. "Indian Women: An Historical and Personal Perspective." *Pupil Personnel Services* 4 (July 1975): 12-22.

Christensen begins by pointing out that the first Anishinabe created by Gitchee Manitou was a woman and discusses the roles of Indian women, the differences between Indian and white women in relation to the women's movement, and the literary views of Indian women. "Accounts of Indian women are based on the biased and one-sided views of . . . the trader, the missionary, and the anthropologist," she says.

148. Churchill, Claire Warner. *Slave Wives of Nehalem*. Portland, OR: Metropolitan Press, 1933.

Author's aim is to reconstruct, from records of explorers, ethnologists, and historians, the daily lives of captured women in tribes on the north Oregon coast. Plots are fictional and romanticized; end notes amplify cultural data in stories with direct quotations from sources on Nehalem, Clatsop, Tillamook, and Nestucca tribal customs.

149. Clark, LaVerne Harvell. "The Girl's Puberty Ceremony of the San Carlos Apache." *Journal of Popular Culture* 10, 2 (1976): 431-48.

Description of events, ceremonial clothing and objects, ritual participants, and mythic sources of the coming out of an Apache girl, usually referred to as "The Gift of Changing Woman." Includes 24 photos of the nine-day ceremony.

150. Coltelli, Laura, ed. "The American Indian Today." *Storia Nordamericana* 5, 1 (1988).

   This special issue focuses on Indian issues. Although no article deals specifically with American Indian women, the articles on the census and history provide important background information on social and cultural contexts of Indian experience.

151. Colton, Mary Russell F. with Edmund Nequatewa. "Hopi Courtship and Marriage, Second Mesa." *Museum Notes* 5, 9 (March 1933): 41-54.

   Hopi traditional courtship is discussed with a detailed description of the marriage ceremony including the wearing of wedding robes, grinding of corn, and hair washing ritual which takes place during the four days of the ceremony. Includes discussion of bride's appearance in her wedding robes from the wedding to her burial in them.

152. Condit, James H. "Woman's Place in Alaska's Development." *Women and Missions* 9 (October 1926): 257-59, 265.

   This is basically a religious tract arguing that the missionaries in Alaska have improved the lot of Indian women. Christian women saw it as their mission "to rescue Native women."

153. Cook, Katsi. "The Woman's Dance: Reclaiming Our Powers on the Female Side of Life." *Native Self-Sufficiency* 6 (1981): 17-19.

   Dance and ceremony are used as metaphors for women's culture, power, relationship to seasonal cycles, health and purification, and general well-being. They reassert traditional values and channels of power in the modern world.

154. Cook, Sherburne F. "The Conflict Between the California Indians and White Civilization: IV. Trends in Marriage and Divorce Since 1850." *Ibero-Americana* 24. Berkeley: University of California Press, 1943.

In this study of Indian marriages and separations, the author cites several case studies which demonstrate the varieties of interpretation of these unions and dissolutions based on whether the marriages were "legal" or "Indian fashion."

155. Cruikshank, Julie. "Becoming a Woman in Athapaskan Society: Changing Traditions on the Upper Yukon River." *Western Canadian Journal of Anthropology* 5, 2 (1975): 1-14.

The disappearance of the traditional female puberty ritual symbolizes a breakdown in society including the loss of skills, values, and discipline learned in the ceremony as well as longevity, toughness, other characteristics of a good life, and the bonding established among women during the ceremonial period. Younger women are deprived of a clear-cut transition from childhood to womanhood, thus creating an extended adolescence.

156. Cruikshank, Julie. "Native Women in the North: An Expanding Role." *North/Nord* 18 (November-December, 1971): 1-7.

Discusses the role of Canadian Indian men and women, the laws which affect Indian women, and women's role in the family as well as at work and in politics.

157. Damas, David. "Demographic Aspects of Central Eskimo Marriage Practices." *American Ethnologist* 2, 3 (August 1975): 409-18.

Marriage among Iqlulik, Netsilik, and Copper Eskimos is related to subsistence and historical factors. Wealth and mobility are seen as assets in the search for marriageable women.

158. De Laguna, Frederica. "Matrilineal Kin Groups in Northwestern North America." In *Proceedings: Northern Athapaskan Conference, 1971.* Vol. 1. A. McFadyen Clark, ed. Ottawa: National Museum of Man Mercury Series, Canadian Ethnology Science Paper No. 27, 1975, 17-145.

There are several theories about the origin of matriliny in the interior of Alaska and Yukon Territory and on the Northwest

Coast. De Laguna reviews six groups of tribes, emphasizing the sib names, crests, and traditions.

159. Devens, Carol. "Separate Confrontations: Gender as a Factor in Indian Adaptation to European Colonization in New France." *American Quarterly* 38, 3 (1986): 461-80.

When the French colonized American Indian lands, they found tribes with systems of balanced gender roles which puzzled and horrified them. When they tried to impose European values and roles upon these tribes, women were significantly less receptive than men because Christian gender patterns increased their work loads and severely undermined their control of production and distribution, and thus eroded their basis for power within their communities. In many cases tribal women in "New France" put up fierce resistance to the imposition of social patterns that deprived them of autonomy and authority; women's adherence to traditional ways strengthened as contact with missionaries and traders continued.

160. Downs, James F. "The Cowboy and the Lady: Models as a Determinant of the Rate of Acculturation among the Pinon Navajo." In *Native Americans Today: Sociological Perspectives*. Howard M. Bahr, Bruce A. Chadwick, and Robert C. Day, eds. New York: Harper and Row, 1972, 257-90.

Downs discusses traditional behavior of Navajo women. The author sees the American myth of the cowboy as offering the Navajo male a culturally acceptable model for individual action, but does not offer Navajo females a model. Navajo females are prevented from fulfillment of aspirations for personal action because they lack even a borrowed model for non-traditional domestic roles or are censured for emulating white female behavior and may even be forced to leave the community.

161. Driver, Harold E. "Culture Element Distributions: Sixteen Girls' Puberty Rites in Western North America." In *Comparative Studies by Harold E. Driver & Essays in His Honor*. New Haven: Human Relations Area Files Press, 1974, 149-76.

Discussion of common elements of puberty rituals in Pacific, Plateau, Great Basin, Yuman, Pueblo, Athabaskan, and California tribes. Focus on the correlation of ritual factors to regional environments and languages, discussion of recent ritual modification. Study is based on quantitative data.

162. Driver, Harold E. "Girls' Puberty Rites and Matrilocal Residence." *American Anthropologist* 71 (October 1969): 905-08.

    Challenges the view that matrilocal residence causes girls' puberty rites to be part of the culture. Author sees agriculturally based residence as post-dating the establishment of female puberty rites which occur in hunter/gatherer and fishing societies throughout North America twenty times more frequently than in farming societies.

163. Driver, Harold E. "Girls' Puberty Rites in Western North America." *Publications in Anthropological Records* 6, 2 (1941): 21-90.

    This is a comparative study of puberty rites among tribes of California and the Athabaskan southwest. Driver includes tables showing distribution of traits and relationships of traits to elements such as language and geography.

164. Driver, Harold E. "Reply to Opler on Apachean Subsistence, Residence, and Girls' Puberty Rites." *American Anthropologist* 74 (October 1972): 1147-51.

    In this article Driver responds to Morris E. Opler's article in the same volume. Author claims Apache matrilocality derives from contact with agricultural-dominated Plains tribes, not Pueblo influence.

165. Dubois, Cora and Dorothy Demetracopoulou. "Wintu Myths." *University of California Publications in American Archaeology and Ethnology* no. 28. Berkeley: University of California, 1931.

    Jenny Curl and Jo Bender are the narrators of traditional stories.

166.   Eastman, Elaine Goodale. "Indian Women at Home." *Indian's Friend* 8, 7 (March 1896): 9-10.

Though Indian women spend the greater part of their lives serving their families, as grandmothers they wield great power in the community which the author sees as detrimental to the "civilization" of tribal people. The grandmother becomes adamantly suspicious of white ways, thus retarding "progress." The author sees it as essential to work with and through women to influence Indian men toward assimilation.

167.   Etienne, Mona and Eleanor Leacock, eds. *Women and Colonization: Anthropological Perspectives*. New York: Praeger, 1980.

This collection of essays contains four essays on North American Indian women, particularly on Eastern tribes--Seneca, Algonkion, Montagnais--focusing on assimilation effects, trade, and resistance to colonization.

168.   Evans, Susan M. *Born For Liberty: A History of Women in America*. New York: The Free Press, 1989.

One chapter is primarily based on Iroquois material and characterizes Indian women as gatherers, nurturers, traders and shamans. The author sees their power as "rooted in kinship relations and economics." Misperceptions by colonists are addressed, and the stereotyping of Indian women as slaves and drudges is explained as the result of whites' "obliviousness to the realities of gender in Indian societies." The author omits all Indian women from 1700 onward.

169.   Ewers, John C. "Deadlier than the Male." *American Heritage* 16 (1965): 10-13.

Four Indian women's stories are given: Other Magpie, Woman Chief, Throwing Down, Running Eagle. The stories are about their exploits as warriors, not complete biographical accounts.

170. Ewers, John C. "Mothers of the Mixed-Bloods: The Marginal Woman in the History of the Upper Missouri." In *Probing the American West*. Kenneth Ross Toole, ed. Santa Fe: Museum of New Mexico, 1962, 62-70.

    Ewers here assumes the duties of women to be inferior; he ignores the division of labor as part of a culture.

171. Farrer, Claire. "Singing for Life: The Mescalero Apache Girls' Puberty Ceremonies." In *Southwest Indian Ritual Drama*. Charlotte J. Frisbie, ed. Albuquerque: University of New Mexico Press, 1980, 125-59.

    Farrer describes the history and meaning of the annual event which celebrates the initial menses of girls in the tribe. Details and photographs of the ritual drama are included along with the mythic origins.

172. Fedorick, Joy Asham. "Mother Tongue: Aboriginal Cultures and Languages." *Canadian Woman Studies* 10, 2 & 3(Summer/Fall 1989): 69-71.

    Language and culture are being maintained through stories and projects which use modern technology to continue the literary voice of Native people.

173. Fiske, Shirley. "Rules of Address: Navajo Women in Los Angeles." *Journal of Anthropological Research* 34 (1978): 72-91.

    Using urban Navajo women as the subjects for research, the author explores what a Navajo must know about the social class, occupation, gender, education and communication situations in order to address people appropriately. Data indicates Navajo women are more formal with Anglos and older Indians, and personal name avoidance is maintained.

174. Flannery, Regina. "The Position of Woman among the Eastern Cree." *Primitive Man* 8 (1935): 81-86.

Flannery's research on the women in the James Bay region of Canada during the 1930s documented economic, socio-domestic, political, and magico-religious culture. Flannery concludes that the status of Cree women is fairly high compared with marginal peoples in other parts of the world.

175. Flannery, Regina. "The Position of Women among the Mescalero Apache." *Primitive Man* 5 (April-July 1932): 26-32.

Discusses arranged marriages as well as economic, social, and religious lives of Mescalero Apache women.

176. Fleming, E. McClung. "Symbols of the U.S. from Indian Queen to Uncle Sam." In *Frontiers of American Culture*. Ray B. Browne, ed. Lafayette, IN: Purdue University Press, 1968, 1-24.

The first part of the chapter discusses the use of the Indian woman to represent America. The Indian princess image began in the 1760s and lasted into the nineteenth century.

177. Fletcher, Alice. "The Indian Woman and Her Problem." *Southern Workman* 28 (1899): 172-76.

While traditional Indian women's lives were filled with hardship, their industries were essential and exalted, ceremonially confirming their position of honor. Turn-of-the-century women, however, no longer have arenas to maintain their honored status, having been relegated to domestic work and deprived of their right to own property. Most importantly, Christian teachings, which identify woman as the source of evil and sin, have belittled and tainted Indian women's character unjustly.

178. Foote, Cheryl J. and Sandra K. Schackel. "Indian Women of New Mexico." In *New Mexico Women: Intercultural Perspectives*. Joan M. Jensen and Darlis A. Miller, eds. Albuquerque: University of New Mexico Press, 1986, 17-40.

The arrival of the first Spanish in 1535 changed life for Indian women. The Spanish considered the Indians a labor force and souls to be saved. Indian women were used as interpreters, domestics and were often sexually abused.

179. French, Laurence. "Social Problems Among Cherokee Females: A Study of Cultural Ambivalence and Role Identity." *American Journal of Psychoanalysis* 36, 2 (Summer 1976): 163-69.

Women are viewed as more likely than men to be involved in social problems because they have a disproportionately high representation in the Cherokee population; they are often victims of male violence. Because they are the major socializing agent of children they are directly involved with problematic children. The breakdown of the traditional Cherokee harmony ethic under the dominance of white society is seen as the cause of the deterioration of women's status and their current state of dependence and vulnerability.

180. Friedl, Ernestine. *Women and Men: An Anthropologist's View*. New York: Holt, Rinehart and Winston, 1975.

A study of food production, trading, ritual, political, kinship and marriage property, child rearing, residency and age roles in African and North American tribal cultures with particular attention to Eskimos and Washo tribes in North America.

181. Frisbie, Charlotte J. *Kinaalda: A Study of the Navajo Girl's Puberty Ceremony*. Middletown, CT: Wesleyan University Press, 1967.

Frisbie provides a record of four ceremonial days--what happens and why. The ceremony is part of the Blessing Way and marks the young woman's entry into adulthood through recreation of a tribal creation myth.

182. Frisbie, Charlotte J. "Traditional Navajo Women: Ethnographic and Life History Portrayals." *American Indian Quarterly* 6, 1-2 (Spring-Summer 1982): 11-33.

Frisbie analyzes ten basic enthnographies and fourteen published life histories of Navajo men and women to reach conclusions about the lives of Navajo women prior to World War II.

183. Gaber, Clark M. "Eskimo Infanticide." *The Scientific Monthly* 64 (1947): 98-102.

Author discusses the practice of infanticide by Yukon and Malamute Eskimos as a response to economic hardship and famine, noting that infanticide is performed by the mother, usually on female babies, deformed newborns, or twins, and sometimes on illegitimate babies, though there is little community censure of girls who bear children out of wedlock. Abortion is not a common practice. Tone of article is extremely ethnocentric.

184. Garbarino, Merwyn S. *Big Cypress, A Changing Seminole Community.* New York: Holt, Rinehart and Winston, 1972.

This is a general study of the Seminoles; it includes a section on social organization that deals in part with women's roles as they have been influenced by changes in tribal economics, education, and social structures.

185. Garbarino, Merwyn S. "Life in the City: Chicago." In *The American Indian in Urban Society.* Jack O. Wadell and O. Michael Watson, eds. Boston: Little, Brown, and Co., 1971, 168-205.

This study includes statements by both male and female American Indians living in Chicago. They talk of housing, education, children, family relationships, and Indian identity.

186. Giles, Albert S., Sr. "Polygamy in Comanche Country." *Southwest Review* 51, 3 (Summer 1966): 286-97.

An undocumented and sexist account of Comanche polygamy as the author observed the practice as a turn-of-the-century trader in Oklahoma.

187. Goddard, Pliny Earle. "Hupa Texts." *University of California Publications in American Archaeology and Ethnology* 1, 2 (1904). Berkeley: University of California Texts, 1904.

Informant Emma Lewis (1901) provides information on Hopi life and stories.

188. Goldenweiser, A. A. "Functions of Women in Iroquois Society." *American Anthropologist* 17 (1915): 376-77.

This account of the minutes of a 1914 meeting reviews the paper presented by Goldenweiser on Iroquois women and their power within the tribe. He believes that the status of women in "primitive societies" is higher than that in other cultures.

189. Gonzalez, Ellice B. *Changing Economic Roles for Micmac Men and Women: An Ethnohistorical Analysis.* Canadian Ethnology Service Mercury Series No. 72. Ottawa: National Museums of Man, 1981.

Study of the changing roles of Micmac male and female roles in Nova Scotia over a 400-year period of increasing European influence.

190. Goudy, Irene. "Yakimas." In *An American Indian Anthology.* Benet Tvedten, ed. Marvin, SD: Blue Cloud Abbey 1971, 63-65.

An account of the Cherokee Green Corn Dance, which is no longer performed as it was a century ago, is discussed by a Cherokee woman.

191. Graham, Jessica D. (Schultz). "In the Lodge of a Matokiks: The Women's Buffalo Society of the Blood Indians." In *Lifeways of Intermontane and Plains Montana Indians.* Leslie B. Davis, ed. Bozeman: Montana State University, 1979.

The author became the first non-Indian member of the Women's Buffalo Society in 1931. She was first accepted by the Blood Indians of Canada. This is an account of the first ceremony in which she participated.

192. Green, Rayna. "Native American Women: Review Essay." *Signs* 6 (Winter 1980): 248-67.

     Green discusses the scholarship and popular literature written about American Indian women since the seventeenth century in the United States and Canada. She organizes the material chronologically, enabling readers to understand the various trends and cycles of interest in Indian women's lives.

193. Griffen, Joyce. "Life is Harder Here: The Case of the Urban Navajo Woman." *American Indian Quarterly* 6, 1-2 (1982): 90-104.

     Based on field research and interviews, this study examines the lives of twenty-two Navajo women in Flagstaff, Arizona, their ties with their families on the reservation, and the role religion plays in their lives.

194. Griffin, Naomi Musmaker. *The Roles of Men and Women in Eskimo Culture*. Chicago: University of Chicago Press, 1930.

     Discusses roles and division of labor. Includes chart of activities indicating whether men or women participate.

195. Grinnell, George Bird. "Cheyenne Woman Customs." *American Anthropologist*, n.s. 4 (January-March 1902): 13-16.

     Customs associated with puberty and childbirth were communicated to Grinnell by older Cheyenne women who recall traditional life before the reservation period.

196. Grumet, Robert Steven. "Sunksquaws, Shamans, and Tradeswomen: Middle Atlantic Coastal Algonquin Women During the 17th and 18th Centuries." In *Women and Colonization: Anthropological Perspectives*. Mona Etienne and Eleanor Leacock, eds. New York: Praeger Publishers, 1980, 43-62.

     Analysis of adaptive strategies of tribal women in one of the first tribes to have extensive contact with European colonies with focus on women's powerful roles in political, spiritual, and economic leadership.

197. Guemple, Lee. "Men and Women, Husbands and Wives: The Role of Gender in Traditional Inuit Society." *Inuit Studies* 10, 1-2 (1986): 9-24.

Relationships between spouses among Belcher Island Inuit people in light of gender and tasks assigned to both men and women.

198. Haas, Mary R. "Men's and Women's Speech in Koasati." In *Language in Culture and Society*. Dell Hymes, ed. New York: Harper and Row, 1964, 228-33.

Discusses male and female differences in vocabulary and pronunciation, noting that sex differentiation in language is not prevalent among young speakers who generally use male vocabulary, but that older women adhere to a female vocabulary.

199. Hagen, Cecil. "Liberated Women? Not Those Lewis and Clark Met on Their Way." *Pacific Northwesterner* 25, 2 (1981): 17-25.

Discusses the harsh realities of the lives of Indian women in the early nineteenth century based on information drawn from the journals of the Lewis and Clark Expedition.

200. Haile, Father Bernard, O.F.M. *Women Versus Men: A Conflict of Navajo Emergence*. Karl W. Luckert, ed. Lincoln: University of Nebraska Press, 1981.

Focusing on the separation of the sexes and the ensuing reconciliation, this text looks at the theme of gender role definition in the origin myth of the Dine people.

201. Hallowell, A. Irving. "Shabwam: A Dissocial Indian Girl." *American Journal of Orthopsychiatry* 8 (April 1938): 329-40.

Interesting account of a young girl who was presumed "crazy" by the tribe and of her subsequent interaction with the author.

The article includes comments about the attitudes toward women and girls in Ojibwa culture. Shabwam was a Saulteaux Indian living east of Lake Winnipeg.

202. Hammond, Dorothy and Alta Jablow. *Women in Cultures of the World*. Menlo Park, CA: Cummings Publishing Company, 1976.

Using a cross-cultural approach, the authors attempt to balance male-based ethnography by analyzing not only the institutional framework of women's roles but the qualitative aspects of women's lives. Study draws data from numerous North American Indian tribes, including Apache, Blackfoot, Cheyenne, Crow, Sioux, Pawnee, Cree, Eskimo, Iroquois, Lummi, Salish, Menomini, Winnebago, Ojibwa, Mojave, Papago, Pomo, and Washo.

203. Hanasy, Laila Shukry. "The Role of Women in a Changing Navajo Society." *American Anthropologist* 59 (February 1957): 101-11.

This study done in New Mexico during 1951-52 suggests that women's roles have been adversely affected by recent social and economic changes.

204. Hansen, Chadwick. "The Metamorphosis of Tituba, or Why American Intellectuals Can't Tell an Indian Witch from a Negro." *New England Quarterly* 47 (1974): 3-12.

Tituba, an important figure in the Salem witch trials, was actually a Carib Indian, though she is usually represented in literature and drama as practicing medicine and magic derived from African sources; historians have thus been misled by their lack of rigorous scholarship to misidentify Tituba as an African.

205. Hanson, Wynne. "The Urban Indian Woman and Her Family." *Social Casework: The Journal of Contemporary Social Work* 61, 8 (October 1980): 476-83.

This is a series of vignettes which demonstrates the difficulty Indian women have adapting to the changes from homemaker to workers in the city. After a brief historical account of the roles of Indian women, the author presents five cases of successful adjustment to urban areas. All have responded positively to external threats to Indian survival.

206. Hartland, Sidney. "Matrilineal Kinship, and the Question of its Priority." *Memoirs of the American Anthropological Association* 4 (1917): 1-87.

   This cross-cultural kinship study draws heavily from North American tribal societies. Author argues matrilineal kinship systems are an early pattern of social order in Algonquin and Siouan tribes and that radical social changes caused primarily by white, particularly missionary programs, resulted in a breakdown of traditional matrilineal kinship systems.

207. Hewitt, J. N. B. "Status of Women in Iroquois Polity Before 1784." *Smithsonian Annual Reports for the Year Ending 30 June 1932*. Washington, DC: Smithsonian Institute, 1933, 475-588.

   Discusses matrilineal features of Iroquois internal organization and kinship relations. Hewitt argues that "the life of a woman was regarded as of double value of that of a man to the community" and points to the change in the power of women as a result of white contact.

208. Hill, Jane H. and Rosinda Nolasquez. *Mulu'wetum: The First People, Cupeno Oral History and Language*. Banning, CA: Malki Museum Press, 1973.

   Recollections and stories of Cupeno people in both English and Cupeno narrated by Rosinda Nolasquez with interpretations by Jane Hill. Includes historical narratives, myths, and animal tales.

209. Hippler, Arthur E. "Additional Perspectives on Eskimo Female Infanticide." *American Anthropologist* 74 (October 1972): 1318-19.

   Discussion of female infanticide among the Netsilik Eskimos.

210. Hoffman, W. J. "The Mide'wiwin or 'Grand Medicine Society' of the Ojibwa." *Bureau of [American] Ethnology Report*, 1885-86. Washington, DC: Government Printing Office, 1891, 149-300.

Early source discussing the types of male and female participation in healing and ceremonies within the Mide'wiwin Society.

211. Honigmann, John J. *Culture and Ethos of Kaska Society*. Yale University Publications in Anthropology, no. 40. New Haven: Yale University Press, 1949.

This study of Dease Lake in British Columbia includes autobiographical sketches with Rorschach analysis, dream interpretation, and discussion in depth of Dorothy Plover's personality and life.

212. Howard, Oliver O. *My Life and Experiences among our Hostile Indians*. Hartford CT: A. T. Worthington, 1907. Rpt. New York: Da Capo Press, 1972.

In this autobiography of Oliver Howard, major general in the U.S. Army, he includes a chapter on "Squaw Men" and a chapter on Sarah Winnemucca. This book provides a military view of Indian women.

213. Hunter, Lois Marie. *The Shinnecock Indians*. Islip, NY: Buys Brothers, 1950.

One chapter, "Only a Squaw," tells of the role of women in Shinnecock culture.

214. Hurtado, Albert L. "Hardly a Farmhouse--A Kitchen Without Them: Indian and White Households in the California Frontier in 1860." *Western Historical Quarterly* 13 (July 1982): 245-70.

This essay examines the variety of household patterns in which Indians held roles as livestock hands, domestic servants, and spouses. The marriage of white men to Indian women and the removal of many Indians from tribal communities to white households had an effect on social and survival patterns. Individual survival was increased in white communities but social integration led to an overall decline in Native populations and breakdown in tribal organization.

215. Ingleis, Gordon R. "Northwest American Matriliny: The Problem of Origins." *Ethnology* 9, 2 (April 1970): 149-159.

The emergence and diffusion of matrilineal societies is traced from Pacific Northwest coastal areas inland. Residence is argued as the primary basis for matriliny; extreme localization, investment of labor and expectation of continued returns year after year, and detailed knowledge of local terrain are all essential for emergence of matriliny.

216. Jacobs, Melville. *Clackamas Chinook Texts*. Bloomington: Indiana University Research Center in Anthropology, Folklore and Linguistics, 1958.

The informant is Mrs. Victoria Howard of West Linn, Oregon. Information was gathered during the period 1929-30. Discusses traditional roles, many incorporating information on the roles and power of women in Chinook society.

217. Jacobs, Melville. "The Romantic Role of Older Women in a Culture of the Pacific Northwest Coast." *Kroeber Anthropology Society Papers* 18 (1958): 79-85.

Jacobs notes that while nubile women are powerless in Northwest coastal tribes, post-menstrual women have significant power and influence and are often portrayed as central figures in narratives.

218. Jaimes, Marie Annette. "Towards a New Image of American Indian Women: The Renewing Power of the Feminine." *Journal of American Indian Education* 22, 1 (October 1982): 18-32.

Jaimes draws on a number of sources to argue for American Indian women's power within Native societies to contradict misleading stereotypes of the squaw and princess.

219. Jake, Lucille, Evelyn James and Pamela Bunte. "The Southern
      Paiute Woman in a Changing Society." *Frontiers* 7, 1 (1983): 44-
      49.

      Two Southern Paiute women (Jake and James) worked with an
      anthropologist (Bunte) on an oral history project which included
      interviews with the two grandmothers. The women reminisced
      about growing up as Paiute women during times of incredible
      changes. Excerpts from the interviews are included.

220. James, George Wharton. "Types of Female Beauty Among the
      Indians of the Southwest." *Overland Monthly* 35, 207 (1900):
      195-209.

      Author argues against ethnocentric imposition of standards of
      beauty on tribal people, recommending interviewing men in a
      tribe to decide on traits of female beauty. Examples are primarily
      "Moki" (Hopi) and Havasupai.

221. Jamieson, Kathleen. "Sisters under the Skin: An Exploration of
      the Implication of Feminist Materialist Perspective Research."
      Canadian Ethnic Studies 13, 1 (1981): 130-43.

      Jamieson analyzes the position of Canadian Indian women
      from a feminist historical perspective. She argues that the social
      and economic positions of Indian women make them more like
      Indian men than like non-Indian women.

222. Jensen, Joan M. and Darlis A. Miller, eds. "Appendix A, Early
      Women in New Mexico." In *New Mexico Women: Intercultural
      Perspectives*. Albuquerque: University of New Mexico Press,
      1986.

      Brief discussion of pre-historic evidence of women's roles notes
      presence of Indian women as early as 12,000 years ago and traces
      evidence of introduction of weaving, corn production, and pottery
      as women's labor areas.

223. Kehoe, Alice B. "The Function of Ceremonial Sexual Intercourse Among the Northern Plains Indians." *Plains Anthropologist* 15, 48 (1970): 99-103.

   Anthropologist Kehoe briefly discusses ritual sexual intercourse and the power relationships between the participants.

224. Kehoe, Alice B. "Old Women Had Great Power." *The Western Canadian Journal of Anthropology* 6 (1976): 68-76.

   Essay examines the two arenas in which Blackfoot women may act--secular and ritual. They gain the respected title, "Old Lady" by rising above domestic activities and entering into tribal ritual, thus gaining power to live long, to acquire wealth, and to enjoy unassailable personal autonomy. While Blackfoot women are recognized as the foundation of tribal society, women whose strength and ability take them beyond the domestic sphere may be publicly honored for their wisdom and as models of proper human life.

225. Keith, Anne B. "The Navajo Girls' Puberty Ceremony: Function and Meaning for the Adolescent." *El Palacio* 71, 1 (Spring 1964): 27-36.

   The Navajo Kinaalda ceremony bestows recognition of adulthood, and traditionally of marriageability, of a young girl and serves as a period of education for her in the ideal attributes of Navajo womanhood. Interpretation of the ceremony is based on interviews with participants and tribal members and includes statements regarding the association of good power and spirits with the girl and her community during and because of the correct performance of the ceremony.

226. Kidwell, Clara Sue. "American Indian Women: Problems Communicating a Cultural/Sexual Identity." *The Creative Woman* 2, 3 (Winter 1979): 33-38.

   Because of the women's liberation movement in mainstream American society, Indian women's roles continue to be viewed as confining and unrewarding because the roles of mother and wife are not highly valued in the dominant society. The misunderstanding of tribal role expectation serves as a barrier to cross-cultural communication and leads to inappropriate imposition of white values on tribal role identification and practices by outsiders. Indian women can benefit from informing people about the status women hold in their tribe and the falsity of widespread stereotypes.

227. Kidwell, Clara Sue. "The Power of Women in Three American Indian Societies." *Journal of Ethnic Studies* 6 (1979): 113-21.

In this study of Indian women's roles Kidwell discusses Ojibwa, Winnebago, and Menominee cultures.

228. Kidwell, Clara Sue. "Power of Women in Three American Indian Societies." In *Looking Back at "A Second Look at a Second Sex."* Berkeley, CA: Women's Center, 1980, 86-95.

Discussion of traditional attitudes and values of Menominee, Ojibwa, and Winnebago, all patrilineal societies in which women's roles are nevertheless essential. Three female anthropologists who studied these tribes--Nancy Lurie (Winnebago), Louise Spindler (Menominee) and Ruth Landes (Ojibwa)--have provided important data on women's roles.

229. Kidwell, Clara Sue. [Review of *Bright Eyes: The Story of Susette LaFlesche, an Omaha Indian* by Dorothy Clarke Wilson]. *Journal of Ethnic Studies* 2 (Winter 1975): 118-22.

Although this is primarily a book review, Kidwell places emphasis on the roles of Indian women.

230. Kimball, Geoffrey. "Men's and Women's Speech in Koasati: A Reappraisal." *International Journal of American Linguistics* 53 (January 1987): 30-38.

Kimball challenges Haas's statement that only middle aged women use the female form of the language; younger women use the male form now. He also challenges Booker's argument that male forms are more basic than female, noting that female male-language users produce it only in passing.

231. Klein, Laura. "Contending with Colonization: Tlingit Men and Women in Change." In *Women and Colonization: Anthropological Perspectives*. Mona Etienne and Eleanor Leacock, eds. New York: Praeger Publishers, 1980, 88-108.

Discussion of how tribal members dealt with fur traders, missionaries, and industrialists with emphasis on women's roles in providing continuity in culture by resisting Euro-American sex-role models.

232. Klein, Laura. "'She's One of Us, You Know': The Public Life of Tlingit Women: Traditional Historical and Contemporary Perspectives." *The Western Canadian Journal of Anthropology* 6 (1976): 164-83.

Traditional literature of the Tlingit shows that women, as well as men, engaged in fishing, trade, war, and prestige competition, and, in fact, the manipulation and accumulation of wealth was a recognized area of expertise for women. Missionary and contemporary influences have not succeeded in diminishing Tlingit women's power; rather, women have transformed their power to areas of craft production, wage work, athletic activities, and community politics, thus broadening their spheres of influence.

233. Kluckhohn, Clyde. "Navajo Women's Knowledge of Their Song Ceremonials." *El Palacio* 45 (November 23-39, December 7, 1938): 87-92.

Based on data collected from forty married and twenty unmarried Navajo women from the Ramah-Atargne area, Kluckhohn assesses the ceremonial knowledge of Navajo women as being correlated to their relationship to men who participate in ceremonies. No women singers or chanters were included in the interview group.

234. Kluckhohn, Clyde. "Navajo Women's Knowledge of Their Song Ceremonials." In *Culture and Behavior*. Richard Kluckhohn, ed. New York: Free Press, 1962, 92-96.

This study showed Navaho women had little knowledge of ceremonies; there were no women singers or curers in the group interviewed.

235. Kroeber, Alfred L. *Handbook of Indians of California*. Washington, DC: U. S. Government Printing Office. Bureau of American Ethnology Bulletin 78, 1925, 63-66.

Included in a short report on the stages a woman goes through to become a shaman is an anonymous personal narrative of a Yurok woman who experienced the process of purification, fasting, dreaming, dancing, and prayer to achieve curing power. The narrative is brief and used to support ethnographic analysis of Yurok religion.

236. Kroeber, Alfred L. "Luiseno Indian Girls in Southern California." *American Anthropologist* n.s., 8 (1906): 31-32.

Brief discussion of how Luiseno female puberty rites differ from Yaman rites.

237. Kunitz, Stephen J. and John C. Slocomb. "The Changing Sex Ratio of the Navajo Tribe." *Social Biology* 23, 1 (Spring 1976): 33-44.

Since the 1940s the ratio of the Navajo Tribe has shifted and there are now more women than men because of declining maternal mortality rates, increasing male mortality rates, and greater out-migration of men than women. The author examines the social and economic consequences of these shifts.

238. LaDuke, Winona. "In Honor of Women Warriors." *off our backs* 11 (February 1981): 3-4.

Anishinabe woman discusses problems facing contemporary Indian women and the historical antecedents of the problems.

239. LaDuke, Winona. "Words from the Indigenous Women's Network Meeting." *Akwesasne Notes* 17, 6 (Winter 1985): 8-10.

   In September of 1985 the Indigenous Women's Network met at Yelm, Washington. This article is a summary of the meeting highlighting issues such as domestic violence, support groups and spiritualism.

240. LaFlesche, Francis. "Osage Marriage Customs." *American Anthropologist*, n.s. 14 (January-March 1912): 127-30.

   Three forms of marriage customs are recorded: traditional first marriage between young men and women negotiated by parents of both families; marriage to a widow in which the woman is approached directly; and secret cohabitation, which is seen as a deliberate disregard for tribal custom; children born to such a union are not considered tribal members.

241. LaFlesche, Suzette. "The Indian Question." *Christian Union* 21, 100 (March 10, 1880): 222-23.

   In this early publication by Suzette LaFlesche, she argues for Indian citizenship and recognition that the American Indian is not a child.

242. Latta, F. F. *Handbook of the Yokuts Indians*. Oildale, CA: Bear State Books, 1949.

   Latta collected information about the San Joaquin Valley Indians from aged Indians and pioneer whites who remembered the "old ways." The volume ends with a lengthy account by Yoi'mut, the last full-blood survivor of the Chunut tribe. She was the historian of her tribe and provided a full account of her life. Yoi'mut died in 1933.

243. Lavalee, Mary Ann. "Yesterday's Indian Women: The Role of Native Women, Past, Present, Future." *Tawow* 1 (Spring 1970): 7.

This is a tribute to the figure of the grandmother in Indian cultures as a model of generosity, strength and continuity.

244. Leacock, Eleanor. "The Changing Family and Levi-Strauss, or Whatever Happened to Fathers?" *Social Research* 44, 2 (Summer 1977): 235-59.

Levi-Strauss ignored the economic reciprocity of earlier societies, particularly Indian societies such as the Iroquois, Cherokee and Wyandot.

245. Leacock, Eleanor. "Matrilocality in a Simple Hunting Economy (Montagnais-Naskapi)." *Southwestern Journal of Anthropology* 11 (Spring 1955): 31-47.

Examples indicate the post-marital residence is determined by women and based on maintaining loving and compatible working groups. Constant movement from band to band is so frequent that patri- or matrilocality does not apply with any consistency, though contemporary trends favor patrilocality while matrilocality dominated in the past; the change is attributable to the greater contribution of male labor in modern times.

246. Leacock, Eleanor. "Montagnais Women and the Jesuit Program for Colonization." In *Women and Colonization: Anthropological Perspectives*. New York: Praeger Publishers, 1980, 25-42.

Studies Jesuit records of Montagnais-Naskapi women's relations to husband and family, work patterns, influence in decision making, changes imposed by missionaries.

247. Leacock, Eleanor. "Women's Status in Egalitarian Society: Implications of Social Evolution." *Current Anthropology* 19 (1978): 247-76.

Traces the change from egalitarian status of women in pre-contact period through the transition to male dominance as the result of the imposition of European economic systems, arguing the oppression of women and reduction of their spheres of activities was caused by complex changes from production for consumption to production of commodities for exchange. Study is based on African, Australian and North American tribal groups.

248. Leacock, Eleanor, and Jacqueline Goodman. "Montagnais Marriage and the Jesuits in the Seventeenth Century: Incidents from the Relation of Paul Le Jeune." *The Western Canadian Journal of Anthropology* 6, 3 (1976): 77-91.

Seventeenth century Jesuit records indicate that among the Montagnais, mature adults of both sexes made decisions about their own lives and activities and women had great power, particularly in food distribution. Jesuits, with their concern for instilling obedience to authority, were committed to destroying the personal autonomy ethic of Native societies and focused on subordination of women to effect a hierarchical system.

249. Lefley, Harriet. "Acculturation, Child Rearing, and Self-Esteem in Two North American Indian Tribes." *Ethos* 4, 3 (Fall 1976): 385-401.

Deals with Mikasuki Seminole of Florida and focuses on the level of positive self-concept or self-esteem of the individuals studied. Mothers and children were studied and the findings were compared with previous studies which demonstrate a relationship between maternal self-esteem and the self-esteem of male and female children.

250. Leighton, Dorthea C. "As I Knew Them: Navajo Women in 1940." *American Indian Quarterly* 6, 1-2 (1982): 43-51.

Leighton reveals the knowledge about women's roles which she gained during five months on the Navajo Reservation. She provides several personal accounts by Navajo women which demonstrate their independence and self-reliance.

251. Lewis, Ann. "Separate Yet Sharing." *Conservationist* 30 (January-February 1976): 17.

This brief summary of the historical and contemporary roles of Iroquois women shows their power within the tribe.

252. Lewis, Claudia. *Indian Families of the Northwest Coast: The Impact of Change.* Chicago: University of Chicago Press, 1970.

This is a study of a Northwest coast Indian community with information on the roles of women, marriage, and the future of the community.

253. Lewis, Oscar. "Manly-Hearted Women Among the Northern Piegan." *American Anthropologist* 43, 1 (January-March 1941): 173-87.

A discussion of characteristics of a female personality type among the Blackfoot describes the manly-hearted woman as excelling in both women's and men's work; economically self-sufficient or holding favorite wife status; demonstrating assertive public behavior, freedom of movement, and social interaction; showing sexual assertiveness; making claims of superior virtue; and having central roles in ceremonies. Manly-heartedness may be achieved at any point in a woman's adult life and such women are both envied and feared by other members of the society.

254. Liberty, Margot. "Hell Came With Horses: Plains Indian Women in the Equestrian Era." *Montana, the Magazine of Western History* 32, 3 (Summer 1982): 10-19.

This essay explores the erosion of women's power in Plains society as a result of the introduction of the horse and the decline in women's roles as major food providers. It also traces the increase of women's power following military defeat of tribes and confinement on reservations.

255. Liberty, Margot. "Plains Indian Women Through Time: A Preliminary Overview." *Lifeways of Intermontane and Plains Indians.* Leslie B. Davis, ed. Bozeman: Montana State University, 1979, 137-50.

Liberty evaluates the changing roles of Plains Indian women through time beginning with a generalized description of the Plains environment and tracing women's status in economics, politics, religion, and personal autonomy. As tribes moved from horticultural to equestrian lifeways, the personal autonomy of Plains women declined.

256. Lincoln, Bruce. "Women's Initiation Among the Navajo: Myth, Rite and Meaning." *Paideuma* [West Germany] 23 (1977): 255-63.

    Sees the Navajo female initiation rite as a rebirth into womanhood and attainment of promised reproductive power through re-enactment of the Changing Woman myth.

257. Lowie, Robert H. "Marriage and Family Life Among the Plains Indians." *Scientific Monthly* 34 (January-June 1932): 462-64.

    Lowie describes the gender roles of Plains Indians by analogy to gender practices in Victorian England, noting failure of women to live up to ideals of modesty and virtue did not result in becoming outcast but did bring loss of prestige and exclusion from certain ceremonies. Lowie also explains polygamous marriage was no disgrace for women and argues against squaw stereotypes noting women's work was continuous and men's less regular but more arduous. Essay is clearly written to popular audience to correct misconceptions and "savage" stereotypes.

258. Lowie, Robert H. "The Matrilineal Complex." *University of California Publications in American Archaeology and Ethnology* 16 (1919-20): 29-45.

    Lowie provides a detailed account of terminology and practice in matrilineal societies.

259. Luchitti, Cathy, in collaboration with Carol Olwell. *Women of the West*. St. George, UT: Antelope Island Press, 1982.

Includes a brief section on the contribution of Indian women to the exploration and cultural traditions of the Western United States.

260. Lurie, Nancy Oestreich. "Indian Women: A Legacy of Freedom." In *Look to the Mountaintop.* Robert Iacopi, ed. San Jose: Gousha Publications, 1972, 29-36.

Lurie discusses some of the myths and legends about Pocahontas, stereotypes of Indian women, women's roles in tribal organization, and contemporary Indian women.

261. Lurie, Nancy Oestreich. "A Papago Woman and a Woman Anthropologist." *Reviews in Anthropology* 7 (Winter 1980): 120.

Lurie discusses the relationship of Ruth Underhill and Papago Maria Chona and the compiling of Chona's autobiography.

262. Manitonquat (Medicine Story). "Daughters of Creation." *Many Smokes* 15, 2 (Fall 1981): 16-19.

Women are seen, by this male author, as the best teachers and guides because of their relation to the creative forces of nature. He points out that Indian peoples particularly honor the roles of women and describes traditional tribal life as a model for harmony which contrasts with the oppressive imbalance of contemporary life.

263. Margolin, Malcolm, ed. *The Way We Lived: California Indian Reminiscences, Stories and Songs.* Berkeley: Heyday Books, 1981.

In this collection several women's views are presented, albeit in short excerpts from longer works. Of particular interest are the accounts about growing up, love and marriage.

264. Marriott, Alice, and Carol Rachlin. "Indians: 1966, Four Case Histories." *Southwest Review* 51 (Spring 1966): 149-60.

Written in a fictional style, these brief case histories trace the adjustment of Arapaho-Cheyennes to city life and their adaptations of traditions to a new environment. Two of the depictions focus on women.

265. Mason, J. Alden. *The Language of the Salinan Indians*. University of California Publications in American Archaeology and Ethnology, Vol. 14. Berkeley: University of California, 1918.

Informant Maria Ocarpia narrates a creation myth and animal stories for the purpose of grammatical study by Mason.

266. Mason, Otis. *Woman's Share in Primitive Culture*. New York: Appleton, 1894.

Deals with roles of women all over the world. Although dated, a good overview of the roles of food-bringer, weaver, skin dresser, potter, artist, and linguist and the importance of women in society and religion.

267. Mathes, Valerie Sherer. "American Indian Women and the Catholic Church." *North Dakota History* 47 (Fall 1980): 20-25.

Mathes reviews the lives of Katherine Tekakwitha and Louise Sighouin and discusses Indian women who joined various sisterhoods of the Catholic church.

268. Mathes, Valerie Sherer. "A New Look at the Life of Women in Indian Society." *American Indian Quarterly* 2, 2 (Summer 1975): 131-39.

Mathes shows that generalizations about the inferiority of Indian women based on works by Catlin, Morgan, Denig and Hodge, all white males, do not take into account the ethnocentrism of the observers or the division of labor in tribes that has been documented in other sources.

269. Mathur, Mary E. Flemming. "Who Cares that a Woman's Work is Never Done. . .?" *Indian Historian* 4, 2 (Summer 1971): 11-16.

Mathur is critical of the dearth of information on the roles of American Indian women as well as the misrepresentation of those roles. She focuses her discussion of women's lives on the Iroquois.

270. Matthiasson, John S. "Northern Baffin Island Women in Three Culture Periods." *The Western Canadian Journal of Anthropology* 6, 3 (1976): 201-12.

Descriptions of Inuit society by anthropologists underestimate the power women have and continue to display and thus, in ethnographic literature, a false view of women's roles is perpetuated. Author argues that colonialism led Inuit women to consolidate their traditional positions of relative equality with men and enhanced their ability to engage in female bonding behavior.

271. Matthiasson, John S. "Northern Baffin Island Women in Three Culture Periods." In Occasional Papers in Anthropology No. 2, *Sex Roles in Changing Cultures*. Ann McElroy and Carolyn Matthiasson, eds. Buffalo: Department of Anthropology, State University of New York, 1979, 61-71.

Study of women's roles in the Pond Inlet area of Northern Baffin Island from pre-contact to the present. This paper is an effort to understand Inuit women beyond the "sexual hospitality" image which has characterized research on Inuit women.

272. Maynard, Eileen. "Changing Sex Roles and Family Structure Among the Oglala Sioux." In Occasional Papers in Anthropology, No. 1: *Sex Roles in Changing Cultures*. Ann McElroy and Carolyn Matthiason, eds. Buffalo: Department of Anthropology, State University of New York, 1979, 11-19.

Description of traditional sex roles of Oglala Sioux on the Pine Ridge Reservation in South Dakota and the changes reservation life have brought to Pine Ridge. Most significantly, women's status has risen and men's roles have declined in importance as government support has increased and male political power has declined.

273. McCartney, Martha W. "Cockacoeske, Queen of Pamunkey: Diplomat and Suzeraine." In *Powhatan's Mantle*. Peter H. Wood, Gregory A. Waselkov, and M. Thomas Hatley, eds. Lincoln: University of Nebraska Press, 1989.

Cockacoeske, a relative of Powhatan, was chief of the Pamunkey Indians in Virginia for thirty years beginning in 1656. Her influence on Indian-white relationships has largely been ignored by historians.

274. McCarty, Darlene. "A Day with Yaha." In *The American Indian Speaks*. John R. Milton, ed. Vermillion: University of South Dakota Press, 1969, 119-25.

Memories of her grandmother Yaha blend the traditional and contemporary experiences.

275. McClellan, Catharine. *My Old People Say: An Ethnographic Survey of Southern Yukon Territory*. 2 vols. Publications in Ethnology 6 (1&2). Ottawa: National Museums of Canada, 1975.

This study of three groups in southern Yukon Territory describes Indian life during the last quarter of the nineteenth century. Of interest are the sections on life cycles and social organization.

276. McClellan, Catharine, Lucie Birckel, Robert Bringhurst, James A. Fall, Carol McCarthy and Janice R. Sheppard. *Part of the Land, Part of the Water: A History of the Yukon Indians*. Vancouver: Douglas and McIntyre, 1987.

In this illustrated account of Yukon life, the anthropological information is supported by commentary by many Indian men and women who participated in the study. Chapter twelve includes statements by over twenty women.

277. McCormack, Patricia A., ed. "Cross Sex Reflections: Native Peoples." *The Western Canadian Journal of Anthropology* 6, 3 (1976): 1-288.

Eleven of the sixteen essays in this issue examine the roles of women within their tribes and in intertribal organizations from the pre-contact period to the 1970s. Adaptation of traditional roles to changing circumstances is a theme throughout the issue.

278. McCullogh, C. W. "Modiste to Miss Navajo." *Arizona Highways* 31, 7 (July 1955): 8-17.

Illustrated article which traces the history of Navajo women's dress from the nineteenth century to the mid-twentieth century.

279. McElroy, Ann. "Canadian Arctic Modernization and Change in Female Inuit Role Identification." *American Ethnologist* 4, 2 (November 1975): 662-86.

This study of two Inuit communities on Baffin Island indicates that significant female role changes are being caused by rejection or revision of the patterns of traditional women's identity factors and activities. Young women increasingly seek wage employment, education, and upward mobility through job and marriage choices, moving toward stronger acceptance of Euro-Canadian values. New roles do not, however, necessarily imply disintegration of family ties or stability, and female adaptability may prove to be a long term strength in sustaining Inuit social networks.

280. McElroy, Ann. "The Negotiation of Sex-Role Identity in Eastern Arctic Culture Change." *The Western Canadian Journal of Anthropology* 6, 3 (1976): 184-200.

The author explores the differences in patterns of male and female adaptation to culture change on South Baffin Island. The study indicates that men's roles have been unstable and discontinuous during the period of European contact, while female roles have remained fairly stable and served as the basis for greater female flexibility and self-esteem.

281. McElroy, Ann. "The Negotiation of Sex-Role Identity in Eastern Arctic Culture Change." In Occasional Papers in Anthropology, No. 2 *Sex Roles in Changing Cultures*. Ann McElroy and

Carolyn Matthiasson, eds. Buffalo: Department of Anthropology, State University of New York, 1979, 49-60.

A study of male and female adaptation to culture change in the Eastern Canadian Arctic from the time of early European contact. McElroy discusses male and female roles and the impact of European contact on their roles.

282. McMurtrie, Douglas C. "A Legend of Lesbian Love Among the North American Indians." *Urologic and Cutaneous Review* (April 1914): 192-93.

McMurtrie relates Fox and Assiniboine tales of a sexual relations between two women to demonstrate the existence of lesbian activity among North American Indians, though he sees it as rare and cautions that tales often exaggerate or are fiction. He sees the liaisons depicted in the tales as characteristic of a "primitive" conception of sexuality.

283. McSwain, Romola Mae. *The Role of Wives in the Urban Adjustment of Navaho Migrant Families to Denver, Colorado*. Navaho Urban Relocation Research Report no. 10, April 1965.

This study includes nine case studies of Navaho migrant women in Denver. The author suggests that wives play a crucial role in the adjustment of Navaho families to urban life.

284. Mead, Margaret. *The Changing Culture of an Indian Tribe*. New York: Columbia University Press, 1932.

In this examination of tribal women during the period of white contact, Mead used the Omaha (called "Antlers" in the study) to show the negative impact of white contact on traditional life.

285. Mead, Margaret, ed. *Cooperation and Competition Among Primitive Peoples*. Boston: Beacon Press, 1961.

This book contains chapters on thirteen cultures in an attempt to develop a systematic approach to the problems of culture and personality. Included in the volume are essays on Eskimos of

Greenland, the Ojibwa of Canada, the Kwakiutl of Vancouver Island, the Iroquois, the Zuni, and the Dakota. Each tribal study includes data on women's roles and status.

286. Medicine, Beatrice. "American Indian Family: Cultural Change and Adaptive Strategies." *Journal of Ethnic Studies* 8 (Winter 1981): 13-23.

By discussing the varieties of kinship systems, marriage patterns, and social organizational structures found in North American Indian tribes, the author distinguishes the concepts of Indian family and of extended family as applicable to Indians from the white application of terms and norms for family definition. She posits that the view of Indian families as dysfunctional is a product of middle-class white ethnocentricity. By contrast, the author argues that tribal social systems provide selective adaptations and interactions within Indian domestic units and communities that have sustained Indian families despite racial oppression.

287. Medicine, Beatrice. "American Indian Women: Spirituality and Status." *Bread and Roses* 2 (November 1980): 15-18.

The mental health needs of American Indian women are severely neglected and need to be addressed regarding such issues of low self-esteem, sexual and intellectual exploitation, family instability, economic stresses, repressed anger, and stress from conflicting expectations of Indian and white worlds.

288. Medicine, Beatrice. "The Anthropologist as the Indian's Image Maker." *Indian Historian* 4 (Fall 1971): 27-29.

Medicine discusses how the Indian image has been created by outsiders and that when the Indian presents his or her own history, there are accusations of subjectivity or ethnocentrism.

289. Medicine, Beatrice. "Child Socialization Among Native Americans: The Lakota (Sioux) in Cultural Context." *Wicazo Sa* 1, 2 (Fall 1985): 23-28.

The impact of gender roles and the learning processes that transmit them within Lakota society are examined. Children learn by means of precept and example how sex roles are defined and enacted. Qualities of womanhood are discussed.

290. Medicine, Beatrice. "Indian Women: Tribal Identity as Status Quo." In *Woman's Nature: Rationalizations of Inequality*. Marion Lowe and Ruth Hubbard, eds. New York: Pergamon, 1983, 63-73.

Medicine discusses women's roles among the Lakota Sioux and explains the contradictions between Native values and the dominant white culture. Indian women are valued for both their biological and economic functions in tribal cultures, but white values have often distorted the traditional roles.

291. Medicine, Beatrice. *The Native American Woman: A Perspective*. Austin, TX: National Educational Laboratory Publishers, March, 1978.

A contemporary perspective by a Lakota woman who has been a spokeswoman for Indian women's rights and who is also an anthropologist. The book includes comments on anthropologists and historians, changes Indian women have undergone, and expectations for the future. There are lengthy quotations and photographs to supplement the text.

292. Medicine, Beatrice. "Role and Function of Indian Women." *Indian Education* 7 (January 1977): 4-5.

These are excerpts about the position of Indian women from Medicine's address to the Eighth National Indian Education Association Convention.

293. Metcalf, Ann. "Navajo Women in the City: Lessons from a Quarter Century of Relocation." *American Indian Quarterly* 6, 1-2 (Spring-Summer 1982): 71-89.

Metcalf reviews the government policy of relocation and then reports on findings from a group of young Navajo women in San Francisco.

294. Metcalf, Ann. "Reservation-Born, City-Bred: Native American Women and Children in the City." In Occasional Papers in Anthropology No. 1. *Sex Roles in Changing Cultures*. Ann McElroy and Carolyn Matthiasson, eds. Buffalo: Department of Anthropology, State University of New York, 1979, 21-33.

Analysis of the changes women have experienced in roles, family structure, and domestic life as a result of moving to urban areas. Metcalf uses census data and field work in San Francisco as a basis for describing Indian life in the city.

295. Metoyer, Cheryl A. "The Native American Woman." In *The Study of Women: Enlarging Perspectives of Social Reality*. Eloise C. Snyder, ed. New York: Harper and Row, 1979.

The chapter on Indian women is a brief part of a longer study on contemporary women.

296. Michelson, Truman. "How Meskwaki Children Should be Brought Up." In *American Indian Life*. Elsie Clews Parsons, ed. Lincoln: University of Nebraska Press, 1967, 81-86.

Discusses how girls are taught traditional skills and self-discipline and prepared for marriage and childbearing so that they will be respected members of their families and communities.

297. Mingwon, Mingwon (Shirley Bear). "Equality Among Women." *Canadian Literature* 124-125 (Spring-Summer 1990): 133-37.

In a brief discussion of the power of women, Mingwon uses myth, history, and language to demonstrate the erosion of female power in indigenous societies.

298. Morris, Clyde P. "Yavapai-Apache Family Organization: In a Reservation Context." *Plateau* 44, 3 (Winter 1972): 105-10.

Contemporary residency patterns of Yavapai-Apache living on the Camp and Middle Verde reservations in Arizona indicate the persistence of traditional matrilocal multi-household family clusters in spite of off-reservation employment.

299. Myres, Sandra L. *Westering Women and the Frontier Experience, 1800-1915*. Albuquerque: University of New Mexico Press, 1982.

Contains one very good chapter, "Land of Savagery/Land of Promise: Women's Views of Indians" (pp. 37-71), which links pioneer women's views to the development of racism in America and contrasts women's views of Indians with the dominant male view. While both white men and women felt superior, because female contact was most often peaceful, women ironically felt less threatened by Indians than white men and were curious about and could identify with Indian women's daily lives despite the prevailing notion that Indians were a threat to Christian values. Focus on white/Indian women encounters.

300. Native American Research Group. *American Indian Socialization to Urban Life*. San Francisco: Institute for Scientific Analysis, 1975.

This report "Native American Families in the City" presents the final findings of a research project conceived and conducted by Native Americans to understand the Indian experience in the city. One hundred and twenty Indian families in Oakland, California, were selected for the study. One-third of the families were headed by a woman.

301. Nelson, A. "Women in Groups: Women's Ritual Sodalities in Native North America." *The Western Canadian Journal of Anthropology* 6, 3 (1976): 29-67.

Among Native American horticulture societies, women's roles as mothers and fertility symbols must be emphasized in order for them to practice collective autonomy in matters of ceremony and ritual power. Study draws data from Hopi, Tewa, Mandan, Iroquois, Pawnee and Navajo cultures.

302. Nicks, Trudy. "Mary Anne's Dilemma: The Ethnohistory of an
      Ambivalent Identity." *Canadian Ethnic Studies* 17, 2 (1985):
      103-14.

      Nicks uses the example of a Metis woman to trace the changes
      and confusions of determining personal identity as well as its
      expression in cultural artifacts.

303. Niethammer, Carolyn. *Daughters of the Earth: The Lives and
      Legends of American Indian Women*. New York: Collier Books,
      1977.

      The cycle of life for women in traditional Indian cultures is
      described and analyzed. Childbirth, childhood, courtship,
      marriage, homemaking, power roles, arts, religious practices,
      aging and death are depicted in cultures in North America. A
      useful bibliography is included.

304. Nowak, Barbara. "Women's Roles and Status in a Changing
      Iroquois Society." In Occasional Papers in Anthropology, No.
      1. *Sex Roles in Changing Cultures*. Ann McElroy and Carolyn
      Matthiasson, eds. Buffalo: State University of New York, 1979,
      95-109.

      The reorganization of Iroquois society after the American
      Revolution affected men and women differently. Although
      women's lives had more stability, as time went on men's roles
      stabilized and women lost much of their former authority in what
      had been a matriarchy.

305. O'Meara, Walter. *Daughters of the Country: The Women of the
      Fur Traders and Mountain Men*. New York: Harcourt, Brace
      and World, 1968.

      Discusses in detail the relationships between Indian women and
      white men on the frontier. O'Meara studied journals, memoirs,
      chronicles, and letters to gather information.

306. Oosten, Jaarich G. "Male and Female in Inuit Shamanism." *Inuit
      Studies* 10, 1-2 (1986): 115-31.

Author argues that male or female identities of shamans were submerged because the shamanistic role demands a transcendence of gender.

307. Opland, David V. "Marriage and Divorce for the Devils Lake Indian Reservation." *North Dakota Law Review* 47 (1971): 317-34.

Analysis of current legal status regulating marriage and divorce and the proposal for a body of domestic law established through tribal code to regulate marriage, dissolution, termination, divorce, counseling, financial and custody arrangements, separations, and annulments and all the procedures for processing each category of legal action.

308. Opler, Morris E. "The Kinship Systems of the Southern Athabaskan-Speaking Tribes." *American Anthropologist* 38 (1936): 620-33.

Study examines the Chiricahua, Mescalero, Jicarilla and Lipan Apache with comparisons to Navajo and Kiowan kinship systems and designation. Attention is given to the common factor that women of all ages may be designated by a single term.

309. Opler, Morris E. "Women's Social Status and the Forms of Marriage." *American Journal of Sociology* 49 (1943): 125-46.

Pawnee, Shoshoni, Ute, and Paiute data is used to discuss the high status of women in societies which practice polyandry. Though not the prevailing mode of marriage in these societies, it was practiced frequently enough to support an argument for a higher degree of independence among women in these tribes. Marriage to multiple partners often dissolved, sometimes due to jealousy, sometimes due to a more culturally sanctioned marriage by one of the mates, but women who engaged in polyandry were likely to retain property, fruits of labor, and children.

310. Ortiz, Bev. "Skills Remembered, Cherished, and Continued: Northern Sierra Miwok Food Preparations and Soaproot Brush

Making." *News From Native California* 4, 3 (Spring 1990): 16-19.

The author interviewed tribal scholar Dorothy Stanley about acorn preparation, manzanita berry cider, and other foods. Stanley also describes making brushes out of soaproot.

311. Oswalt, Robert L. ed. *Kashaya Texts*. University of California Publications in Linguistics 36. Berkeley: University of California Press, 1964.

Essie Parrish is one of six informants who provide information for the study of language.

312. Oxendine, Joan. "The Luiseno Girls' Ceremony." *Journal of California and Great Basin Anthropology* 2, 1 (1980): 37-50.

Discussion of California's patrilineal Luiseno society, and the girls' puberty ceremonies, based on information from late nineteenth and early twentieth century male anthropologists.

313. Paper, Jordan. "The Forgotten Grandmothers: Amerindian Women and Religion in Colonized North America." *Canadian Women Studies/Les Cahiers de la Femme* 5, 2 (Winter 1983): 48-51.

Briefly discusses the roles of women in pre-contact cultures, the significance of which were obscured in the observations of male biased missionaries, travellers and ethnologists.

314. Paper, Jordan. "The Post-Contact Origin of an American Indian High God: The Suppressing of Feminine Spirituality." *American Indian Quarterly* 7, 4 (Fall 1983): 1-24.

Focuses on Algonkin linguistic family and traditional religious concepts and points out that most Indian cultures considered both male and female generative powers but that terms such as "Great Spirit" have tended to negate the female role in creation and religion.

315. Parezo, Nancy J., Kelley A. Hays, and Barbara F. Slivac. "The Mind's Road." In *The Desert is No Lady*. Vera Norwood and Janice Monk, eds. New Haven: Yale University Press, 1987, 146-73.

The authors ask how gender and ethnicity shape the aesthetic response to the Southwest. They look at the sexual division of labor in the production of art with emphasis on the Puebloans and Navajo. Changes were introduced by Europeans as tourists and traders, and the shifts caused changes in both designs and quality. Illustrations depict the place of landscape in the art of Indian women of the Southwest, and a chart shows the division of labor prior to 1880.

316. Parkman, E. Breck. "The Maien." *National Women's Anthropology Newsletter* 5, 2 (1981): 16-22.

The Maien was a female secret society of the Coast Miwok. According to Robert Thomas, great-great-grandson of the last chief, the Coast Miwok traditionally had a male chief and two female leaders, a "woman chief" and a "maien." Members of the Maien society participated in initiation ceremonies and "world renewal" ceremonies.

317. Parsons, Elsie Clews, ed. *American Indian Life*. Lincoln: University of Nebraska Press, 1967.

This collection of anthropological essays includes a traditional tale about a Crow woman, a study of Meskwaki traditional education of children, a brief biography of an Iroquois woman, and a story about an Arvik woman.

318. Parsons, Elsie Clews. "Mothers and Children at Zuni, New Mexico." *Man* 19 (1919): 168-73.

Parsons begins by pointing out that girls are more desirable than boys at the Zuni Pueblo and goes on to recount a number of rituals associated with pregnancy, childbirth, and childrearing.

319. Parsons, Elsie Clews. "Notes on the Zuni, Part II." *Memoirs of the American Anthropological Association* 4 (1917): 229-327.

    Parsons discusses the roles of Zuni women in communal and personal ceremonialism, particularly discussing marriage and birthing rituals in relation to female kinship. She also discusses proper household etiquette and women's clothing and includes a traditional tale concerning courtship and marriage.

320. Parsons, Elsie Clews. *A Pueblo Indian Journal 1920-1921.* Memoirs of the American Anthropological Association, No. 32, 1925, 5-123.

    Recorded by Crow Wing, this journal contains information about Hopi domestic and village life on a day-to-day basis and contains many descriptions of female Katsina figures and ceremonial events.

321. Parsons, Elsie Clews. "The Social Organization of the Tewa of New Mexico." *Memoirs of the American Anthropological Association* 36 (1929): 1-309.

    This comprehensive ethnography of the Tewa includes a lengthy analysis of betrothal and marriage practices, and a discussion of household composition, and inheritance of property and houses. Survey of homes in Santa Clara, San Juan, San Ildefonso, Nambe, and Tequque indicates dominance of female ownership.

322. Parsons, Elsie Clews. "Tewa Mothers and Children." *Man* 24 (October 1924): 148-51.

    Tewa birth and childrearing customs, taboos, and rituals are presented. Discussion of practices related to birthing and early childhood such as dealing with abnormal behavior in children, curing childhood illness, and encouraging development.

323. Parsons, Elsie Clews. "Waiyautitsa of Zuni, New Mexico." *Scientific Monthly* 9 (November 1919): 443-57.

Focuses attention upon differentiation of the sexes at Zuni by tracing the "typical" experiences of a girl growing up on the Zuni Pueblo.

324. Peet, Stephen D. "The Indian Woman As She Was." *American Antiquarian and Oriental Journal* 27 (1905): 348-50.

The stereotype of the Indian woman as beast of burden and drudge is challenged on the basis of traditional division of labor and her work is compared to turn-of-the-century farm wives in a favorable light since she did not till, milk cows, tend chickens, wash clothes, sew clothing for social and church events, cook elaborate meals, wash dishes, etc. Her work is seen as productive and efficient, based on need rather than rigid norms.

325. Perdue, Theda. "Cherokee Women and the Trail of Tears." *Journal of Women's History* 1, 1 (Spring 1989): 14-30.

Discusses the Cherokee as matrilineal and matrilocal, yet the women had little voice in negotiations with the U.S. government after about 1785. In 1839 the U.S. government forced the removal of the Cherokee Nation west of the Mississippi River to Oklahoma. The Treaty of New Echota was signed by men, indicating that by that time the power of Cherokee women had declined. In 1785 Nancy Ward had been a spokesperson for her people.

326. Perdue, Theda. "Southern Indians and the Cult of True Womanhood." In *The Web of Southern Social Relations: Essays on Family Life, Education and Women*. Walter J. Fraser, Jr., R. Frank Saunders, Jr., and Jon L. Wakelyn, Jr., eds. Athens: University of Georgia Press, 1985, 35-51.

Mission schools among the Cherokee, Choctaws, and Chickasaws successfully molded women to the ideals of southern womanhood--purity, submissiveness to fathers and husbands, domesticity, morality, spirituality--and thoroughly undermined traditional female roles and power because tribal men began to expect all women to be submissive, even those not sent to mission schools, and passed laws to undermine matrilineal

kinship and exclude women from the political process. Cherokee
Catherine Brown is discussed as a model of the womanhood cult
among the southern tribes.

327. Perry, Richard J. "Matrilineal Descent in a Hunting Context: The
     Athapaskan Case." *Ethnology* 28 (January 1989): 33-51.

     Contrary to the general patterns, there is evidence that proto-
     Athapaskan Subarctic social organization was characterized by
     matrilineal descent and matrilocal residence. Given the
     mountainous environment and absenteeism of the male hunter,
     the predominant emphasis on mother-child bonding is related to
     the specific pattern of subsistence.

328. Pesavento, Wilma J. "Ball Games of Native American Women of
     the Plains." ERIC ED 121 766, 1976.

     Traditional ball games are described and analyzed in terms of
     individual tribal characteristics in twelve Plains tribes extending
     over a wide area. Players included young girls as well as grown
     women. Double ball and shinny were the dominant forms of
     games played by females.

329. Porter, Tom. "Traditional Women's Role as Outlined by Bear
     Clan Chief, Tom Porter." *Akwesasne Notes* 19, 3 (Late Spring
     1987): 32.

     Porter argues that women carry the burden of caring for Indian
     families and that the mothers are responsible for leading the
     Medicine Societies. This is a brief tribute to the women in
     Porter's life.

330. Powers, Marla N. "The Americanization of Indian Girls." *Society*
     24 (January/February 1987): 83-86.

     Discussion of an exhibit at the Voorhees Simmerli Art
     Museum, Rutgers University.

331. Powers, Marla N. "Oglala Women." *Society* 25 (March/April
     1988): 81-85.

Discussion of Oglala Sioux women, illustrated with photographs from the 1950s. Powers gives brief biographies of the women to illustrate the changes in Sioux women's lives.

332. Powers, Marla N. *Oglala Women: Myth, Ritual, and Reality.* Chicago: University of Chicago Press, 1986.

An anthropological study based on 25 years of study on the Pine Ridge reservation in South Dakota. Powers argues that Sioux women have far more power and authority than has been depicted by earlier anthropologists and historians.

333. Powers, Marla N. "Research Debunks Image of Native American Women." *New Directions for Women* 15, 2 (March-April 1986): 8.

Based on research among the Oglala Sioux, the author debunks popular stereotypes of Indian women, particularly those portrayed in photography and film. Powers emphasizes Indian women's participation in the political and economic arenas.

334. Quinn, Naomi. "Anthropological Studies of Women's Status." *Annual Review of Anthropology* 6 (1977): 181-225.

Drawing on cross-cultural data, including studies of women in North American Indian societies, this article discusses marriage, child rearing, and economic and domestic authority among women, concluding that sedentary, intense agriculture tends toward reduced status for women. Author calls for reassessment of male biased generalizations about inferior status of women. Useful bibliography.

335. Quintero, Nita. "Coming of Age the Apache Way." *National Geographic* 157 (February 1980): 262-71.

A photo essay on the Apache woman's puberty ceremony. Includes discussion of ceremonial sponsors, food exchange, role of mountain spirits, and significance of rituals to Apache women's roles.

336. Randle, Martha Champion. "Iroquois Women, Then and Now." In *Symposium on Local Diversity in Iroquois Culture*. William N. Fenton, ed. Bureau of American Ethnology Bulletin no. 149, 1951, 169-80.

Concludes that culture shock was felt more by males. Iroquois women have retained ancient security and efficiency.

337. Red Horse, John, August Shattuck, and Fred Hoffman. *The American Indian Family: Strengths and Stresses*. Isleta, NM: American Indian Social Research and Development Associates, 1981.

Proceedings of 1980 Conference on the American Indian family held in Phoenix, Arizona. The volume includes papers as well as discussions and recommendations.

338. Red Horse, John G., Ronald Lewis, Marvin Feit, and James Decker. "Family Behavior of Urban American Indians." *Social Casework* 59, 2 (February 1978): 67-72.

It is necessary to understand the extended family networks of American Indians in order to formulate human service delivery and public policy. Cases are used to illustrate three distinct lifestyle patterns of American Indian families.

339. Reichard, Gladys A. *Spider Woman: A Story of Navajo Weavers and Chanters*. Santa Fe: Rio Grande Press, 1968. Originally published New York: Macmillan, 1934.

This first person ethnographic narrative by an anthropologist traces her experience living on the Navajo reservation and learning techniques of weaving from Navajo women. The text includes detailed descriptions of weaving techniques, designs, women's lore, women's ceremonial activities, a traditional wedding, a curing ritual, herbal medicine, and details of day to day life centered on women's work. Primary source of information is the Red Point family, particularly Maria Antonia and her daughters Altnaha and Marie.

340. Reiter, Rayna, ed. *Toward an Anthropology of Women*. New York: Monthly Review Press, 1975.

A cross-cultural collection of essays which applies feminist theory to anthropological study of cultures, this text attempts to address the male bias in the anthropological study which has misinterpreted female roles in cultures. One essay "Iroquois Women: An Ethnohistoric Footnote," by Judith K. Brown, examines the relationship between the position of women and their economic role in food production and distribution.

341. Richards, Cara E. "Matriarchy or Mistake: The Role of Iroquois Women through Time." In *Cultural Stability and Cultural Change*. Verne R. Ray, ed. Seattle: American Ethnological Society, 1957, 36-45.

Analyzes power positions of the sexes in Iroquois society, showing the gradual increase in the power of women and loss by the men through social change and time.

342. Richards, Cara E. "Onondaga Women: Among the Liberated." In *Many Sisters: Women in Cross Cultural Perspective*. Carolyn Matthiasson, ed. New York: Free Press, 1974, 401-20.

The high status of Iroquois women is documented by Richards's account of a woman born in 1900 on the reservation. In the composite picture of a reservation woman, Richards reveals the power of Onondaga women.

343. Riley, Glenda. "Some European (Mis) Perceptions of American Indian Women." *New Mexico Historical Review* 59, 3 (July 1984): 237-66.

Review essay which traces the eighteenth and nineteenth century biased and sexist views of Indian women communicated by European explorers, travellers and commentators. Most texts describe Indian women as unfortunate workhorses who become cruel brutes as a result of mistreatment by their husbands. Riley analyzes the ethnocentric and superficial misinterpretations of over forty Europeans from various countries, including Germany,

France, Denmark, Poland, Norway, and England. Notes provide a good source on narratives by Europeans.

344. Riley, Glenda. *Women and Indians on the Frontier, 1825-1915.* Albuquerque: University of New Mexico Press, 1984.

One chapter analyzes the preconceptions about Indian women prevalent during the westering movement which prevented understanding of Native women's feelings, attitudes, actual roles, and accomplishments, derived from or recorded by whites, including pioneer women, who frequently gave accounts of threatening, savage women. This book also includes some discussion of the portrayal of Indian women by early sentimental novelists and the impact of popular literature on the attitude of whites toward Native women. This volume does demonstrate, through pioneer women's diaries and letters, the capacity for some women to form empathetic views of Native women as their contact increased. Includes historic photos of Indian women from several tribes.

345. Rodekohr, Janet. "The Native American Woman: Is she the Tie that Binds her People Together." *AAUW Journal* 69 (1976): 16-18.

Using research on the history and current society of the Omaha tribe, Rodekohr examines the stresses and potentials for Indian women both in urban and reservation settings and argues that they succeed in overcoming the anxieties of coping in two cultures when a solid family and network of friends supports their ambitions.

346. Roscoe, Will, comp. *Living the Spirit: A Gay American Indian Anthology.* New York: St. Martin's Press, 1988.

Several writers examine historical and contemporary views of homosexuality in American Indian communities. Writers such as Paula Gunn Allen and Beth Brant discuss lesbianism and provide literary examples derived from the oral tradition as well as contemporary accounts.

347. Rothenberg, Diane. "The Mothers of the Nation: Seneca Resistance to Quaker Intervention." In *Women and Colonization*. Mona Etienne and Eleanor Leacock, eds. New York: Praeger, 1980, 67-87.

   Seneca women resisted the late seventeenth-century Quaker missionary economic program which was based on capitalist ideology and was designed to transform Seneca society into a male dominated system and deny women their traditional control of agricultural production and political authority.

348. Rust, Horatio N. "A Puberty Ceremony of the Mission Indians." *American Anthropologist* n.s., 8, 1 (1906): 28-32.

   Description of a four-day female puberty ceremony held to prepare young women for marriage in Yuman society.

349. Sanday, Peggy R. "Toward a Theory of the Status of Women." *American Anthropologist* 75, 5 (1973): 1682-1700.

   Cross-cultural data suggests female status is directly related to female control of production and demand for female produce as well as the degree of emphasis placed on maternity and fertility as sacred function. Crow and Iroquois data is included in this study.

350. Sanders, Douglas. "Indian Women: A Brief History of Their Roles and Rights." *McGill Law Journal* 21, 4 (1975): 652-72.

   The traditional rights of Indian women are seen as varying from culture to culture and serve as context for focus on the *Lavell vs. Canada* case which failed to grant Indian status to a Metis woman and has become the symbol of Indian reaction against legal discrimination against Indian women. Also discusses the Cannard case and the potential for an effective political movement by Indian women.

351. Sapir, Edward and Morris Swadish. *Nootka Texts. Tales and Ethnological Narratives*. William Dwight Whitney Linguistic Series. Philadelphia: Linguistic Society of America, 1939.

Female mythic figures are prominent in this collection of tales from western Vancouver Island. They include Crow Girl and Pitch Woman. Ethnological narratives include a story of a girl who received her power from the sea in a vision and through ritual performance.

352. Sapir, Edward, ed. *Takelma Texts*. University of Pennsylvania Anthropological Publications from the University Museum 2, 1 (1900): 1-267.

Collected on the Siletz reservation of Western Oregon in 1906, from Frances Johnson (Gwisqwashan), one of a handful of Takelma speakers still living, this bilingual collection includes numerous coyote tales and other animal stories, medicine formulas, and a brief section of personal narratives.

353. Sapir, Edward, ed. *Yana Texts*. New York: Kraus Reprint, 1964.

Yana woman Betty Brown narrates traditional texts in her Native language which are presented with both literal and literary English translations. Several of the narratives focus on women, marriage, and childbirth, and one concerns the dream of the narrator about a visit to her deceased mother in a land of flowers.

354. Schlegel, Alice. "The Adolescent Socialization of the Hopi Girl." *Ethnology* 12 (October 1973): 449-62.

Sees Hopi female adolescence as a time of crisis, strained relations, moodiness, and unpredictability, complicated by fear of rejection by a lover. Study of the period of socialization into womanhood.

355. Schlegel, Alice. *Hopi Indian Widowhood*. Working Paper 17-4. Tucson, AZ: Southwest Institute for Research on Women, University of Arizona, 1983, 35-54.

Schlegel found that between 1860 and 1939 there were fewer widows than widowers among the Hopi and Hopi women received a great deal of familial support. Widows' social position was not affected by their changed role from married woman to widow. The community setting and sex roles in the Hopi society and in Hopi marriage are analyzed to explain the position of widows in the society.

356. Schlegel, Alice. "Male and Female in Hopi Thought and Action." In *Sexual Stratification: A Cross-Cultural View*. Alice Schlegel, ed. New York: Columbia University Press, 1977, 245-69.

Discusses high status and authority of women resulting from their roles as the source and keepers of human life and partners in maintaining the home and community. Argues that Hopi sex roles provide a balance and shared authority in all spheres of Hopi life.

357. Schlegel, Alice. *Male Dominance and Female Autonomy: Domestic Authority in Matrilineal Societies*. New Haven: Human Relations Area Press, 1977.

Matrilineal kinship and the problem of domestic authority is analyzed in sixty-six cultures worldwide, including Cochiti, Hopi, Crow, Pawnee, Delaware, Tlingit and Yavapai. Degrees of male authority over female are discussed in terms of spousal and sibling relationships with societies where brothers and spouses have relatively equal influence favoring women's autonomy in the household. Data also refutes claims of a decline in matrilineal descent systems.

358. Schlegel, Alice. "Sexual Antagonism Among the Sexually Egalitarian Hopi." *Ethos* 7, 2 (Summer 1979): 124-41.

Schlegel examines the husband-wife and brother-sister relationships within the institutions of the household. The cultural context includes joking, patterned castration threats, adultery, and belief in witchcraft, all of which serve to either ameliorate or exacerbate the conflicts.

359. Schlissel, Lillian, ed. *Women's Diaries of the Westward Journey*. New York: Schocken Books, 1989.

Comments by pioneer women on the strangeness of Indian women, barter with Indian women, and details of how Indian women cooked and cared for children.

360. Scott, Leslee M. "Indian Women as Food Providers and Tribal Counselors." *Oregon Historical Quarterly* 42 (1941): 208-19.

Women as food providers and figures of authority are interrelated subjects; their usefulness as food providers led to their tribal influence. Women were responsible for the basic essentials of food and shelter.

361. Scully, Vincent. "In Praise of Women: The Mescalero Puberty." *Art in America* 60 (July-August 1972): 70-77.

Ceremony celebrating coming of age of girls has been combined with the Mountain Spirits dance and is described in detail.

362. Sharp, Henry S. *Chipewyan Marriage*. Canadian Ethnology Service Paper No. 58. Ottawa: National Museum of Man Mercury Series, 1979.

This is a study of the kinship system of the Mission Chipewyan and the conflict inherent in the system. Sharp discusses changes in the marriage system and adoption within the groups based on fieldwork during the 1960s and 1970s. As the Chipewyan have moved from traditional bush life to village life, the changes have been apparent in kinship as well as other social relationships.

363. Sharp, Henry S. "Man:Wolf: Woman:Dog." *Arctic Anthropology* 13, 1 (1976): 25-43.

Sharp analyzes the metaphorical use of Man, Wolf, Woman, and Dog in the Chipewyan culture and demonstrates the relationships between language, myth, and behavior. The Chipewyan origin myth posits that sexual relations between a woman and a dog brought forth the first people. The relationships between dogs and wolves are examined to illustrate the confusion inherent in the contradictions between myth and reality.

364. Sharp, Henry S. "The Null Case: The Chipewyan." In *Woman the Gatherer*. Frances Dahlberg, ed. New Haven: Yale University Press, 1981, 221-44.

Account of the position of women among Chippewyan and Athapaskan-speaking people of the Northwest Territories, Manitoba, Saskatchewan, and Alberta. The dependence on men for food production results in women being devalued.

365. Shepardson, Mary T. "The Status of Navajo Women." *American Indian Quarterly* 6, 1-2 (Spring-Summer 1982): 149-69.

Compares the status of Navajo women in three periods: traditional society before stock reduction (1868-1933), during and after stock reduction (1933-early 1950s), and present day (1980s). She postulates that Navajo women lost status with stock reduction but have regained it through education and wage work.

366. Shimony, Annemarie. "Women of Influence and Prestige Among the Native American Iroquois." In *Unspoken Words: Women's Religious Lives in Non-Western Cultures*. Nancy Auer Falk and Rita M. Gross, eds. San Francisco: Harper & Row, 1980, 243-59.

The traditional role of Iroquois women in the Longhouse religion is examined by observation of contemporary Iroquois social organization. Shimony clarifies the positions of chief's matron and fortuneteller and provides details about women's participation in the Longhouse. Shimony concludes that women do not dominate Iroquois religious life but that they have great powers which place them in complementary positions in relation to men.

367. Shipley, William. *Maidu Texts and Dictionary*. University of California Publications in Linguistics, vol. 33. Berkeley: University of California, 1963.

Informant is Maym Gallagher of Payner Creek, California. Includes her autobiography, bilingual texts of historical incidents, animal tales, and Gallagher's interviews with other informants. Autobiography focuses on childhood experiences.

368. Sirdofshy, Arthur. "An Apache Girl Comes of Age." *Travel* 138 (July 1972): 40-43.

In the Apache Sunrise Dance, Winona Crawford dances three days to celebrate becoming a woman. Illustrated.

369. Smith, Sherry L. "Beyond Princess and Squaw: Army Officer's Perceptions of Indian Women." In *The Women's West*. Susan Armitage and Elizabeth Jameson, eds. Norman: University of Oklahoma Press, 1987, 63-75.

Using correspondence and other historical records, levels of friendship and intimacy of U.S. Army officers with Indian women is analyzed in order to demonstrate that, while attitudes of racial superiority among officers were the norm, not all interaction with Indian women was violent or exploitative.

370. Smith, Sherry L. *The View from Officers' Row*. Tucson: University of Arizona Press, 1990.

American army views of the Indian tribes they fought against are revealed in this study which includes the views of officers' wives as well. A general tone of respect toward Indians, and particularly curiosity toward them, dominates the text. Male and female views of Indian women are expressed primarily in personal document, since official reports do not generally include commentary on Native women.

371. Smithson, Carma Lee. *The Havasupai Woman*. Salt Lake City: University of Utah Press, 1959.

Data were obtained from three men and six women; emphasis is on the life cycle of the Havasupai woman. Discusses the limitations of social and economic roles within the patrilineal culture.

372. Smits, David D. "'We Are Not to Grow Wild': Seventeenth-Century New England's Repudiation of Anglo-Indian Intermarriage." *American Indian Culture and Research Journal* 11, 4 (1987): 1-31.

Smits examines the factors which discouraged or precluded European settlers from marrying Indian women. Many sources document the high percentage of male settlers and the scarcity of English brides. Among several reasons interracial marriages did not take place, Smits argues that ethnocentrism manifested itself in religious obsessions and fears about the collapse of the social order should such unions take place.

373. Speck, Frank G. *Catawba Texts*. 1934; Rpt. New York: AMS Press, 1969.

Informants about Catawba culture include three women: Mrs. Samson Owl, Mrs. Margaret Wiley Brown, and Mrs. Sally Gordon.

374. Speck, Frank. "The Question of Matrilineal Descent in the Southeastern Siouan Area." *American Anthropologist* n.s., 40 (1938): 1-12.

This essay argues that Catawba and Tutelo and other southeastern Siouan tribes do not share a unilateral matrilineal clan descent system with the neighboring Cherokee and Creek and related tribes and posits that their social formation probably centered on the social nucleus of the town tribe characteristic of the southeastern area at large.

375. Spicer, Edward H. *People of Pascua*. Kathleen M. Sands and Rosamond B. Spicer, eds. Tucson: University of Arizona Press, 1988.

This ethnographic history of a Yaqui community in Arizona in the late 1930s and early 1940s includes sixteen biographies of Yaqui including women of three generations.

376. Spindler, Louise S. *Menomini Women and Culture Change*. Memoirs of the American Anthropological Association 91, 64, 1, part 2 (February 1962): 1-113.

    Study of acculturation of Menomini Indian women living in Wisconsin. Spindler found five levels of acculturation from a Native oriented group to an elite acculturated group.

377. Spindler, Louise S. "Women in Menomini Culture." In *The North American Indians: A Sourcebook*. Roger C. Owen *et al.* London: Macmillan, 1967, 598-605.

    Comments on the role of women among the Menominis of the Upper Great Lakes area in such areas as child training, menstruation, gaining power, witchcraft, ceremonies, and change since European contact.

378. Spindler, Louise and George Spindler. "Changing Women in Men's Worlds." In Occasional Papers in Anthropology, No. 2 *Sex Roles in Changing Cultures*. Ann McElroy and Carolyn Matthiasson, eds. Buffalo: Department of Anthropology, State University of New York, 1979, 35-47.

    Discussion of four societies in which change in women's roles has occurred as a result of acculturation: Blood Indians of Alberta, Menomini of Wisconsin, Mistassini Cree of Quebec, and peasant-oriented German villages.

379. Spindler, Louise S. and George Spindler. "Male and Female Adaptations in Culture Change." *American Anthropologist* n.s., 60, 2 (April 1958): 217-33.

    Compares the psychological adaptations of adult males and females in the rapidly changing Menomini tribe of Wisconsin. Women are seen as more conservative, less anxious about culture change, and more concerned about immediate daily needs than their male counterparts.

380. Spindler, Louise and George Spindler. "A Modal Personality Technique in the Study of Menomini Acculturation." In

Studying Personality Cross Culturally. Bert Kaplan, ed. Evanston, IL: Harper & Row Publishers, 1961, 479-92.

Discussion of the extension of collection and analysis of acculturation to include Menomini women as well as men and the implementation of the modal personality techniques Rorschach data. Three basic categories are used: Native oriented, peyote culture, and transitional.

381. Spott, Robert and A. L. Kroeber. *Yurok Narratives*. University of California Publications in American Archaeology and Ethnology 35, 9 (1943): 143-256.

Collaborative study of Yurok stories, a few myths but primarily historical and recent stories. Each story is followed by interpretation of the cultural context and significance. Several stories focus on marriage negotiation and bride protest, others on slave status, a female doctor who cannot master her power, and other women with curing powers.

382. Stephen, A. M. "Notes on Marriage among the Navajos, Navajo Dress and Navajo Dwellings." *Our Forest Children* 3 (1890): 222-23.

Concerned about the growing influence of white culture on Navajos, the author describes the traditional marriage ceremony and social practice relating to marriage, the jewelry and clothing, and the hogan architecture of the Navajos to record this information for posterity.

383. Steward, Julian H. "Shoshoni Polyandry." *American Anthropologist* n.s., 38 (January-March 1936): 561-64.

Shoshoni polyandry is not based on an excess of marriageable males, but rather on the practice of equal contribution of males and females to the household and a social structure in which the relationship of both sexes to plural marriage was almost identical. The common unit of polyandry was fraternal, and polyandry was practiced primarily among northern Shoshonis.

384. Stewart, Omer Call. "Northern Paiute Polyandry." *American Anthropologist* n.s., 39, 1-3 (January-March 1937): 368-69.

    A cultural survey in 1936 indicates the presence of polyandry among five of the eleven Northwestern Paiute bands, those now located in Burns, Oregon, and at Pyramid Lake, McDermitt, Winnemucca, and Owyhu, Nevada. Few cases exist and indications are that polyandry was not a common feature of Northern Paiute social life and was not institutionalized.

385. Sutter, Virginia. "Today's Strength from Yesterday's Tradition-- The Continuity of the American Indian Woman." *Frontiers* 6, 3 (1981): 53-57.

    Discusses the history of Northern Arapaho women who numbered 740 in 1877 and now number 3000. Their survival is attributed to the historical value accorded women and to their ability to acculturate to change brought by the Europeans while still maintaining tribal traditions.

386. Swentzell, Rina and Tito Naranjo. "Nurturing the *Gia* at Santa Clara Pueblo." *El Palacio* 92, 1 (Summer/Fall 1986): 35-39.

    "Gia" is synonymous with "mother," but also is used to refer to any nurturer, including the Earth. An example of a "gia" from Santa Clara--Khuun Tsawi--is used to demonstrate the important role of women. The authors give profiles of five Pueblo women who exemplify different aspects of "gia."

387. Swindlehurst, Captain Fred. "The Cree Squaw." *The Indian's Friend* 37, 4 (March 1925): 2, 5.

    Describes the Cree woman of Hudson's Bay as a child all her life. Clearly reflecting the racism of the period, the author refers to "papooses" as "olive-colored lumps of beauty," and to Indian women as "a willing slave and a beast of burden," yet he claims to admire Indian women.

388. Taylor, Dabney, "The Major's Blackfoot Bride." *Frontier Times* 43, 1 (December-January 1969): 26-29.

The courtship and marriage of a Blood woman, Natawistacha, and Major Alexander Culbertson of the American Fur Company is recalled by their granddaughter. She describes Natawistacha as adventuresome and recounts how her grandmother helped Audubon in his scientific study and bird watching and earned his respect for her work and her artistry as a beadworker. She also aided in negotiations between her tribe and explorers mapping out a route for a railroad to the Pacific coast. The author pays special note to the records of whites who praised "Natty" for her mastery of "civilized" ways and compares her to Sacajawea.

389. Terrell, John Upton and Donna M. Terrell. *Indian Women of the Western Morning: Their Life in Early America*. New York: Dial Press, 1974.

This book provides a look at the various roles of American Indian women with examples from different cultural groups. The text includes many pan-Indian tribal generalizations, but it is important as one of only a few books directly focused on Indian women.

390. Thometz, Judy. "The Earth Mother." *Many Smokes* 15, 2 (Fall 1981): 8-11.

Beginning with a Chippewa creation myth and terms used by Zunis and Iroquois to describe the earth, the article compares American Indian concepts of the earth .as Mother to those in Polynesia and in the ancient Middle East. A new age approach connects tribal images of the Earth Mother to the characteristics and qualities of living women.

391. Thompson, Laura and Alice Joseph. *The Hopi Way*. Lawrence, KS: Haskell Institute, 1944.

This book includes discussion on matrilineal organization and clans among the Hopi and includes material on women's participation in ceremonies and social roles.

392. Titier, Mischa. "The Problem of Cross-Cousin Marriage among the Hopi." *American Anthropologist* 40, 1 (January-March 1938): 105-11.

    The mock battle Hopi women on the groom's side of the marriage wage against male relations as part of a traditional wedding is seen as ritualized expression of resentment on the part of the women, second-cousins, from whom the groom would traditionally have chosen a wife.

393. Tobias, Cynthia, Bette Ide, and Margarita Kay. *Identifying Anglo, Mexican-American and American Indian Respondents for a Study of Recent Widows: Suggestions for Future Researchers.* Working Paper No. 23. Southwest Institute for Research on Women. Tucson: University of Arizona, 1987.

    A short paper which discusses the mechanisms--advertisements, letters, church referrals--to secure the names of widows to interview in Tucson, Arizona. The majority of American Indian referrals came through church contacts. The study is useful for scholars seeking participants for specific studies.

394. Tomkin, Merle, Carol Stern and Margie Bowker. "Listening to Native American Women." *Heresies 13: Feminism and Ecology* 4, 1 (1981): 17-21.

    Rocky Olguin, of Zapotaca descent, a participant in the 1980 "Longest Walk," describes Indian women as victims of "suppression, depression, oppression, and repression" as a result of assimilationist government policies and the erosion of traditional Indian life. Lois Red Elk (Dakota), an activist in the American Indian Movement, addresses issues of misunderstanding of lesbian women and threats to Indian survival. Madonna Thunder Hawk discusses the role of Women of All Red Nations in challenging threats to the survival of Indian people, particularly misuse of Indian lands and mineral holdings.

395. Trigger, Bruce G. "Iroquoian Matriliny." *Pennsylvania Archaeologist* 48 (1978): 55-65.

Trigger uses historical and archaeological evidence to determine that men's and women's roles among the Iroquois complemented one another and that matrilocal residence was a result of activity patterns following the adoption of horticulture.

396. Tsosie, Rebecca. "Changing Women: The Cross-Currents of American Indian Feminine Identity." *American Indian Culture and Research Journal* 12, 1 (1988): 1-37.

   Indian women writers are challenging stereotypes and "affirming their own concepts of femininity and 'Indianess.'" Tsosie analyzes Indian women's autobiographies, novels, and poetry to demonstrate the range of Indian women's experience and creativity. Includes discussion of works by Joy Harjo, Luci Tapahonso, Leslie Silko, Louise Erdrich, Paula Gunn Allen, and personal narrative authors Helen Sekaquaptewa, Mountain Wolf Woman, Maria Campbell, Anna Shaw and others.

397. Van Kirk, Sylvia. *Many Tender Ties: Women in Fur-Trade Society in Western Canada, 1670-1870.* Watson & Dwyer Publishing, 1980.

   Discusses Indian wives of fur traders and their contributions to the trade, their status before and after the coming of white women to trapping territories, abuse, dress, and influence on their daughters.

398. Van Leeuwen, Mary Stewart. "A Cross Cultural Examination of Psychological Differentiation in Males and Females." *International Journal of Psychology* 13, 2 (1978): 87-122.

   Focuses on the concept of differentiation and examines sex difference studies done on Eskimo and American Indians as well as other groups. The "ecological model" as well as "social conformity" and "biological" models are explained.

399. Voeglin, C. F. *The Shawnee Female Deity.* 1936; Rpt. New Haven: Yale University Publications in Anthropology, 1970.

Discusses the female creator called Our Grandmother by the Shawnee.

400. Wagner, Jean K. "The Role of Intermarriage in the Acculturation of Selected Urban American Indian Women." *Anthropologica* 18, 2 (1976): 215-29.

Wagner examines the effect of intermarriage on degrees of acculturation for urban Indian women in social, cultural, and personal identity, identifying three major categories of women: tradition-oriented, transitional, and American middle-class. She identifies a broad range of roles and attitudes toward Indian identification with blood quantum and personal preference and contact with their tribes, influencing the factors of the dominant society adopted by the women studied.

401. Wallace, Anthony F. C. "Women, Land, and Society: Three Aspects of Aboriginal Delaware Life." *Pennsylvania Archaeologist* 17 (1947): 1-35.

A history of Delaware culture (1600-1763) reconstructed through primary texts. Discusses power of women and the application of the term "women" to the Delaware, arguing that it was complimentary, meaning "mother, grandmother, or mother of nations."

402. Waterman, T. T. and A. L. Kroeber. *Yurok Marriages*. University of California Publications in American Archaeology and Ethnology, 335, (1943): 1-14.

Analysis of Yurok marriages as recorded in 1909 genealogies from Northwestern California. Marriages are categorized as full or half depending on whether or not the man pays for his wife. Only about 25% of the marriages did not involve payment.

403. Weist, Katherine M. "Plains Indian Women: An Assessment." In *Anthropology on the Great Plains*. W. Raymond Wood and Margot Liberty, eds. Lincoln: University of Nebraska Press, 1980, 255-71.

Weist cites examples of the views about Plains Indian women perpetuated by anthropologists, discusses some of the reasons for the paucity of material about Plains Indian women, and analyzes the materials that are available.

404. Welter, Barbara, ed. *The Woman Question in American History*. Hinsdale, IL: Dryden Press, 1973.

Welter includes one chapter on American Indian women, excerpts from *Daughters of the Country*, by Walter O'Meara. It is unfortunate that only O'Meara's narrow view is presented.

405. Weslager, C. A. "Further Light on the Delaware Indians as Women." *Journal of the Washington Academy of Science* 37 (15 September 1947): 298-304.

Discussion and clarification of the meaning of "feminization" of the Delaware by the Five Iroquois Nations. Discusses the controversy over the subjugation of the Delaware Indians by the Five Nations in the 1700s.

406. Westermeyer, Joseph. "Sex Roles at the Indian-Majority Interface in Minnesota." *International Journal of Social Psychology* 24 (September 1978): 189-94.

This article addresses the pattern and distribution of bias against Indian men relegated to custodial positions by women in influential roles and suggests remedial measures such as returning to a more traditional system of sex-roles, and returning authority in Indian communities to Indians so that men and women will share more equally in influential roles.

407. Whitaker, Kathleen. "Na Ih Es: An Apache Puberty Ceremony." *Masterkey* 45, 1 (January-March 1971): 4-12.

Illustrated account of a girl's puberty ceremony at the San Carlos Apache reservation in Arizona. Each phase of the ceremony is discussed in this transition to womanhood.

408. White, Leslie A. "The Pueblo of Santo Domingo, New Mexico."
      Memoirs of the American Anthropology Association 45 (1935):
      7-210.

      This comprehensive ethnography of Santo Domingo, at the
      time the most conservative of the Rio Grande pueblos, includes
      discussions of marriage and child rearing practices, including
      sanctions on marriage with women from other tribes, and burial
      customs regarding exo-marriage women. General discussion of
      matrilineal kinship system. Text also includes a version of the
      turkey-maiden tale.

409. Williams, Alice. "Maria Seymour: Native Language Instructors
      Program." *Canadian Woman Studies* 10, 2 & 3 (Summer/Fall
      1989): 75-78.

      The teaching of Native languages in Canadian schools has
      revitalized culture and maintained traditions.

410. Wilson, Maggie. "Naming Beverly's Baby." *Native Peoples* 1, 1
      (Fall 1987): 2-5.

      Illustrated account of the naming ceremony for a 20-day old
      son in the Hopi village of Shungapavi.

411. Wilson, Terry P. "Osage Indian Women During a Century of
      Change, 1870-1980." *Prologue: The Journal of the National
      Archives* 14 (Winter 1982): 185-201.

      An argument against the prevailing view that Osage women
      were merely chattel in their society, this essay points out
      traditional matrilineal residence, a equitable division of labor
      between men and women, the rigorous maintenance of personal
      hygiene by women, and the resistance to white cultural
      dominance by Osage mothers as evidence of the high status of
      women in traditional Osage culture. Wilson also discusses the
      impact of marriage to white men, boarding schools, legal
      interference by the BIA, frauds perpetrated to wrest oil and
      mineral income from Osages, violence done to Osage women by
      white men to gain their resource rights, and the Osage woman

who fought the U.S. government for the right to vote in tribal elections and hold tribal offices.

412. Winnemucca, Sarah. "The Pah-Utes." *Californian* 6 (1882): 252-56.

Winnemucca provides information on foods, the courage of the people, the oral language, traditions, ranking systems and customs affecting Indian girls, and the ceremony of courtship.

413. Witherspoon, Gary. *Language and Art in the Navajo Universe.* Ann Arbor: University of Michigan Press, 1977.

Defining both language and culture as symbolic codes, the author uncovers Navajo metaphysical assumptions through methods traditionally associated with philology. One section of his text addresses classification of sex in relation to other elements of Navajo life such as color, direction, kinship, and the role of gender in the creation myth.

414. Witherspoon, Gary. *Navajo Kinship and Marriage.* Chicago: University of Chicago Press, 1975.

Based on data collected in fifty contiguous subsistence residential units and drawing on the experiences and knowledge of both Navajo men and women, Witherspoon develops a study of Navajo social systems from a Navajo viewpoint. As a Navajo speaker and linguist, the author pays particular attention to interpretation of Navajo kin terms, and determines that the solidarity of the mother and child is seen by Navajos as the ideal relationship between and among all people.

415. Witt, Shirley Hill. "The Brave-Hearted Women." *Akwesasne Notes* 8 (Early Summer 1976): 16-17.

Witt relates the strength of Indian women to traditional positions within tribes.

416. Wittstock, Laura Waterman. "Native American Women in the Feminist Milieu." In *Contemporary Native American Addresses.*

John R. Maestas, ed. Provo, UT: Brigham Young University, 1976, 373-76.

A Seneca woman describes the powerful traditional roles of women in the Iroquois Confederacy and urges that Indian women of all tribes act within tribal context to assert their power.

417. Wittstock, Laura. "Native American Women: Twilight of a Long Maidenhood." In *Comparative Perspectives of Third World Women: The Import of Race, Sex and Class*. Beverly Lindsay, ed. New York: Praeger, 1980, 207-27.

The author examines the colonial policy of channeling Native women toward domestic work and later U.S. policy of relocation and their effects on Indian women's perceptions of their roles. The essay argues that urban Indian women identify strongly with the women's movement but rural Indian women continue to identify themselves through arts and other manifestations of the domestic sphere. Indian women generally prefer to bring about changes within tribal context to working in the political arena.

418. Wyman, Leland C. "Navajo Girls' Puberty Rite." *New Mexico Anthropologist* 15 (1943): 3-12.

A detailed account of the ceremony describes each step in the ritual reenactment of the Changing Woman myth. Actions, paraphernalia, food preparations, consecration of the hogan and food, molding and painting of the girl are all explained.

419. Yazzie, Ethelou. "Navajo Wisdom." In *Contemporary Native American Addresses*. John R. Maestas, ed. Provo, UT: Brigham Young University, 1976, 263-76.

Yazzie discusses the Navajo creation narrative and curing rituals. Figures from these traditional stories include Changing Woman, Spider Woman, and Salt Woman. The importance of women in Navajo culture is emphasized.

420. Yehwehnode (Twylah Nitsch). "Woman." *Many Smokes* 15, 2 (Fall 1981): 13.

Wolf Clan Mother of the Seneca, Yehwehnode, relates a legend which exemplifies the honor and respect given to women and analyzes its significance for the endurance of her tribe.

421. Young, M. Jane. "Women, Reproduction and Religion in Western Puebloan Society." *Journal of American Folklore* 100, 398 (Oct.-Dec. 1987): 436-45.

Argues that ritual behavior of Puebloan men is imitative of reproductive power of women. Stresses the importance of women to the ceremonial life of Western Pueblos.

422. Ywahoo, Dhyani. *Voices of Our Ancestors: Cherokee Teachings From the Wisdom Fire.* Barbara DuBois, ed. Boston: Shambhala, 1987.

Compiled from a series of the lectures by the author, an Eastern Cherokee, the intent of this is to teach the principles of Cherokee spiritual and moral mysteries to the public. Each of the three major philosophical principles--will, love and active intelligence--is illustrated with seven examples related to individual, family, national and world harmony. The text makes cross-cultural comparisons to tenets of European and Asian belief systems and appears to be closer to "New Age" philosophy than traditional tribal views. Author is founder of the Sunray Meditation Society dedicated to planetary peace.

Politics and Law

POLITICS AND LAW

423. "A Woman's Ways." *Native Self-Sufficiency* 4, 3-4 (September 1981).

   An interview with Judy Swamp, a Mohawk activist.

424. "An Indian Woman for Sheriff." *Indian's Friend* 42, 5 (September 1930): 4.

   Ida Scott, an Omaha woman running for sheriff in Thurston County, Nebraska, is campaigning on the promise to rid the area of bootleggers, many of whom are Indian women, according to her. She expects support of Omahas and Winnebagos, especially from Indian women voters, and may appoint women deputies.

425. "B.C. Native Women's Society." *Canadian Woman Studies* 10, 2 & 3 (Summer/Fall 1989): 141-42.

   Discussion of an organization formed in 1968 to respond to the Indian Act and its discriminatory actions toward women.

426. "Hopi Prototypes of the 'Suffragettes.'" *Indian's Friend* 21, 8 (April 1909): 10.

   Legend describes a "strike" by Hopi women who moved away from their men to a distant mesa until men conceded them mastery of the household. This story is seen as the source of the recognition of the rights of women in Hopi society where women own property and men labor for them.

427. "Indian Suffragettes." *Indian's Friend* 25, 6 (March 1913): 11.

Dawn Mist, a daughter of a chief of the "Glacier National Park Indians" and her group of "mounted maidens" ride in the Washington, D.C., Women's Suffrage pageant of 1913, replete in tribal costumes, and camp out in tepees in the capital.

428. "Indian Women Join the Struggle." *Leader Post* (15 November 1967): 39.

Brief summary of a conference sponsored by the Department of Indian Affairs and the University of Saskatchewan. The keynote speaker was Mary Ann Lavalee, and sixty delegates discussed drinking, illegitimacy, school drop-outs, delinquents, and women's role in maintaining the family.

429. *Indian Women Plan for the Seventies*. Report of the Associated Country Women of the World's National Seminar of American Indian Women, August 8, 1970, Ft. Collins, Colorado. ERIC ED 103 176.

Indian women selected for the grass roots activism in their tribal communities met to discuss such issues as Indian and non-Indian values, alcoholism and drug abuse, education, community development, and family communication.

430. "Indian Women Want to Help Themselves." *Indian's Friend* 39, 2 (November 1926): 1.

The Eagle Feather Club in Spokane, Washington, is described as an organization of Indian women for the discussion of women's problems and the study of methods for the advancement of Indian women.

431. "Leaders of their People: Native Women Working for the Future." *Indian Truth: Special Issue on Native Women*. Marg Emery and Ann Larner, eds. 239 (May-June): 9-10.

Indian women active in health care, government, the arts, education, and law are profiled.

432. "Marriage Plot Against Indian Boys and Girls Discovered."
     Indian's Friend 26, 2 (November 1913): 8.

     When a disreputable white banker's plot to marry off two sons
     and a daughter of a Creek Indian whose land is worth over a
     million dollars to dishonest non-Indian spouses in order to
     swindle the family out of its land and oil rights was discovered,
     the family sent the children to boarding schools, the daughter to
     Arizona and the boys to Carlisle, to protect them.

433. "Native American Women Denied Voice at International
     Women's Year Conference." *Akwesasne Notes* 7, 3 (Early
     Autumn 1975): 33.

     Native American women who were not part of the 1975 official
     United Nations Conference in Mexico City attended the
     International Women's Year Tribune to discuss the subjugation
     of women of color in the Americas as well as elsewhere in the
     world.

434. "Native Women's Association of Canada." *Canadian Woman
     Studies* 10, 2 & 3 (Summer/Fall 1989): 133-35.

     This article profiles this association in Canada which promotes
     Native women's rights.

435. "Navajo Organizer Leads Fight Against Uranium." *Native Self-
     Sufficiency* 4, 3-4 (September 1981).

     Interview with Elsie Peshlakai, Native American organizer
     from New Mexico.

436. "Pauktuutit." *Canadian Woman Studies* 10, 2 & 3 (Summer/Fall
     1989): 137-39.

     This women's association created in 1984 focuses on issues
     such as child sexual abuse, family violence, midwifery, and child
     care.

437. "Quebec Native Women's Association." *Canadian Woman Studies* 10, 2 & 3 (Summer/Fall 1989): 143-45.

Discussion of an association founded in 1974 to support Native women in education, social services, training, and employment.

438. *Report on the National Seminar of American Indian Women and the North American Indian Women's Association.* August 2-8, 1970, Fort Collins, Colorado. Colorado State University. Washington, DC: US Government Printing Office, 1970. ERIC ED 065 772.

This meeting of 68 Indian women representing 43 tribes was held at Colorado State University to provide an opportunity for Indian women to discuss the needs of Indian communities and to stimulate more women to take leadership roles.

439. "Women Go to War on Indian Laws." *Akwesasne Notes* 2, 1 (1970): 47.

A Montreal conference of Indian women castigates supporters of the Canadian Indian Act which deprives Native women who marry white men of all tribal rights.

440. Alberta Native Women's Society. *Report of the First Alberta Native Women's Conference.* Edmonton: Alberta Native Woman's Society, 1968.

Complete program, addresses, recommendations, evaluations, and list of attendees. The women attending addressed health concerns, Canadian politics, water issues, and Metis issues.

441. Allan, Chris. "Baby By-the-Falling Waters Joins the Fight." *Akwesasne Notes* 3, 2 (March 1971): 27.

Kahn-Tineta Horn, a Mohawk activist, attracted negative response from non-Indians when she gave birth to Kanawahere ("By-the-Falling Waters") outside of marriage.

442. Atwood, Barbara Ann. "Fighting Over Indian Children: The Uses and Abuses of Jurisdictional Ambiguity." *UCLA Law Review* 36, 6 (August 1989): 1051-1108.

Rules for decisions of child custody between state and tribal courts are ambiguous and work hardships on all participants in proceedings. Increasing mobility and marriage outside the tribe is causing more conflict of authority in custody cases as numbers of divorces and legal conflicts rise. Based on cases cited and current national policy, the author recommends a "preferred" role of tribal courts in order to protect participants from "the anguish of prolonged jurisdictional competition."

443. Berman, Susan. "Working for My People: Thorpe's Daughter Indian Activist." *Akwesasne Notes* 3, 2 (March 1971): 27.

Brief account of Grace Thorpe's active involvement with D.Q. University near Davis, California. Thorpe is a member of the Sauk and Fox tribe and the daughter of Jim Thorpe. She participated in the occupation of Alcatraz and was a founding member of the National Indian Women's Action Corps.

444. Bernstein, Alison. "A Mixed Record: The Political Enfranchisement of American Indian Women During the Indian New Deal." *Journal of the West* 23 (July 1984): 13-20.

John Collier's Indian New Deal did not effectively utilize women in developing programs. Though he relied on Gertrude Bonnin for advice, there were other Indian women who might have played significant roles, Ella Deloria and Ruth Muskrat, for instance, and he generally failed to recognize the existing political influence of Indian women. On the positive side, the Collier programs included education for women in nursing and clerical work and their effect was to give Indian women a platform for work in social welfare and education, in local organizations, and state politics.

445. Bomberry, Dan, ed. "Sage Advice from a Long Time Activist: Janet McCloud." *Native Self-Sufficiency* 6 (1981): 4-5, 20.

Janet McCloud (Tulalip) talks about strategies for survival in the modern world and urges Indian women not to emulate white models because their own tribal traditions offer models that give women more empowerment.

446. Bonney, Rachel A. "The Role of Women in Indian Activism." *Western Canadian Journal of Anthropology* 6, 3 (1976): 243-48.

The roles of Indian women in modern intertribal organizations may be a continuation of some traditional women's roles relating to tribal education, health, rights, survival, sovereignty, and pride rather than a manifestation of women's or individual rights.

447. Brady, Victoria, Sarah Crome, and Lyn Reese. "Resist: Survival Tactics of Indian Women." *California History* 63 (Spring 1984): 140-51.

Throughout the years of European colonization in California, Indian women developed a variety of methods of passive resistance, in some cases moving to areas isolated from white influence, in other cases escaping from mission schools, hiding children from whites who wanted them as workers or to put them in schools, preserving traditional women's customs, supporting women shamans, and learning to develop markets for their baskets.

448. Broussand, C. "Mohawk Beauty with a Mission." *Look* 28 (28 January 1964): 91-94.

This is a brief, illustrated account of Kahn Tineta Horn, a Canadian Mohawk woman who was active as a spokesperson for her people.

449. Bysiewicz, Shirley and Ruth Van de Mark. "The Legal Status of Dakota Indian Women." *American Indian Law Review* 3 (1975): 255-312.

This essay examines the status of Dakota women from traditional times through the imposition of reservation administrative policies through the effects of federal legislation.

The laws of domestic relations and inheritance which severely discriminate against Indian women are discussed in terms of legal cases, and the growing political strength of Dakota women today is illustrated in income, educational, and occupational terms and by examples of women in tribal offices. Despite abuse and oppression, Dakota women are actively fighting discrimination and asserting their legal rights.

450. Cardinal, Harold. "Native Women and the Indian Act." In *Two Nations, Many Cultures: Ethnic Groups in Canada*. Jean Leonard Elliot, ed. Scarborough, Ontario: Prentice-Hall, 1979, 44-50.

Discusses the challenges to the Canadian Indian Act of 1951, which violated Native women's rights set forth under the Canadian Bill of Rights.

451. Caskanette, A. and P. Terbasket. "The Lovesick Lake Native Women's Association." *Canadian Woman Studies* 10, 2 & 3 (Summer/Fall 1989): 93-94.

A group of Metis women organized in 1982 to work with the youth of the community by providing economic and social support.

452. Chehak, Gail. "An Urban Perspective." *Native Self- Sufficiency* 4, 3-4 (September 1981).

Chehak is a Klamath Indian activist involved with issues facing urban Indian women.

453. Chrystos. "Nidishenok (Sisters)." *Maenad: A Woman's Literary Journal* 2, 2 (Winter 1982): 23-32.

Discussing the lesbian-heterosexual split, Chrystos takes a critical view of separatism, arguing that it divides and hurts women.

454. Corrizan, Samuel W. "A Note on Canadian Indian Marriage Law." *The Western Canadian Journal of Anthropology* 4, 2 (1974): 17-27.

Using the nine Canadian Dakota reservations in Manitoba and Saskatchewan as the basis for his study, the author examines the differences between Native and national law regarding marriage, noting some Dakota marriages correspond to Canadian law while others could subject some Dakotas to bigamy charges. Citing nineteenth century recognition of Native marriage laws, the author advocates national development of multi-cultural marriage laws.

455. Cruikshank, Julie. "Native Women in the North: An Expanding Role." *North/Nord* 18 (November-December 1971): 1-7.

This article discusses the role of Canadian Indian men and women, the laws which affect Indian women, and women's role in the family as well as at work and in politics.

456. Emery, Marg. "Indian Women's Groups Span a Broad Spectrum." *Indian Truth: Special Issue on Indian Women*. Marg Emery and Ann Laquer, eds. 239 (May-June): 8

Brief histories of three Indian women's organizations--North American Indian Women's Association, Ohoyo, and Women of All Red Nations--along with goals and activities.

457. Flaherty, Martha. "I Fought to Keep My Hair." *Nunavut* 5, 6 (June 1986): 4-6.

An Inuit woman recalls resisting white policy to cut Native children's hair when they were removed from their village to Resolute Bay. Lack of food and the difficulties of hunting are also discussed.

458. Giese, Paula. "Free Sarah Bad Heart Bull (and the Other Custer Defendants)." *North Country Anvil* 13 (October/November 1974): 64-71.

The story of Sarah Bad Heart Bull, who was arrested at a demonstration in Custer, South Dakota, protesting the light sentence given to the murderer of her son. Includes a transcription of a radio interview with Bad Heart Bull.

459. Giese, Paula. "Secret Agent Douglass Durham and the Death of Jancita Eagle Deer." *North Country Anvil* (March/April 1976): 1-15.

Thwarted in their attempts to gain an official investigation into the hit-and-run "accident" of Jancita Marie Eagle Deer (Rosebud Sioux), the American Indian Movement spokeswoman's account of her personal history and death is intended as an epitaph for an Indian woman brutalized and exploited by a federal agent posing as an AIM activist.

460. Goodwill, Jean C. "A New Horizon for Native Women in Canada." In *Citizen Participation: Canada, a Book of Readings*. James A. Draper, ed. Toronto: New Press, 1971, 362-70.

Goodwill discusses the increased involvement in politics and education by Canadian Indian women in order to retain their heritage and preserve their rights.

461. Gouge, Saxon. "Let's Ban the Word 'Squaw.'" *Ohoyo: Bulletin of American Indian--Alaska Native Women* 9 (July 1981).

Gouge, an Ojibwa woman, urges the abandonment of the word "squaw" with its demeaning connotation of enslavement and drudgery and suggests tribal people use their own language to avoid negative terms for Indian peoples and roles.

462. Gray, Cynthia. "A Question of Sovereignty: Patricia Monture v. the Queen." *Canadian Woman Studies* 10, 2 & 3 (Summer/Fall 1989): 146-47.

Patricia Monture has filed a suit that she should not be required to take an oath to support the Queen because she is a member of a sovereign nation.

463. Green, Leanne. "Foster Care and After." *Canadian Woman Studies* 10, 2 & 3 (Summer/Fall 1989): 41-43.

Account of a child who went through the foster care system after being removed from the loving home of her grandparents.

464. Green, Rayna. "Native American Women: The Leadership Paradox." *Women's Educational Equity Communications Network News and Notes* 1 (Spring 1980): 1, 4.

Green discusses the paradox of the growing assumption of positions in the professions by Indian women and their continuing poor status in the areas of health, education, and economics. Racism, sexism, and classism deny many Indian women access to equal status and perpetuate problems. Because the number of Indian women who have attained leadership and professional status is small, they bear a disproportionate burden within and outside their communities.

465. Hansen, Karen Tranberg. "Ethnic Group Policy and the Politics of Sex: The Seattle Indian Case." *Urban Anthropology* 8, 1 (Spring 1979): 29-47.

Hansen discusses the American Indian Women's Service League, a Seattle organization begun in 1958. The group of women was successful in making changes but when forced to restructure to gain federal funding, the power of the women diminished and the association's influence on policy declined.

466. Hauptman, Laurence M. "Alice Jemison: Seneca Political Activist." *Indian Historian* 12, 2 (Summer 1979): 15-22, 60-62.

Alice Jemison (1901-1964) was an activist against the BIA through her organization, the American Indian Federation. Hauptman has examined government records and Congressional testimony to document the contributions of this Seneca woman to the struggle of her people.

467. Herzog, Kristin. "Women, Religion, and Peace in an American Indian Ritual." *Explorations in Ethnic Studies* 7, 1 (January 1984): 16-38.

Herzog examines the epic of Dekanawida and the role of women in the history, politics and religion of the Iroquois League.

468. Jamieson, Kathleen. "Multiple Jeopardy: The Evolution of a Native Women's Movement." *Atlantis* 4, 1 Part 2 (1979): 157-78.

Traces the history of Native women's political involvement in Canada, beginning with their effective barring from political life by the Indian Act (1869-1951), enfranchisement in 1960, and the challenges to the Indian Act in the 1970s.

469. Jamieson, Kathleen. *Indian Women and the Law in Canada: Citizen Minus.* Ottawa: Canadian Government Publishing Centre, 1978.

The Indian Act ruled that an Indian who married a non-Indian ceased to be an Indian under Canadian law. The legislation affected Indian women economically and politically and the non-Indian status was extended to her children. Indian men, however, could confer Indian status on non-Indians through marriage, and in no case lost their legal status as Indian. This study examines the impact of the Indian Act on Indian women in Canada and analyzes the case of Jeanette Lavell who challenged the Canadian law.

470. Jamieson, Kathleen Macleod. "Human Rights: Indian Women Need Not Appeal." *Branching Out: Canadian Magazine for Women* 6, 2 (1979): 11-13.

Discusses the fight by Indian women married to non-Indian men to regain their legal status as Indians in Canada.

471. Knack, Martha C. "Contemporary Southern Paiute Women and the Measurement of Women's Economic and Political Status." *Ethnology* 28 (1989): 233-48.

Contemporary Southern Paiute women's roles are in large part the result of an historical process, regional development, and interactive relations in the Great Basin and must be analyzed in terms of colonialism as well as traditional roles, rights and duties. Sanday's variables--material control, solidarity groups, demand for goods, and political participation--are a useful initial index.

472. Koester, Susan H. "'By the Words of thy Mouth Let Thee Be Judged': The Alaska Native Sisterhood Speaks." *Journal of the West* 27, 2 (April 1988): 35-44.

Four Tlingit women organized the Alaska Native Sisterhood in 1920, first to support the Alaska Native Brotherhood, and later to serve as a political voice for Native people of Alaska.

473. LaChapelle, Caroline. "Beyond Barriers: Native Women and the Women's Movement." In *Still Ain't Satisfied! Canadian Feminism Today*. Maureen Fitzgerald, Connie Guberman, and Margie Wolfe, eds. Toronto: Women's Press, 1982, 257-64.

Written by an Ojibwa woman, this essay explores the reasons why few Native women are active in the Canadian women's movement. An historical overview of the plight of Native women focuses on the discriminatory Indian Act which deprives Indian women of Indian status if they marry non-status or non-Indian men, and the author urges more involvement and gives strategies for Indian women's unity and action.

474. Lindstrom, Vieno. "Constitutional Law, Santa Clara Pueblo vs. Martinez: Tribal Membership and the Indian Civil Rights Act." *American Indian Law Review* 6, 1 (Summer 1978): 205-16.

Analysis of a suit brought by Santa Clara Pueblo member Julia Martinez on behalf of her daughter who cannot be accorded tribal status because her father is not a Santa Clara tribal member. The case accuses the membership ordinance of contravening the equal protection and due process provisions of the Indian Civil Rights Act of 1968.

475. Marshall, Karen. "Caretakers of the Earth." *Women of Power* 14
      (Summer 1989): 42-44.

      Photographic essay on the Navajo women in the Big Mountain
      area of the reservation who are facing relocation as a result of
      Public Law 93-531.

476. Miller, Dorothy L. "Native American Women: Leadership
      Images." *Integrateducation* 15, 1 (January/February 1978): 37-
      39.

      Miller discusses the world views of Native Americans and non-
      Native Americans as they impact on the roles of Indian men and
      women. Indian women face a dual challenge in leadership roles
      both within their tribes and within American society in general.

477. Miller, Lischen M. "Native Women of Alaska." *Pacific Monthly* 7,
      8 (1902): 60-61.

      Alaska Native women are seen as having the political equality
      that the women's suffrage in white culture in America is seeking.
      They are, in fact, described as more politically powerful than
      men, but the author argues that they would be happier if they
      accepted male dominance.

478. Nahanee, Theresa. "Canadian Women Demand Equal Rights."
      Indian News 15 (January 1973): 1, 6-7.

      Reports on a meeting of Canadian Indian women concerned
      with their status accorded by the Canadian government.

479. O'Connor, Shirley, Patricia Monture, and Norissa O'Connor.
      "Grandmother, Mothers and Daughters." *Canadian Woman
      Studies* 10, 2 & 3 (Summer/Fall 1989): 38-39.

      Two Native women discuss the Ontario Native Women's
      Association and the need for Native women to be involved in
      improving the lives of Native women.

480. Ortiz, Roxanne Dunbar. "Land and Nationhood: The American
      Indian Struggle for Self-Determination and Survival." *Socialist
      Review* 12, 63-64 (May/August 1982): 105-20.

      The U.S. Government provoked the formation of American
      Indian nationalism in the eighteenth and nineteenth centuries as
      a response to threats to their existence. Nationalism as a survival
      mechanism reasserted itself again in the 1950s in response to
      termination policy and led to the formation of AIM and militant
      action on the part of Indians in the 1960s and 1970s.

481. Pascoe, R. "Canadian Indian Women Fight For Tribal Rights."
      MS 11 (October 1982): 19.

      The new Canadian constitution, which promises to eliminate all
      sexual discrimination, should prevent the loss of rights Indian
      women face under the Indian Act which deprives Canadian tribal
      women of Indian status and rights when they marry non-Indians.
      However the 15,000 women and 45,000 children who have lost
      Indian rights since 1920 will not be reinstated by the new
      constitution.

482. Payne, Diane. "Each of my Generations is Getting Stronger: An
      Interview with Janet McCloud." *Indian Truth: Special Issue on
      Native Women*. Marg Emery and Ann Laquer, eds. 239 (May-
      June): 5-7.

      Janet McCloud (Yet Si Blue), a Tulalip woman, discusses her
      active role in Northwest fishing rights disputes and comments on
      the support she has received from other Indian women. She also
      advocates reactivating puberty rituals in order to ensure continued
      traditional education of tribal women.

483. Platiel, Rudy. "Kahn-tineta Wants Her Sister Evicted." *Akwesasne
      Notes* 3, 7 (1971): 38.

      Kahn-tineta Horn, a 29-year-old Mohawk activist who
      characterizes herself as a racist in favor of apartheid, is fighting
      to evict all non-Indians from her reserve, including her sister who
      has lost Indian status under the Canadian Indian Act. Response

to her efforts are mixed with many residents expressing the opinion that residency policy should be left to the tribal leaders.

484. Sainte-Marie, Buffy. "Victims No More." *Akwesasne Notes* 8, 5 (Midwinter 1976-77): 29.

This is a personal statement from Cree singer Buffy Sainte-Marie in which she advises Indians to be proud of their Indianness.

485. Sanders, Douglas. "Indian Women: A Brief History of Their Roles and Rights." *McGill Law Journal* 21, 4 (1975): 652-72.

Based on data from the Lavell case, the author suggests that the "preconditions of the women's movement" do not yet exist in Canadian Indian communities. He notes that Indian communities need to be recognized as culturally different collections and white norms should not be imposed on them. He prefaces this discussion with a brief history of women's traditional roles and rights and white misunderstanding of and misinterpretation of women's rights.

486. Silmar, Janet, ed. *Enough is Enough: Aboriginal Women Speak Out*. Toronto: The Women's Press, 1987.

Native women from the Tobique Reserve in New Brunswick became politically active to improve living conditions and succeeded in changing the Canadian Indian Act which eroded Native women's rights. The book is a collection of personal narratives from women who experienced discrimination and acted to improve their legal and economic status. Silmar provides biographical sketches of the women included in the volume.

487. Sugar, Fran. "Entrenched Social Catastrophe: Native Women in Prison." *Canadian Woman Studies* 10, 2 & 3 (Summer/Fall 1989): 87-89.

A profile of an 18-year-old offender demonstrates the effect of the criminal justice system on Native women.

488. Tellinghuisen, Roger A. "The Indian Child Welfare Act of 1978: A Practical Guide with [Limited] Commentary." *South Dakota Law Review* 34, 3 (1989): 660-99.

There is evidence that Indian children removed from their homes under the Indian Child Welfare Act of 1978 who grew up in non-Indian homes experienced cultural crisis during teenage years. The author argues for policy that restores Indian parents' rights and rights of tribes regarding Indian children. Current law does not serve the interests of Indian children and often leads to tragedy. Cases are cited.

489. Temkin, Merle, Carol Stern, and Margie Bowker. "Listening to Native American Women." *Heresies* 13, 4, 1 (1981): 17-21.

Interviews with Native American women who are active in environmental and energy issues.

490. Thorpe, Dagmar. "Native American Women Win Historic Rights Case." *MS* 12 (December 1983): 17.

Dann sisters win Shoshone case which validates the tribe's claim to more than one-third of the state's land, 24 million acres, which these two women ranchers asserted had been taken illegally by the U.S. government.

491. Thorpe, Dagmar. "Native Political Organizing in Nevada: A Woman's Perspective." *Native Self-Sufficiency* 4, 34 (September 1981): 14-15.

Thorpe is the founder of Native Nevadans for Political Education and Action and argues that political organizing is crucial for the survival of Indian people. She focuses on the Western Shoshone and the Treaty of Ruby Valley. Other women active in Nevada are Debra Harry, Janet Moose, and Pearl Dann.

492. Thorpe, Dagmar. "Traditional Shoshone Sisters Win Wonder Women Award." *Akwesasne Notes* 16, 1 (Midwinter 1984): 12.

Mary and Carrie Dann, Western Shoshone sisters, received awards from the Wonder Woman Foundation in 1983 for their defense of tribal rights. Their case, *US vs. Dann*, argued that the Western Shoshone owned eighteen million acres of eastern Nevada.

493. Turpel, Aki-kwe/Mary Ellen. "Aboriginal Peoples and the Canadian Charter of Rights and Freedoms." *Canadian Woman Studies* 10, 2 & 3 (Summer/Fall 1989): 149-157.

Using Canadian law and legal principles, Turpel argues for the rights of Native peoples in an ethnocentric legal system.

494. Wallis, Michael. "Hail to the Chief: Wilma Mankiller is the First Woman to be Elected Cherokee Nation Chief." *Phillip Morris Magazine* (October 1989): 37-39.

This forty-three-year-old grandmother and political activist is the first woman chief of the Cherokee tribe and the first woman to lead a "major Indian tribe." She sees herself as a model to young Indian women. A brief biography is included.

495. Wauneka, Annie D. "The Dilemma for Indian Women." *Wassaja* 4 (September 1976): 8.

Wauneka asserts that Indian women's first priorities are "equal treatment, opportunity and recognition of the Indians and Tribal Government." She believes that women's roles cannot be assessed until the legal status of all Indians is reaffirmed and strengthened.

496. Whyte, John D. "The Lavell Case and Equality in Canada." *Queen's Quarterly* 81, 1 (1974): 28-41.

The author feels that the Supreme Court's decision in the 1973 Lavell case failed to clarify the main issues of the case, which were "the legitimacy of administration of the Native peoples of Canada," and "the constitutional value of equality of the sexes."

497. Williams, Walter L. "Twentieth Century Indian Leaders: Brokers and Providers." *Journal of the West* 23, 3 (July 1984): 3-6.

The impact of Native American women in national leadership roles is largely overlooked. Gertrude Bonnin is cited as an important figure influencing modern Indian struggles for power because of her part in conceiving pan-Indian identity. Current studies of Indian women's roles are seen as beginning to rectify the dearth of information on Indian women.

498. Witt, Shirley Hill. "The Brave-Hearted Women: The Struggle at Wounded Knee." *Civil Rights Digest* 8, 4 (1976): 38-45.

Anna Mae Picton Aquash, a Micmac from Shukenacadie, Nova Scotia, who was killed on the Pine Ridge reservation during the second battle of Wounded Knee, is a symbol of the activist Indian women who have been harassed, jailed, beaten, and killed for their commitment to Indian causes. Biography, traditional oratory regarding the power of tribal women, diary entries, political statements, an autopsy report, and a tribute to Picton Aquash are included.

499. Wittstock, Laura. "On Women's Rights for Native Peoples." *Akwesasne Notes* 7, 3 (1975): 39.

Statement by a Seneca woman who was acting director of the American Indian Press Association. Wittstock argues that women's roles must be defined tribally, not by outside agencies or government policies such as the Indian Civil Rights Act.

500. Women of All Red Nations. *W.A.R.N.* Porcupine, SD: We Will Remember Group, 1978.

Reports on the conference of Women of All Red Nations (W.A.R.N.) and includes articles on personal experiences of American Indian women concerning contemporary issues.

501. Yamasaki, April. "Canada Confronts a 100-Year-Old Injustice." *MS* 8 (January 1980): 23.

Discusses a challenge to the 1869 Canadian Indian Act which forced Indian women who married white men to give up their status as Indians and leave their reservations.

502. Zitkala-Sa [Gertrude Bonnin]. "America, Home of the Red Man." *The American Indian Magazine* 6 (Winter 1919): 165-67.

A response to a remark that the author, a Native American, was a "foreigner."

503. Zitkala-Sa [Gertrude Bonnin]. "Americanize the First American: A Plan of Regeneration." Library of American Indian Affairs, Microfilm reel 125, no. 160.

This pamphlet blasts the reservation system and argues for Indian enfranchisement and improved living conditions.

504. Zitkala-Sa [Gertrude Bonnin]. "Editorial Comment." *The American Indian Magazine* 6 (July-September 1918): 113-14.

Commentary on a Society of American Indians conference in favor of abolishing BIA schools.

505. Zitkala-Sa [Gertrude Bonnin]. "Editorial Comment." *The American Indian Magazine* 7 (Summer 1919): 61-63.

Commentary on Indian soldiers in World War I and the campaign for Indian citizenship.

506. Zitkala-Sa [Gertrude Bonnin]. "Editorial Comment." *The American Indian Magazine* 6 (Winter 1919): 161-62.

Argues for Indian citizenship.

507. Zitkala-Sa [Gertrude Bonnin]. "Editorial Comment." *The American Indian Magazine* 7 (Spring 1919): 5-9.

Commentary on Indian land issues in Utah and South Dakota.

508.   Zitkala-Sa [Gertrude Bonnin]. "Letter to Chiefs and Headmen of the Tribes." *The American Indian Magazine* 6 (Winter 1919): 196-97.

Bonnin exhorts tribal leaders to emphasize education and not to sell tribal lands.

509.   Zitkala-Sa [Gertrude Bonnin]. "Indian Gifts to the Civilized Man." *The American Indian Magazine* 6 (July-September 1918): 115-16.

Discusses American Indian contributions to mainstream American cultures, and particularly Indian participation in World War I.

510.   Zitkala-Sa [Gertrude Bonnin]. "A Year's Experience in Community Service Work Among the Ute Tribes of Indians." *The American Indian Magazine* 4 (October-December 1916): 307-10.

Bonnin discusses her community organizing efforts on the Uintah-Ouray reservation in Utah, and concludes that Indian community workers can provide the best service to their own people.

511.   Zitkala-Sa [Gertrude Bonnin], Charles H. Fabens, and Matthew K. Sniffen. *Oklahoma's Poor Rich Indians: An Orgy of Graft and Exploitation of the Five Civilized Tribes--Legalized Robbery.* Publication of the Indian Rights Association, 2nd series, no. 127. Philadelphia: Indian Rights Association, 1924.

Based on five weeks of field work in eastern Oklahoma in 1923, this is a study of the corruption draining the resources of the Five Civilized Tribes resulting from the shifting of jurisdiction from the Department of Interior to local courts. County judges, guardians, lawyers, bankers, and merchants are accused of "shamelessly and openly" robbing the tribes through withholding of food supplies, falsified leases, kidnapping of girls and women, false marriage records, and other abuses.

Health, Education, and Employment

HEALTH, EDUCATION, AND EMPLOYMENT

512. "An Illustrated Souvenir Catalog of the Cherokee National Female Seminary." *Journal of Cherokee Studies* 10, 1 (Spring 1985).

 This special issue traces the history of the Cherokee National Female Seminary in Tallequah from 1850-1906.

513. "An Osage Cattle Queen of Oklahoma." *Indian's Friend* 23, 12 (August 1911): 2.

 Credited with being the richest member of the Osage tribe, June Applebee, an adopted member of the tribe, at the age of fifty, widowed and struggling to feed her fifteen children, gained permission to claim all motherless calves from herds being grazed on Osage land by Texas cattlemen. This became the basis for her huge herd and her success.

514. "An Up-To-Date Heroine of the Wyandottes." *Indian's Friend* 22, 1 (September 1909): 10-11.

 Lyda Conley, the first Indian woman to be admitted to the bar in Kansas, is praised for challenging the U.S. government's sale of an Indian burial ground in Kansas City for development purposes. The sale violated the 1855 treaty, which is the basis of Conley's case.

515. "Indian Woman Carries the Mail." *Indian's Friend* 24, 10-11 (June-July 1912): 12.

Mary Fisher (Maush-gwon ah-quod oke), from Bois Fort, is the first full-blood Indian woman to become a mail carrier. She delivered mail for six months in 1910 during one of the coldest winters on record.

516. "Indian Woman Lawyers." *Indian's Friend* 20, 6 (February 1908): 5.

Julia Cyr, a Winnebago Indian who represents the Winnebagos and Omahas, and Lyda Conley, who gained fame for defending the Wyandotte claim to cemetery property in Kansas City, are profiled briefly.

517. *Indian Women Today.* Window Rock, AZ: Southwestern Indian Women's Conference, September 24-25, 1975. ERIC ED 125 818.

Indian women gathered to discuss job equality, attitudes towards the women's movement, education and the Indian woman, extending the role of Indian women, and other Indian women's issues. They attended workshops on funding, legal issues, self-identity, aging, and tribal government relations.

518. "Interview with Barbara Moore, on Sterilization." *Akwesasne Notes* 11, 2 (May 1979): 11-12.

Barbara Moore relates the circumstances under which she was sterilized without her knowledge or agreement. This interview was conducted in Germany where this Sioux woman was representing the Pan-Indian delegation to the Society for Threatened Peoples.

519. "Killing Our Future: Sterilization and Experiments." *Akwesasne Notes* 9, 1, (Early Spring 1977): 4-6.

Comprehensive report of abuse by the Indian Health Service against Indian women and children. During a three year period 3400 Native women were sterilized. This pattern was repeated in Canada, and statistics from New York City show the majority of sterilizations were performed on minority women. The GAO report also showed that Indian children were frequently subjected to medical experiments.

520. "Sterilization of Young Native Women Alleged at Indian Hospital." *Akwesasne Notes* 6 (Early Summer 1974): 22.

In a report from Claremore, Oklahoma, *Notes* cites statistics which show that 48 Native women were sterilized in one month in a small Indian Health Service hospital. Most of the women were in their twenties. Other discriminating policies of the Indian Health Service are cited.

521. "The Case of Mary Grey-Eyes." *Time* 72 (November 10, 1958): 60.

A cooperative health project coordinated by Cornell University and the Navajo tribe integrated contemporary American medicine and traditional Navajo curing practices at a hospital in Many Farms, New Mexico, on the Navajo reservation. The cooperation of physicians and medicine men is illustrated by the case of Mary Grey-Eyes who is successfully cured of meningitis and lightening disease.

522. "Wilma Mankiller on Economic Development." *Native Self-Sufficiency* 8, 4 (Spring 1987): 12-13.

Mankiller, the Principal Chief of the Cherokee Nation, addresses the issues tribes face in attempting to develop resources and create jobs. She discusses housing, bingo, utilities, and the mistakes tribes have made by not following indigenous forms of Indian economy.

523. "Woman's Work in Indian Homes." *Indian's Friend* 6, 12 (August 1894): 9-10.

The writer, based on observations of Indian tribes in the Dakota Territory, urges white women to welcome Indian women into their homes which serve as models for "civilized" domesticity. She sees the presence of white women among Indians as purifying and morally uplifting and that it may lead to Indian men according Indian women more respect.

524. A-------, Filomena. "An Indian Girl's Letter." *Indian's Friend* 11, 8 (April 1899): 11-12.

Written by a student at the Sherman Indian Institute, an Indian boarding school, this letter gives details of school activities including Thanksgiving and Christmas festivities, class events, socials, and Christian society activities.

525. Abbott, Devon. "'Commendable Progress': Acculturation at the Cherokee Female Seminary." *American Indian Quarterly* 11, 3 (Summer 1987): 187-201.

The Cherokee Female Seminary opened in 1851 to educate young Cherokee women in the classics and religion. After 1900, students assumed more responsibility for maintenance and the focus of classes became oriented more to domestic skills. Nothing was taught of tribal traditions and the school served to facilitate acculturation.

526. Abbott, Devon Irene. "Medicine for the Rosebuds: Health Care at the Cherokee Female Seminary, 1876-1909." *American Indian Culture and Research Journal* 12, 1 (1988): 59-71.

The Cherokee Female Seminary was founded in 1851 at Park Hill in the Cherokee Nation. In spite of a concerted effort to educate the "Cherokee Rosebuds," students were exposed to unsanitary conditions which resulted in numerous health problems.

527. Aboriginal Women's Council of Saskatchewan. "Child Sexual Abuse: Words from Concerned Women." *Canadian Woman Studies* 10, 2 & 3 (Summer/Fall 1989): 90-91.

Child sexual abuse and violence against women have created a cycle of abuse which threatens to destroy a generation of Indian children.

528. Ager, Lynn Price. "The Economic Role of Women in Alaskan Eskimo Society." In *A World of Women.* Erika Bourguignon, ed. New York: Praeger, 1980, 305-17.

This chapter focuses on women's traditional and contemporary contributions to the economy of Eskimo society. Although the activities have changed in modern times, women continue to contribute to the economy through crafts and processing of game. Women's status continues to be seen as equal to men's in economic value.

529. Alexander, Jo, *et al. Women and Aging: An Anthology by Women*. Corvallis, OR: Calyx Books, 1986.

A multi-genre anthology which includes works by Mary TallMountain and Gail Tremblay.

530. Almquist, Elizabeth M. "Labor Market Gender Inequality in Minority Groups." *Gender and Society* 1, 4 (December 1987): 400-14.

Comparisons of minority women in the work force with each other and men within the same group. Researchers posit that gender inequality is smallest among the most disadvantaged minority groups, which includes American Indians. The more males are discriminated against by employers, the more they discriminate against women, but there is more equal sharing of resources among minority men and women.

531. American Association of Retired Persons. *A Portrait of Older Minorities*. Washington, DC: AARP, 1986.

This is a brochure which includes a brief section on Native American elderly. The statistics provided confirm the low economic status of Indian elderly and the poor quality of health care available to them.

532. Armstrong, Robert L. and Barbara Holmes. "Counseling for Socially Withdrawn Indian Girls." *Journal of American Indian Education* 10, 2 (January 1971): 4-7.

Reports on a 1968-69 study at Phoenix Indian High School. Students suffered from many of the same problems as teenagers everywhere, but the less obvious problem of social withdrawal

seemed widespread among the students. Girls exhibited loneliness
and low self-esteem more than boys. Group counseling was
successful in changing attitudes and behavior problems.

533. Attneave, Carolyn and Agnes Dill. "Indian Boarding Schools and
      Indian Women: Blessing or Curse?" *Proceedings of the
      Conference on the Educational and Occupational Needs of
      American Indian Women 1976*. Washington, DC: U.S.
      Department of Education, 1980, 211-31.

      An overview of the history and changing functions of Indian
      boarding schools including data gathered from women of three
      generations who were educated in BIA boarding schools and their
      assessments of the effects of that experience.

534. Bailey, Flora. "Suggested Techniques for Inducing Navajo Women
      to Accept Hospitalization During Childbirth and for
      Implementing Health Education." *American Journal of Public
      Health and the Nation's Health* 38, 10 (October 1948): 1418-23.

      Based on the traditional beliefs and practices of Navajos
      pertaining to the reproductive cycle, the author advocates
      inculcating procedures that are compatible with Native medical
      beliefs and techniques into the clinical health programs on the
      reservation. Recommended techniques include herbal baths,
      Native foods, Native delivery position, ritual assistance, close post-
      partum physical contact with infant, and nursing on demand.

535. Beauvais, F., E. R. Oetting, and R. Edwards. "Boredom, Poor Self
      Image, Lead Young Indian Girl to Drugs." *NIHB Health
      Reporter* 3, 2 (1982): 5-9.

      Uses the experiences of an 11-year-old Alaskan Indian girl to
      illustrate the frequent abuse of drugs and alcohol by young
      Indians on many reservations.

536. Benyon, L. K. "Burden of Widowhood." *Canadian Magazine* 29
      (May 1907): 23-24.

A fur trader describes the funeral of a young woman of the Carrier tribe, focusing particularly on the "cruel, barbarous, and savage" treatment of the young widow who is beaten and bashed by the dead man's mother and enslaved to his family for two years. Melodramatic account.

537. Bertoli, F., C. S. Rent, and G. S. Rent. "Infant Mortality by Socio-Economic Status for Blacks, Indians and Whites--A Longitudinal Analysis of North Carolina." *Sociology and Social Research* 68 (April 1984): 364-67.

Based on data from the Lumbee of North Carolina, this study posits Indian infants have a mortality rate four times higher than whites, and both Indian and black children at ten years of age have a mortality rate two times higher than white children. Maternal education level is seen as a major factor in infant survival and recent reduction in mortality rates is due to better postnatal health care and high educational attainment by Indian women.

538. Blanchard, Evelyn Lance. "Organizing American Indian Women." *Proceedings of the Conference on Educational and Occupational Needs of American Indian Women*. Washington, DC: U.S. Department of Education, 1980, 123-40.

A look at the traditional social organization of Indian tribes as a basis for building organizational models for Indian women in contemporary society. Recognizes the need for simultaneous organization of men.

539. Bloom, Joseph D. "Migration and Psychopathology of Eskimo Women." *American Journal of Psychiatry* 130 (April 1973): 446-49.

Author theorizes that Eskimo women migrate to the cities because of dissatisfaction with their low standing in the Native culture. The uprooting and often unsatisfactory integration into the city results in increased psychological problems for Eskimo women.

540. Bock, Phillip K. "Patterns of Illegitimacy on a Canadian Indian Reserve, 1860-1960." *Journal of Marriage and Family* 26, 2 (May 1964): 142-48.

Among the Micmacs of Eastern Canada fluctuations in the number of illegitimate births is related to changing social and economic circumstances which affect the community and individual behaviors.

541. Bollinger, Charles C., Thomas C. Carrier, and William J. Ledger. "Intrauterine Contraception in Indians of the American Southwest." *American Journal of Obstetrics and Gynecology* 106, 5 (March 1970): 669-75.

This study, which focuses primarily on "non-English speaking, illiterate, and indigent" Navajo women, shows a 77 percent success rate in IUD birth control but notes complications including abdominal bleeding, pelvic infection, and uterine perforation. Despite these problems, the IUD is recommended as the best method for family planning for women with poor access to medical facilities.

542. Braudy, Susan. "'We Will Remember' Survival School: The Women and Children of the American Indian Movement." *MS* 5 (July 1976): 77-80, 94, 120.

Women involved in the American Indian Movement tell of their desires to educate their children in the traditions of their people.

543. Brown, Judith K. "Economic Organization and the Powers of Women among the Iroquois." *Ethnohistory* 17 (Summer-Fall 1970): 151-67.

This is a study of the relationship between the position of Iroquois women and their economic status. Their high status reflects their control of the tribe's economic organization.

544. Campbell, Gregory R. "The Political Epidemiology of Infant Mortality: A Health Crisis Among Montana American

Indians." *American Indian Culture and Research Journal* 13, 3 & 4 (1989): 105-48.

The author studied the relationship between social disadvantage and infant mortality among Indians in Montana between 1979 and 1987. Statistical analyses show differentials in population according to tribe, age, socioeconomic status, and gender.

545. Carter, Sybil. "Indian Mothers and Their Work." *Indian's Friend* 11, 8 (April 1899): 11.

Lace-making is introduced as a trade industry for women among the Ojibway, Sioux, and Kiowa tribes. The "beauty and purity" of the lace is seen as a means of contradicting the stereotype of the lazy, dirty squaw.

546. Child Study Association of America. *The Indian Girl: Her Social Heritage, Her Needs and Her Opportunities*. Washington, DC: U.S. Government Printing Office, c. 1934.

A brief pamphlet which outlines the problems Indian girls may have at government schools and how teachers and administrators in those schools can help the girls adjust. The pamphlet assumes the girls will need to know how to adjust to white society.

547. Coleman, Michael C. "Motivators of Indian Children at Mission and U.S. Government Schools, 1860-1918: A Study Through Published Reminiscences." *Montana: The Magazine of Western History* 40, 1 (Winter 1990): 30-45.

Study of seven Indians' educational experiences which includes Zitkala-Sa and Helen Sekaquaptewa. Coleman discusses the conflicts the students experienced with Christianity and with school rules as well as their motivation for attending school.

548. Conte, Christine. "Ladies, Livestock, Land, and Lucre: Women's Networks and Social Status on the Western Navajo Reservation." *American Indian Quarterly* 6, 1-2 (Spring-Summer 1982): 105-24.

Conte looks at the role of Navajo women in the western part of the reservation in terms of production, consumption, and distribution of resources. She is interested in the impact of economic development on the status of Navajo women.

549. Cook, Katsi. "A Native American Response: The Circle." In *Birth Control and Controlling Birth: Women Centered Perspectives*. Helen Holmes, Betty B. Hoskins, and Michael Gross, eds. Clifton, NJ: Humana Press, 1980, 251-58.

Cook draws attention to the relationship between women and Earth, emphasizing the destruction of Earth by mining and exploitation which characterizes contemporary life. She uses the history and prophecies of the Hodenosaunee, Hopi, Navajo, and Sioux to explain the Native response to birth and midwifery. Cook is Mohawk and a member of the Central Council of Women of All Red Nations.

550. De Peltquestanque, Estaiene M. "Indian Nurses and Nursing Indians." *American Indian Magazine* 3 (July-September 1915): 169-74.

The author urges nurses to volunteer for service in Indian reservation medical systems and praises Indian nurses for their work though she laments the lack of professional education given to Indian private nurses.

551. Deary, Mary. "Native Community Care: Counseling and Development." *Canadian Woman Studies* 10, 2 & 3 (Summer/Fall 1989): 127-29.

Interviews with Mary Ann Morrisseau, Carol Eshkakagan, and Hilda Corbiere, all participants in Native Community Care: Counseling and Development.

552. Deloria, Ella C. "Health Education for Indian Girls." *Southern Workman* 53 (February 1924): 63-68.

The Indian girl of the twentieth century lives in a very different environment from her grandmother's. A more sedentary, modern life requires health education and attention to training to prepare young women for the new freedoms they have.

553. Devereux, George. "Mohave Indian Obstetrics: A Psychoanalytic Study." *American Imago* 5, 2 (July 1948): 95-139.

Study of myths and rituals surrounding pregnancy and childbirth among the Mohave which includes analysis of the possible psychological reasons for certain taboos.

554. Devereux, George. "Mohave Orality: An Analysis of Nursing and Weaning Customs." *Psychoanalytic Quarterly* 16 (1947): 519-46.

Analysis of the customs and myths of nursing with reference to myths of the Mohave. Devereaux discusses fellatio and cunnilingus as practiced by the Mohave and relates these practices to nursing.

555. Devereux, George. "The Social and Cultural Implications of Incest Among the Mohave Indians." *Psychoanalytic Quarterly* 8, 4 (1939): 510-33.

Devereaux provides myths which support Mohave taboos against incest. In spite of the prohibitions, there are instances of incest which Devereaux discusses and analyzes.

556. Dillingham, Brint. "Indian Women and Indian Health Services Sterilization Practices." *American Indian Journal* 3, 1 (January 1977): 27-28.

Brief article about the forced sterilization of Indian women.

557. Doran, C. M. "Attitudes of 30 American Indians towards Birth Control." *Health Services Reports* 87, 7 (August-September 1972): 658-64.

A survey of Navajo women indicates six degrees of attitudes towards contraception ranging from the idea that birth control is part of the Anglo world and not to be discussed or used, to the full acceptance and practice of contraception by college-educated Navajo women.

558. Dorris, Michael. *The Broken Cord*. New York: Harper & Row, 1989.

Dorris, a Modoc Indian, writes the story of his battle to solve his oldest adopted son's health and learning problems caused by fetal alcohol syndrome. He discusses the effects on and responses by his wife, Chippewa writer Louise Erdrich, as well as the difficulties faced by the rest of their family. Erdrich writes the foreword to the book.

559. Edwards, E. Daniel, Margie E. Edwards, and Geraldine M. Dains. "Modeling: An Important Ingredient in Higher Education for American Indian Women Students." *Journal of the National Association for Women Deans, Administrators and Counselors* 48 (Fall 1984): 31-35.

American Indians have traditionally performed as role models for their people and in the academic world can continue that role in recruiting American Indian women and aiding them in attaining success in academic achievement. This article discusses the characteristics and behaviors desirable in role models for American Indian women.

560. Erikson, Erik H. "Observations on the Yurok: Childhood and World Image." *University of California Publications in American Archaeology and Ethnology*, 35 (1943): 257-301.

This broad study includes a case history of a woman shaman, description of a woman's puberty ritual, psychological analysis of several women, examinations of mother/daughter relationships, modesty, menstruation, and curing experiences.

561. Farris, John J. "Ethanol Metabolism and Memory Impairment in American Indian and White Social Drinkers." *Journal of Studies on Alcohol* 39 (November 1978): 1975-79, 20-33.

American Indian women metabolize alcohol significantly more rapidly than white women of similar age, education, weight, and drinking history; however, the two groups show a similar decrease in memory due to alcohol, indicating they were equally affected.

562. Farris, Lorene. "The American Indian." In *Culture/ Childbearing/Health Professionals*. Ann L. Clarke, ed. Philadelphia: F. A. Davis Co., 1978.

Farris is a Cherokee from Oklahoma and a nurse who has focused on maternal and child nursing. In this chapter she provides background on Indians in America and then discusses the family, attitudes toward children, marriage, birthrate, and childbearing.

563. Farris, Lorene Sanders. "Approaches to Caring for the American Indian Maternity Patient." *American Journal of Maternal Child Nursing* 1, 2 (March/April 1976): 80-87.

The author is the vice president of the American Indian Nurses Association and argues that medicine and nursing have almost totally ignored studies of social and behavioral scientists in the curricula of nursing schools. Maternal mortality, diabetes, and obesity are conditions which affect American Indian women in greater numbers than the rest of the population.

564. Finley, Cathaleen. *Free to Choose: A Career Development Project for Tribal Girls*. Madison: University of Wisconsin--Extension, December 1977. EDRS, ED 152 447.

A curriculum developed to enhance Native American girls' employment skills and possibilities.

565. Fischler, R. S. "Child Abuse and Neglect in American Indian Communities." *Child Abuse and Neglect* 9, 1 (1985): 95-106.

Discusses child abuse and neglect among American Indians, which have been found to happen at the same rates as in other U.S. population groups. However, less is known about both the exact nature of this phenomenon among American Indians or effective treatment strategies. Comments upon the role of the non-Indian health professionals in the prevention and treatment of child abuse and neglect.

566. Fleming, Marilyn B. "Problems Experienced by Anglo, Hispanic and Navajo Indian Women College Students." *Journal of American Indian Education* 22, 1 (October 1982): 7-17.

Fleming used the Mooney problem checklist to study women in a community college nursing program to determine the relationships between problems and ethnicity. She concludes that there is little relationship between problems and ethnicity but acknowledges that the study only includes students who had remained in school and did not evaluate those who had dropped out.

567. Forslund, M. A. "Drinking Problems of Native American and White Youth." *Journal of Drug Education* 9 (1979): 21-27.

Compares the alcohol use of 638 Native American and white high school students from Wyoming and finds more alcohol abuse among American Indian students. A significantly higher proportion of Indian students had passed out, experienced sickness, memory loss, and been "in trouble" as a result of their abuse of alcohol.

568. Frederickson, Vera Mae, ed. "School Days in Northern California: The Accounts of Six Pomo Women." *News From Native California* 4, 1(Fall 1989): 40-45.

Two accounts (Priscilla Hunter and Florence Anderson) are reprinted from *Shelme Ke Janu, Talk from the Past*. The other four (Elsie Allen, Salome Alcantra, Edna Guerrero, and Francis Jack) are transcribed from tapes made in 1987. Indian children couldn't attend public schools until the 1920s, so many of the older women were sent to the Indian boarding school. The youngest, Priscilla Hunter, was born in 1947 and attended public schools.

569. Gilmore, Melvin R. "Notes on Gynecology and Obstetrics of the Arikara Tribe." *Michigan Academy of Science, Arts and Letters, Papers* 14 (1930): 71-81.

     Information recorded in 1926 from Stesta-Kata, an eighty-six-year-old midwife of Arikara, tells of the life of an Arikara girl through childhood, puberty, pregnancy, and childbirth.

570. Gold, Dolores. "Psychological Changes Associated with Acculturation of Saskatchewan Indians." *Journal of Social Psychology* 71 (April 1967): 177-84.

     Based on interviews and tests on four groups of twenty women each, significant differences are found in the behavior and attitudes of urban and reservation women. Higher acculturation rates in urban women are correlated with higher education and socio-economic level and demonstrated in deferred gratification patterns.

571. Goodwill, Jean Cuthand. "Indian and Inuit Nurses of Canada: Profile." *Canadian Woman Studies* 10, 2 & 3 (Summer/Fall 1989): 117-23.

     The organization of Indian and Inuit Nurses of Canada was formed in 1974 to pay special attention to the health status of Native people. Several nurses are profiled.

572. Goodwill, Jean. "A New Horizon for Native Women in Canada." In *Citizen Participation: Canada, a Book of Readings*. James A. Draper, ed. Toronto: New Press, 1971, 362-70.

     Goodwill discusses the increased involvement in politics and education by Canadian Indian women in order to retain their heritage and preserve their rights.

573. Graves, T. D. "The Personal Adjustment of Navajo Indian Migrants to Denver, Colorado." *American Anthropologist* 72, 1 (February 1970): 35-54.

While this study focuses on Navajo males, it includes data on the influence of wives on drinking patterns, noting that women exert a significant measure of control in keeping their spouses drinking within bounds, particularly in situations where the male is unemployed or underpaid and highly motivated to get drunk.

574. Green, Rayna. "American Indian Women Meet in Lawrence." *Women's Studies Newsletter* 7, 3 (Summer 1979): 6-7.

Indian women meet to plan strategies to counteract their invisibility as scholars and the general lack or inaccuracy of scholarship on Indian men and women.

575. Griffin, Naomi Musmaker. *The Roles of Men and Women in Eskimo Culture*. Chicago: University of Chicago Press, 1930.

Discusses roles and division of labor. Includes chart of activities indicating whether men or women participate.

576. Hammond, Dorothy and Alta Jablow. *Women: Their Economic Role in Traditional Societies*. Reading, MA: Addison-Wesley Publishing, Module in Anthropology No. 35, 1973.

The authors discuss the assignment of women's work as a matter of tradition rather than biology or predisposition. They acknowledge that the work of women always gets attention but that it does not elicit the public esteem accorded the work of men.

577. Harris, LaDonna. "American Indian Education and Pluralism." *Contemporary Native American Addresses*. John R. Maestas, ed. Provo, UT: Brigham Young University, 1976.

A recognized Comanche spokeswoman, Harris calls for multicultural education, including the incorporation of Indian languages and literatures into school curricula. Her discussion of issues in Indian education draws heavily on her own and her daughter's self-images as formed through knowledge of Indian cultures.

578. Hayes, Terry L. "Some Factors Related to Contraceptive Behavior Among Wind River Shoshone and Arapaho Females." *Human Organization* 36, 1 (Spring 1977): 72-76.

Includes information on Indian use of and attitudes toward contraception--information of interest to medical personnel and social services personnel interested in family planning.

579. Herzberg, Nancy Karen. *A Journey of a Thousand Miles Begins With a Single Step: The Story of the Passamaquoddy Women's Project.* Perry, ME: Passamaquoddy Tribal Vocational Education Program, 1986.

Report on a project funded by the Women's Bureau/Department of Labor to provide assertiveness training, self-awareness, pre-vocational training, and job assistance to women on two reservations in Maine.

580. Hewett, Priscilla. "Quilicum: A West Coast Indian Restaurant. *Canadian Woman Studies* 10, 2 & 3 (Summer/Fall 1989): 137-39.

A restaurant in Vancouver is run by Indians and serves Native food.

581. Hildebrand, Carol L. "Maternal Child Care Among the Chippewa: A Study of the Past and Present." *Military Medicine* 135 (1970): 35-43.

Pregnancy taboos, birth customs, infant and child care, diet, puberty rites, sanitary conditions, and the influence of the Public Health Service affect the maternal and infant mortality rates and health of children of the Chippewa.

582. Hilger, M. Inez. "Chippewa Pre-Natal Food and Conduct Taboos." *Primitive Man* 9 (July 1936): 46-48.

Reports information collected in Minnesota, Wisconsin, and Michigan during the 1930s. Examines restrictions placed on women during pregnancy.

583. Hippler, Arthur E. "Additional Perspectives on Eskimo Female
      Infanticide." *American Anthropologist* 74 (October 1972):
      1318-19.

      Discussion of female infanticide among the Netsilik Eskimos.

584. Hodgson, Maggie. "The Nechi Institute on Alcohol and Drug
      Education: The Eagle Has Landed." *Canadian Woman Studies*
      10, 2 & 3 (Summer/Fall 1989): 101-04.

      Native sponsored treatment has proved to be successful in
      curbing Indian alcoholism.

585. Holmes, Helen B., Bethy B. Hoskins, and Michael Gross, eds.
      Birth Control and Controlling Birth. Clifton, NJ: The Humana
      Press, 1980.

      Included in this analysis of the history, ethics, and policy on
      contraception are comments on the Native philosophy of
      medicine, American Indian midwifery, the forced sterilization of
      Indian women, and Indian women's health care. Mohawk Katsi
      Cook is the dominant voice on Indian women's health attitudes in
      the text.

586. Hostbjor, Stella. "Social Services to the Indian Unmarried
      Mother." *Child Welfare* 40, 5 (May 1961): 7-9.

      Study based on Indian unmarried mothers in Sisseton, South
      Dakota. During a one-year period there were thirty-three out-of-
      wedlock births in a community of 2300. There were more children
      put up for adoption than there were adoptive homes available,
      causing social workers to have a difficult time advising those
      mothers.

587. Hunt, Jojo. "American Indian Women and Their Relationship to
      the Federal Government." *Proceedings of the Conference on the
      Educational and Occupational Needs of American Indian
      Women*. Washington, DC: U.S. Department of Education,
      1980, 293-312.

Discussion of the variety of legal and social relationships with the federal government--reservation, terminated tribes, urban, non-recognized tribes--on the education and employment of Indian women.

588. Hunter, Kathleen I., Margaret W. Linn, and Shayna R. Stein. "Sterilization Among American Indian and Chicano Mothers." *International Quarterly of Community Health Education* 4, 4 (1983-1984): 343-52.

In a comparative analysis of Muccosukee and Seminole women and children and Chicano women having five or more children, the rate of sterilization is three times higher among Indian women. Indian women report higher factors of pregnancy complication which may account for their higher rate of tubal ligations.

589. Hurlburt, Graham and Eldon Gade. "Personality Differences Between Native American and Caucasian Women Alcoholics: Implications for Alcoholism Counseling." *White Cloud Journal* 3, 2 (1984): 35-39.

Compares Native American and Caucasian female alcoholics using the Eysenck Personality Questionnaire with the goal of finding effective, culture-specific methods of alcoholism counseling for Native American women.

590. IHCP. "The Indian Health Careers Program: Preparing Our Youth to Serve Nations." *Canadian Woman Studies* 10, 2 & 3 (Summer/Fall 1989): 125-26.

Concern about Native health care prompted the creation of IHCP to train Natives in medical fields.

591. Jacobs, Sharon. "Yukon Indian People: Education as Empowerment." *Canadian Woman Studies* 10, 2 & 3 (Summer/Fall 1989): 81-83.

This is a personal account which argues for improved educational opportunities for Yukon Indian people.

592. Jarvis, Gayle Mark. "The Theft of Life." *Akwesasne Notes* 9, 4 (Autumn 1977): 30-33.

The issue of sterilization of Indian women is discussed with specific examples given of young women who were sterilized without their permission. Physician Connie Uri (Choctaw/Cherokee) urged a study of the Indian Health Service which showed Indian women were frequently coerced to be sterilized. Indian women are also concerned about issues concerning their children and issues of adoption and foster care.

593. Jensen, Joan M. "Native American Women and Agriculture: A Seneca Case Study." *Sex Roles* 5, 3 (1977): 423-41.

Examination of the impact of European colonization on modes of production, households, and ideology of Seneca women. Despite loss of control of agricultural production, attitudes from the time of subsistence agriculture have survived and women have continued to maintain status and power into modern times. Study broadens to observe that though many North American tribal women have entered the cash economy, a large number of them do so from their homes through craft production, agriculture, and community-based work.

594. Jensen, Joan M. *With These Hands: Women Working the Land.* Old Westbury, NY: The Feminist Press, 1981.

The first section of this book focuses on American Indian women and their connections to the land and agriculture production. Translated oral accounts of Sky Woman and Corn Woman, songs, and autobiographical accounts by Buffalo Bird Woman, Mary Jemison, and Anna Moore Shaw are included.

595. Jensen, Joan M. *Women's Work Along the Southwest Border: A Significant Aspect of Labor History.* Southwest Institute for Research on Women. Tucson: University of Arizona, 1981.

This summary of research on women's work along the border between Mexico and the United States includes material on Anglo, black, Hispanic, and Native American women. Jensen identifies non-wage labor, market work in the home, and wage work.

596. Joe, Jennie R. "Cultural Influences on Navajo Mothers With Disabled Children." *American Indian Quarterly* 6, 1-2 (Spring/Summer 1982): 170-90.

Joe studied the circumstances and parental reactions to thirty disabled children from the Navajo Reservation. She provides details of the cases and concludes that the families have managed well in adapting to often "unexplainable" occurrences.

597. Johnson, S. "Cirrhosis Mortality Rates Among American Indian Women: Rates and Ratios." *Currents in Alcoholism* 7 (1979): 455-63.

Females account for nearly half the total cirrhosis deaths among Indians, compared to about one third among whites and blacks. Cirrhosis also accounts for about one out of every four deaths among Indian women in the 35-44 age group.

598. Jordan, Scott W., Robert A. Munsick, and Robert S. Stone. "Carcinoma of the Cervix in American Indian Women." *Cancer* 23, 5 (May 1969): 1227-32.

This is a comparative study of New Mexico white and Indian women's incidence of cervical cancers which indicates that a lower frequency among Native women is due, at least partly, to delay in first births relative to earlier first births among white women.

599. Kachel, Douglas. "The Rosebud Sioux Confront Domestic Violence and Women's Issues." *Akwesasne Notes* 21, 3 (Summer 1989): 11.

The White Buffalo Calf Society is working with Indian women and children who are victims of abuse and are confronting government agencies who often overlook domestic violence.

600. Kidwell, Clara Sue. "Status of Native American Women in Higher Education." In *Proceedings of the Conference on Educational*

and Occupational Needs of Native American Women.
Washington, DC: U.S. Department of Education, 1980, 83-122.

Indian women in higher education can look to the past for
models of women who have played roles different from those
dictated by stereotypes. Contemporary women form a significant
pool of resources for the development of stability and progress in
Indian communities, and emphasis on the status of women
educators will facilitate the strengthening of Indian tribes.

601. Krepps, Ethel. "Equality in Education for Indian Women."
      Wassaja: The Indian Historian 13, 2 (June 1980): 9-10.

Ethel Krepps, secretary of the Kiowa tribe, sees traditional
focus of women's role in family management, poverty, and the
insecurity of some Indian men as causes for the inadequate
education of Indian women. The result, she notes, is poor self
image, excessive drinking, and psychological problems. She urges
that education of women become a tribal priority, since women
are increasingly needed in responsible public positions within
tribes.

602. Kunitz, Stephen J. "Navajo and Hopi Fertility, 1971-1972." *Human
      Biology* 46, 3 (September 1974): 435-51.

The lower birth rate of Hopis and the tendency of Hopi
women to end their childbearing earlier as compared to Navajos
seems to be related to the more constricted Hopi land base and
an accelerated pattern of demographic change.

603. Kunitz, Stephen J. "Underdevelopment, Demographic Change and
      Health Care on the Navajo Indian Reservation." *Social Science
      and Medicine* 15 (Spring 1981): 175-92.

In an historical study of health care on the Navajo reservation,
Kunitz includes a section on fertility and contraceptive use.
Generally, Kunitz argues, health care is at the level of an
underdeveloped nation.

604. Kunitz, Stephen J. and J. C. Slocomb. "The Use of Surgery to Avoid Childbearing among Navajo and Hopi Indians." *Human Biology* 48, 1 (February 1976): 9-21.

While various methods of birth control are used by Hopi women with varying degrees of success, surgical means for averting childbearing--including abortions, tubal ligations and hysterectomies--appear to play an important role.

605. Kuttner, Robert E. and Albert B. Lorincz. "Promiscuity and Prostitution in Urbanized Indian Communities." *Mental Hygiene* 54, 1 (January 1970): 79-91.

Prostitution remains an Indian problem in the ghettos of urban centers. Stages between promiscuity and prostitution and the attitudes of women are discussed, and a close association with alcoholism and poverty is argued, with prostitution seen as geared toward sustenance rather than as a commercial venture.

606. LaFlesche, Susan. "My Work as a Physician Among My People." *Southern Workman* (August 1892): 133.

LaFlesche describes patient treatment, travel to attend patients, the volume of work, and the health of the Omaha people she serves as the first Indian physician, noting that practicing medicine on an Indian reservation is often different from practice in white society.

607. LaFromboise, Teresa D. "Professionalization of American Indian Women in Postsecondary Education." *Journal of College Student Personnel* 25, 5 (September 1984): 470-72.

American Indian women are the most under-represented minority attending universities and those who do attend face pressures both from the institution and their families that require skill development to manage successfully, including assertiveness training, problem solving, budget management, and cognitive restructuring of stereotypical socialization messages.

608. LaRoque, Emma. *Defeathering the Indian*. Agincourt, Canada: Book Society of Canada, 1975.

LaRoque is a Cree-Metis woman born in 1950. She describes her book as "a commentary on education based on personal experience."

609. Larson, Janet Karsten. "'And Then There Were None': Is Federal Policy Endangering the American Indian 'Species'?" *Christian Century* 94, 3 (January 26, 1977): 61-63.

The argument that Indian women are seeking sterilization is false. They are often pressured by male doctors or coerced into sterilization through fear of losing federal aid. The rising number of involuntary sterilizations is leading to charges of genocide, and long-overdue reforms in Indian Health Service policies are under consideration.

610. Leland, Joy. "Women and Alcohol in an Indian Settlement." *Medical Anthropology* 2, 4 (Fall 1978): 85-119.

The author describes two elements of the impact of alcohol in the lives of a Nevada Indian community: their drinking behavior and their techniques for coping with men's drinking. Women seldom drink and do not fit the drunken Indian stereotype. Coping with men's drinking has a much more negative impact on their lives than does direct consumption of alcohol.

611. Liberty, Margot. "Population Trends Among Present-Day Indians." *Plains Anthropologist* 69, 20 (April 1975): 225-30.

Demographic analysis of Omaha populations in both reservation and urban settings indicates migration to cities has not significantly altered women's attitudes toward childbearing or birthrates. Large families, averaging four children, seem to be a response to past experience which at times destroyed as much as three fourths of the tribe.

612. Lin, Ruey-lin. "A Profile of Reservation Indian High School Girls." *Journal of American Indian Education* 26, 2 (January 1987): 18-28.

Lin explores the psychosocial characteristics of Indian girls in nine high schools in the area of Billings, Montana. The results of comparisons with Indian boys and white students indicated that the Indian girls were the most troubled in terms of family and school relationships.

613. Lockett, Clay. "Midwives and Childbirth Among the Navajo." *Plateau* 12, 1 (July 1, 1939): 15-17.

Because approximately seventy five percent of Navajo births take place in the hogan, the traditional dwelling, midwifery is a thriving service. The activities of the midwife at a Navajo birthing are described from her arrival at the hogan to the burial of the afterbirth.

614. Malloch, Lesley. "Indian Medicine, Indian Health: Study Between Red and White Medicine." *Canadian Woman Studies* 10, 2 & 3 (Summer/Fall 1989): 105-12.

In this comparison of Indian and non-Indian concepts of health, medicine, and values, Malloch interviewed elders and young people and discusses appropriate treatments.

615. Matchett, William Foster. "Repeated Hallucinatory Experiences as a Part of the Mourning Process Among Hopi Indian Women." *Psychiatry* 35 (1972): 185-94.

Non-psychotic Hopi women, during mourning, repeatedly hallucinate the presence of a recently deceased family member. Degree of volition in bringing about the visitation varies from subject to subject. Three case examples are cited. Analysis infers the visitations function to ease otherwise intolerable losses and are tolerated, though not openly encouraged, in the society.

616. Mathes, Valerie Sherer. "Native American Women in Medicine and the Military." *Journal of the West* 21, 2 (April 1982): 41-48.

Countering the stereotypical portrayal of Indian women as slaves and drudges is evidence from tribes from every region of the superior status of Indian women in comparison to nineteenth century white women. Author documents the lives of several medicine women from Plains and Pacific tribes and focuses on Susan LaFlesche, an Omaha woman who had a medical degree and established health programs. Three women chiefs in New England and numerous female warriors are cited as examples of women who led their tribes in both peace and war. Includes a useful bibliography.

617. McCammon, Charles S. "A Study of Four Hundred Seventy-Five Pregnancies in American Indian Women." *American Journal of Obstetrics and Gynecology* 61, 5 (May 1951): 1159-66.

Based on a study of Navajo women, there is no significant difference between Indian and white birthing experiences in pregnancy symptoms, rate of birth complications, or duration of labor, though Indian women report a lower incidence of nausea and vomiting during early pregnancy than non-Indians.

618. McClain, Carol Shepard, ed. *Women as Healers: Cross Cultural Perspectives*. New Brunswick, NJ: Rutgers University Press, 1989.

Includes original case studies on women in traditional and non-traditional healing roles around the world including women from North America.

619. McDonald, Thomas. "Group Psychotherapy with Native American Women." *International Journal of Group Psychotherapy* 25, 4 (October 1975): 410-20.

Group therapy is described as a "listening place" where Indian women learn they are not alone in facing the problems of relocation to an urban environment, accept themselves and become less judgmental of others, and develop techniques for effective decision making.

620. McGill, Marsha Ann and Emma Mitchell. "California Indian Women's Clubs Past and Present." *News From Native California* 4, 3 (Spring 1990): 22.

In three brief sections, the authors discuss the Pomo Women's Club which was established in 1940 and disbanded in 1957 and the Pomo Inter-Clan Women's Coalition which was founded in 1986 to offer support to Indian families in the Bay Area. In San Diego the United Indian Women's Club was established in 1968 to raise money for scholarships for Indian students.

621. Medicine, Beatrice. "The Interaction of Culture and Sex-Roles in the Schools." In *Proceedings of the Conference on the Educational and Occupational Needs of American Indian Women*. Washington, DC: U.S. Department of Education, 1980, 141-58.

Ethnographic records mask the adaption and adjustments in child training which Native peoples have made as survival strategies and project images of past behaviors to which contemporary children are expected to conform. Recognition of the changing roles of women is needed to understand the contemporary lifestyles of Native women.

622. Medicine, Bea. "Issues in the Professionalization of Native American (Indian) Women." In *NIE/AERA Planning Conference, May 26-27, 1977, Washington, DC Appendix D*. Washington, DC: U.S. Department of Health, Education and Welfare, National Institute of Education, 1978, 105-19.

Discusses the problems of Native American women as they enter college, attend graduate school, and begin their professional years.

623. Medicine, Beatrice. "Native American (Indian) Women: A Call for Research." *Anthropology and Education Quarterly* 19, 2 (1988): 86-92.

Poses questions about the educational status and experience of American Indian women and discusses the possibilities for research in this area.

624. Medicine, Beatrice. "Native American Women Look at Mental Health." *Plainswoman*, 6 (1982): 7.

The mental health needs of Indian women are neglected and need to be addressed regarding such issues of low self-esteem, sexual and intellectual exploitation, family instability, economic stresses, repressed anger, and stress from conflicting expectations of the Indian and white worlds.

625. Medicine, Bea. "The Professionalization of Native American (Indian) Women: Towards a Research Agenda." *Wicazo Sa Review* 4, 2 (Spring 1988): 31-42.

Analysis of data in three categories--undergraduates, graduate students, and early professional years--suggests that Native American women continue to adhere to tribal traditions to create and use networking to support a broad variety of needs. They also need placement in a context that takes into account their tribal affiliation. Medicine argues strongly for both gender and ethnic sensitivity in the professionalization of Native women.

626. Metcalf, Ann. "From Schoolgirl to Mother: The Effects of Education on Navajo Women." *Social Problems* 23 (June 1976): 535-44.

This study found that boarding school experiences of Navajo girls had detrimental effects on their adult self-esteem and maternal attitudes.

627. Miller, Helen S. and Ernest D. Mason. *Contemporary Minority Leaders in Nursing: Afro-American, Hispanic, Native American Perspectives*. Kansas City, MO: American Nurses' Association, 1983.

Biographical sketches, photographs, and personal statements of ten Native American nurses are included to demonstrate the contribution of minority health professionals.

628. Milligan, B. Carol. "Nursing Care and Beliefs of Expectant Navajo Women, Part 1." *American Indian Quarterly* 8, 2 (Spring 1984): 83-101.

The Navajo have many prescriptions and proscriptions to serve pregnant women, and it is imperative that providers of health services be aware of these beliefs. Milligan analyzes the behavior and beliefs of both traditional and more modern Navajo women.

629. Milligan, B. Carol. "Nursing Care and Beliefs of Expectant Navajo Women, Part 2." *American Indian Quarterly* 8, 3 (Summer 1984): 199-210.

Continuation of study on pregnancy beliefs and health care among Navajos.

630. Mitchell, Irene B. "Bloomfield Academy." *Chronicles of Oklahoma* 49, 4 (1971-72): 412-26.

Founded as boarding school for Chickasaw girls in 1852, by 1880s Bloomfield Academy was a finishing school, but it did not neglect Chickasaw cultural heritage.

631. Murphy, Sharon. "Women in Native American Journalism." In *Native American Press In Wisconsin and the Nation*. James P. Danky, Maureen E. Hady, and Richard Joseph Morris, eds. Madison: University of Wisconsin Library School, 1982, 65-69.

Survey of American Indian women journalists in the past and present. Key women in Native newspapers are cited.

632. North American Indian Women's Association. *Special Needs of Handicapped Indian Children and Indian Women's Problems*. Washington, DC: Social Services, Bureau of Indian Affairs, May 1978.

This is a project report on data gathering, interviews, and recommendations. The report deals with physical and mental handicaps, child abuse, abuse of Indian women, school-age parenthood, solo parenthood, unwanted pregnancies, malnutrition, and alcoholism. Indian women were trained to gather the information for the report. Although it is a collection of statistics and often unanalyzed information, the report is interesting for its comments on contemporary Indian women's experiences.

633.   Oakland, Lynne and Robert L. Kane. "The Working Mother and Child Neglect on the Navajo Reservation." *Pediatrics* 51, 5 (May 1973): 849-53.

This study argues that the significant factors in child neglect are the mother's marital status and the size of the family, not the mother's age, education, or employment outside the home. Findings are based on records of forty-nine subjects at the Indian Health Service hospital in Shiprock on the Navajo reservation.

634.   Ohoyo Resource Center. *Words of Today's American Indian Women: Ohoyo Makachi*. Wichita Falls, TX: Ohoyo Resource Center, 1981.

Presentations by American Indian and Alaskan Indian women from the April 1981 Ohoyo Resource Center Conference on Educational Equity Awareness, as well as other selected Conference speeches. *Ohoyo* is the Choctaw word for *woman*; *Ohoyo Makachi* is translated as *"women speak."*

635.   Olsen, Karen. "Native Women and the Fur Industry." *Canadian Woman Studies* 10, 2 & 3 (Summer/Fall 1989): 55-56.

The fur trade greatly changed the roles of Indian women; in recent times Indian women have been active in trapping and believe their involvement is a part of the Native way of life.

636.   Opler, Morris E. "Cause and Effect in Apachean Culture, Division of Labor, Residence Patterns, and Girls' Puberty Rites." *American Anthropologist* 74 (October 1972): 1133-46.

Explanation for Apachean matrilocal residence is linked to agriculture and labor and is seen as a system which ensures protection of women. The women's puberty ritual is seen as another form of expressing the Apache women's secure and respected role in her culture.

637. Ortiz, Roxanne Dunbar. "Colonialism and the Role of Women: The Pueblos of New Mexico." *Southwest Economy and Society* 4, 2 (Winter 1978/1979): 28-46.

Discusses Pueblo women in relationship to the means of production. The influences of Spanish colonialism and the Department of the Interior have shaped the management of resources as well as intruded on traditional economic systems.

638. Owen, F. Carrington. "Improving Nursing Skills--A Program for Indian Women." *Nursing Outlook* 19 (1971): 258-59.

Preparing Indian women for auxiliary careers is promoted by a program in the Pine Ridge Hospital for licensed practical nurses and nurse aides. The program is sponsored by the Indian Health Service with the goal of improved care for Indian patients and higher levels of self-confidence and awareness of patient needs in the participants.

639. Parker, William Thornton. "Concerning American Indian Womanhood--An Ethnographical Study." *Annals of Gynaecology and Paediatry*. Boston: Annals Publishing Co., 1892.

Convinced of the imminent demise of Native cultures in North America, Parker, a gynecologist, discusses maternity and childrearing among the Ojibwas, Navajos, Algonquins, Dakotas, Paiutes, Shoshones, Apaches, Cheyennes and Nez Perce, based on written communications from colleagues working for the U.S. Indian Service or as military doctors. Parker argues for the similarity of all tribal groups on the basis of his data on women's menstrual, childbirth, and post-partum customs and suggests a connection between American Indian tribes and the ancient Israelites.

640. Perrone, Bobette, H. Henrietta Stockel, and Victoria Krueger. *Medicine Women, Curanderas, and Women Doctors*. Norman: University of Oklahoma Press, 1989.

In this study of traditional and institutional medicine, three contemporary Native American medicine women present their views on traditional healing. Navajo Annie Kahn, who teaches at Navajo Community College and also is a consultant to mental health agencies, emphasizes the use of traditional healing techniques and benefits of liaison between Navajo and non-tribal health practices. Apache Tu Moonwalker is a herbalist and basketmaker. Cherokee Dhyaani Ywahoo is the "keeper of the Priestcraft" for her nation charged with keeping the sacred crystals of her tribe. Interviews include biographical information and thematically focus on concepts of healing in relation to preserving tribal identity. The book argues the credibility of women as healers--their skills, spirituality and reputations--achieved through the values and institutions of their respective cultures.

641. Pool, Carolyn Garrett. "Reservation Policy and the Economic Position of Wichita Women." *Great Plains Quarterly* 8, 3 (Summer 1988): 158-71.

This is a case study of changes in the economic position of Wichita women during the last half of the nineteenth century. Reservation policies imposed new expectations on division of labor and power within the tribe. Women were usually deprived of previous autonomy and influence within the family and tribe.

642. Powers, Marla N. "Menstruation and Reproduction: An Oglala Case." *Signs* 6, 1 (1980): 54-65.

Examination of the relationship between Oglala female puberty ceremonies and menstrual taboos indicates that menstruation is not a symbol of defilement but rather practices associated with menstruation function to emphasize the importance of the female reproductive role.

643. Rabeau, Erwin S. and Angel Reaud. "Evaluation of Public Health Service Providing Family Planning Services for American Indians." *American Journal of Public Health* 59 (1969): 1331-38.

An analysis of family planning methods used by 75,450 Indian women ages 15-44 includes measurement of acceptance of contraceptive services, reduction of births, and an appraisal of the impact of the program on health, abortion trends, and infant mortality. Cost factors are also discussed.

644. Reid, Jeannie, *et al.* "Nutrient Intake of Pima Indian Women Relationship to Diabetes Mellitus and Gall Bladder Disease." *American Journal of Clinical Nutrition* 24 (1971): 1281-89.

Dietary histories of 277 women between 25 and 44 show that their calorie intake is high and fat levels low with beans, meat and tortillas staple foods. No significant dietary differences were found between nutrient intakes for women with or without disease.

645. Remie, Cornelius. "Towards a New Perspective on Netjilik Inuit Female Infanticide." *Inuit Studies* 9, 1 (1985): 67-76.

This article challenges previous data on Netjilik Inuit female infanticide on the basis that earlier studies ignored demographic data, varying rates in female infanticide among Nejilik sub-groups, the intrusion of Euro-Canadians into the central Arctic, and the impact of differing ecological pressures on Netjilik Inuit culture.

646. Romaniuk, A. "Modernization and Fertility: The Case of the James Bay Indians." *Canadian Review of Sociology and Anthropology* 11 (1974): 344-59.

Increase in fertility among Canadian Cree Indians of six villages is seen as the result of shorter periods of lactation, improved medical care, fewer pregnancy risks, a more sedentary lifestyle and fewer prolonged spousal separations.

647. Rosenblum, Estelle H. "Conversation with a Navajo Nurse." *American Journal of Nursing* 80, 8 (August 1980): 1459-61.

This interview with a Navajo registered nurse covers many elements of traditional culture as well as discussion of cultural sensitivity on the part of nurses as essential for successful treatment of Indian patients and the importance of the effective treatment of children.

648. Rothenberg, Diane. "Erosion of Power: An Economic Basis for the Selective Conservatism of Seneca Women in the Nineteenth Century." *Western Canadian Journal of Anthropology* 6, 3 (1976): 106-22.

Seneca women's opposition to change from female to male agriculture and from communal to private land ownership in the nineteenth century is seen not as female conservatism but as deliberate resistance to the threat of having their means of support wrested from their control and their power base undermined.

649. Russell, Scott C. and Mark B. McDonald. "The Economic Contributions of Women in a Rural Western Navajo Community." *American Indian Quarterly* 6, 3-4 (Fall-Winter 1982): 262-82.

Examines changes in the economy in the Western Navajo community of Shonto. Women have had more access to wage labor since the 1960s, but in this community they continue to be involved in animal husbandry and domestic activities.

650. Sakokwonkwas. "Pregnancies and Mohawk Tradition." *Canadian Woman Studies* 10, 2 & 3 (Summer/Fall 1989): 115-16.

The actions of both women and men in pregnancy are important in ensuring a safe pregnancy and delivery.

651. Sample, L. L. and Albert Mohr. "Wishram Birth and Obstetrics." *Ethnology* 19, 4 (1980): 427-45.

While looking at birth with some awe and fear, the traditional Wishram employed a number of practices to deal with the problems of birthing, including the professional midwife and the pit-roast practice in which the mother was kept warm in a shallow pit covering coals.

652. Scheirbeck, Helen Maynor. "Current Educational Status of American Indian Girls." *Proceedings of the Conference on the Educational and Occupational Needs of American Indian Women.* Washington, DC: U.S. Department of Education, 1980, 63-82.

   Historical overview of statistics on Indian girls's education leads to analysis of reservation and urban schooling for Indian females and a call for a more adequate system of tracking the education of Indian girls.

653. Scott, Leslee M. "Indian Women as Food Providers and Tribal Councilors." *Oregon Historical Quarterly* 42 (1941): 208-19.

   In Pacific Northwest tribes, women traditionally prepared, cooked, and preserved food, dug roots, made dyes, and wove baskets and cloth. Owing to their roles as providers, they held high status and a large measure of independence. Women were consulted in tribal decisions and treated with deference. Matrons of superior character achieved influence similar to male leaders, and women controlled food distribution.

654. Slemenda, Charles W. "Sociocultural Factors Affecting Acceptance of Family Planning Services by Navajo Women." *Human Organization* 37, 2 (Summer 1978): 190-94.

   Women who lack family or spousal financial and emotional support show the highest rate of contraceptive use. Women who refuse contraceptives tend to be more traditional, live farther from clinics, and show less contact with western culture.

655. Slocomb, John C. and Stephen J. Kunitz. "Factors Affecting Maternal Mortality and Morbidity Among American Indians." *Public Health Reports* 92, 4 (July-August 1977): 349-56.

   Causes of Navajo maternal mortality include a high incidence of toxemia and hemorrhage, low levels of monitoring of labor and delivery, and lack of intensive care units and blood banks. Authors argue for development of maternal health programs with emphasis on preventive services.

656. Slocomb, John C., Charles L. Odoroff, and Stephen J. Kunitz. "The Use Effectiveness of Two Contraceptive Methods in a Navajo Population: The Problem of Program Dropouts." *American Journal of Obstetrics and Gynecology* 122, 6 (July 15, 1975): 717-26.

A study of Navajo women using IUD and oral contraceptives between 1966 and 1971 indicates that the IUD users are two to three times more successful in preventing pregnancy than the oral contraceptive users because users of oral birth control have high (41%) dropout rates.

657. Smoke, Dawn. "Too Many Doors Have Been Slammed." *Women and Environments* 9, 2 (Spring 1987): 12-13.

The author is coordinator of the Native Women's Resource Center in Toronto and writes of the problems Indian women have getting housing in the city. Many Indian women leave the reserve to better their lives only to encounter hostility and racism when they attempt to find a place to live.

658. Speck, Dara Culhane. *An Error in Judgement: The Politics of Medical Care in an Indian/White Community.* Vancouver: Talonbooks, 1987.

In 1979 an eleven-year-old Indian girl died in Albert Bay, British Columbia, of an undiagnosed ruptured appendix. This event symbolized the ongoing patterns of neglect of Native health care, colonialism, and Canadian racism. Speck describes the events of Renee Smith's death, the inquest, and the significance of the event within the context of Indian health care in Canada.

659. Straley, Wilson. "Indians Didn't Let the Women Do (All) the Work." *Hobbies* 47 (October 1942): 99.

The author quotes both J. N. B. Hewitt and James Mooney on the work of Indian women to support the argument that women did not do the work in the production of stone artifacts.

660. Sullivan, Deborah A. and Ruth Beeman. *Utilization and Evaluation of Maternity Care by American Indians in Arizona*. Tucson: Southwest Institute for Research on Women, University of Arizona, 1982.

The report focuses on 110 American Indians in Arizona, showing the Indians have less parental care, a higher incidence of new born problems, and higher incidence of communication problems with health caretakers.

661. Szasz, Margaret Connell. *Indian Education in the American Colonies, 1607-1783*. Albuquerque: University of New Mexico Press, 1988.

"Indian Women between Two Worlds: Moor's School and Coeducation in the 1760s" is a discussion of Moor's Indian Charity School in Connecticut, a rare, co-educational school of the eighteenth century. Eleanor Wheelock founded the school which later moved to New Hampshire and was the nucleus for Dartmouth College. The education of girls was focused on serving "their husbands' needs."

662. Szasz, Margaret Connell. "'Poor Richard' Meets the Native American: Schooling for Young Indian Women in Eighteenth Century Connecticut." *Pacific Historical Review* 49, 2 (May 1980): 215-35.

Education of Indian girls was initiated in Connecticut in the mid-1700s in order to train them to serve their husbands' needs and promote a Calvinistic view of life in their families. Case histories of several young Indian women are given; all show the disruptive influence of schooling and the disappointment of educators whose expectations were not met. Indian women with a veneer of colonial culture were overcome by the prejudice of colonial society and the suspicion of their own communities.

663.   Trennert, Robert A. "Educating Indian Girls at Nonreservation
       Boarding Schools, 1878-1920." *Western Historical Quarterly* 13,
       3 (July 1982): 271-90.

       As a major part of the U.S. policy to acculturate Indians, tribal
       youth were sent to distant boarding schools. Girls were separated
       from boys except in the classroom and emphasis in their
       education was on domestic skills. Education of women was
       considered important, not for their personal benefit, but to
       prevent future mates from "backsliding" and to ensure they would
       pass on their new skills and attitudes to their children. A few
       schools developed programs in office skills and nursing in the late
       1800s. Little emphasis was put on academics. Many girls rebelled
       against the system by running away or by returning to traditional
       life when they returned home.

664.   Trennert, Robert A., Jr. *The Phoenix Indian School: Forced
       Assimilation in Arizona, 1891-1935*. Norman: University of
       Oklahoma Press, 1988.

       In this discussion of the Phoenix Indian School, Trennert often
       gives examples of the experiences of the girls there. Most
       interesting is information on how social structures were enforced
       and how useless much of the curriculum was for the young
       women.

665.   U.S. Department of Education. *Proceedings of the Conference on
       the Educational and Occupational Needs of American Indian
       Women, October 12-13, 1976*. Washington, DC: U.S.
       Department of Education, 1980.

       Proceedings of this conference include ten background essays
       ranging from the impact of boarding school education, to the
       effects of transition away from the reservation, to health problems
       of Indian women. Includes conference recommendations and
       chairperson's report.

666.   U.S. Department of Labor. *American Indian Women and
       Programs of the Federal Government: Report of a Symposium
       of Indian Women Leaders*. Washington, DC, January 10-11,

1977. Washington, DC: Employment Standards Administration, Women's Bureau, 1978.

Report of a meeting between Native American women leaders and federal officials for the purpose of communicating about such topics as housing, education, employment, business and community development, and criminal justice.

667. U.S. Department of Labor. *Native American Women and Equal Opportunity: How to Get Ahead in the Federal Government*. Washington, DC: U. S. Government Printing Office, 1979.

This is a publication of the Women's Bureau that resulted from a federal training seminar for American Indian women. Includes "Native Women in the World of Work" by Shirley Hill Witt. Record of the proceedings of a seminar on women's employment in U.S. government agencies which discusses affirmative action, eligibility as applied to Indian women, implementation, enforcement, employment opportunity complaints, networking, and employment services available to Indian women.

668. U.S. Women's Bureau. "Bulletin #297." *Handbook on Women Workers*. Washington, DC: U.S. Government Printing Office, 1975.

Chapter 1, section 10: "Minority Race Women in the Work Force--American Indians, Aleut, and Eskimo Women" is the only reference to Indian women.

669. Uhlmann, Julie M. "The Impact of Modernization on Papago Indian Fertility." *Human Organization* 31, 2 (Summer 1972): 149-61.

Analysis of the fertility levels of Papago women in Tucson and in rural reservation areas indicates a reduced number of children for urban women primarily due to the excess of unmarried females in their reproductive years in the city.

670.   Van Kirk, Sylvia. *Many Tender Ties: Women in Fur Trade Society,*
        1670-1870. Norman: University of Oklahoma Press, 1980.

        Discusses the role of Indian women as intermediaries between
        Indian males and white fur traders during the period 1725-1825,
        and the advantages and disadvantages of that position.

671.   Van Kirk, Sylvia. "The Role of Native Women in the Creation of
        Fur Trade Society in Western Canada, 1670-1830." In *The*
        Women's West. Susan Armitage and Elizabeth Jameson, eds.
        Norman: University of Oklahoma Press, 1987, 53-62.

        Discussion of the relatively high status held by Native women
        as spouses and partners of fur traders. Native women were valued
        for their skills and mediation with local tribes but lost spousal
        preference with the opening of fur trading areas to white women.

672.   Van Kirk, Sylvia. "Women and the Fur Trade." *The Beaver*
        (Winter 1972): 4-21.

        Role of Indian women during the 1800s as liaison between
        Indian and white culture during the fur trading period. Van Kirk
        discusses the advantages (economics and familiarity with
        languages) and the disadvantages (mixed-blood children and
        abandoned Indian wives).

673.   Wallach, Edward E., Alan E. Beer, and Celso-Ramon Garcia.
        "Patient Acceptance of Oral Contraceptives. 1. The American
        Indian." *American Journal of Obstetrics and Gynecology* 97, 7
        (April 1967): 984-91.

        Oral contraceptives are considered a satisfactory method of
        family planning for "indigent and deprived" Navajo Indian women.
        The article outlines the methodology and medical procedures
        undertaken during the study and provides tables and charts on
        pregnancy rates, births, dosages, treatment cycles, and side effects.

674.   Wanatee, Adeline. "Education, the Family and the Schools." In
        The Worlds Between Two Rivers: Perspectives on American
        Indians in Iowa. Gretchen M. Bataille, David M. Gradwohl,

and Charles L. P. Silet, eds. Ames: Iowa State University Press, 1978, 100-03.

Wanatee writes of the super-imposition of white culture on Mesquakie education. She is concerned about Indian students losing both their Native language and their culture through education.

675. Wanepuhnud Corporation. "Wanepuhnud Trainees: Personal Narratives." *Canadian Woman Studies* 10, 2 & 3 (Summer/Fall 1989): 95-100.

Established in 1977, the Wanepuhnud Corporation provides training and employment opportunities for Native women. Personal narratives illustrate the importance of this organization.

676. Whiteman, Henrietta V. "Insignificance of Humanity, 'Man is Tampering with the Moon and the Stars': The Employment Status of American Indian Women." In *Proceedings of the Conference on the Educational and Occupational Needs of American Indian Women*. Washington, DC: U.S. Department of Education, 1980, 37-61.

American society's acquisitiveness and ethnocentrism has resulted in an oppressive and intolerable situation for American Indian women and is intensifying the low status of tribal women as it gains momentum in technology. Implementation of the concept of equality is urged.

677. Whiting, Verde M. "Tribal Career Women." *Independent Woman* 19 (December 1940): 382-84.

Whiting argues the case for the centrality of Indian women in contemporary tribal life citing examples of women recognized for their contributions to music, art, literature, public programs, folklore, education, public policy, and tribal politics and viewing them as career women.

678. Williams, Agnes F. "Transition From the Reservation to an Urban Setting and the Changing Roles of American Indian Women."

Proceedings of the Conference on Educational and Occupational Needs of American Indian Women. Washington, DC: U.S. Department of Education, 1980, 251-84.

This essay traces the changing roles of Native women from pre-contact times to the present, with statistical tables on employment, demographics, and education as a basis for focus on the shift from reservations to cities and analysis of the stresses and adaptation strategies employed by Native women in urban settings.

679.   Williams, Susan M., Janice L. View, and Lourdes R. Miranda. *The Economic Status of American Indian Women: A Navajo Study.* Washington, DC: National Institute for Women of Color, 1984.

Study limited to Navajo reservation women who live in a wage economy. Comparisons are made with economic conditions of Navajo men.

680.   Willoughby, Nona Christensen. "Division of Labor Among the Indians of California." *Reports of the University of California Archaeological Survey* 60 (1963): 1-79.

Text and illustrations indicate the women, as well as men, participated in hunting, fishing, cordage production, shamanism, wood collecting, and moccasin making, and they predominated in food preparation, gathering, clothing production and household article making.

681.   Wilson, J. Donald. "A Note on the Shinhwauk Industrial Home for Indians." *Journal of the Canadian Church Historical Society* 16, 4 (1974): 66-71.

Describes the philosophies of Indian schools in the Saulte Ste. Marie area founded by the assimilationist missionary E. F. Wilson, who believed Indian children had to be kept away from their parents in order to progress.

682. Witt, Shirley Hill. "Native Women in the World of Work: An Overview." In *Native American Women in Equal Opportunity: How to Get Ahead in the Federal Government*. Washington, DC: Government Printing Office, 1979, 8-15.

An overview of Native women in education and other work areas that argues success in work depends on the ability to take the best of traditional tribal life and the white world and to function realistically in both cultures. Includes statistics on employment and income.

683. Witt, Shirley Hill. "Native Women Today: Sexism and the Indian Woman." *Civil Rights Digest* 6 (Spring 1974): 29-35.

Discusses the origins of "squaw" and other stereotypes. Facts and statistics on roles of traditional and contemporary Indian women in education, employment, and health are presented.

684. Wolman, Carol S. "The Cradleboard of the Western Indians: A Baby Tending Device of Cultural Importance." *Clinical Pediatrics* 9, 5 (May 1970): 306-08.

A woman doctor traces the use of cradleboards in the Great Basin and Southwest from 200 A.D. to the contemporary period, commenting on their convenience to Native mothers, their usefulness in protecting the infant, and noting that lack of movement does not retard children's motor skills. The only medical drawback she notes is a prevalence of hip-dislocation which she speculates may be congenital, particularly among Navajos.

685. Wood, Rosemary. "Health Problems Facing American Indian Women." In *Proceedings of the Conference on the Educational and Occupational Needs of American Indian Women*. Washington, DC: U.S. Department of Education, October 1980, 159-83.

Wood traces health problems and health services for American Indians from pre-Columbian America to today's health systems and focuses on American Indian women as health care professionals.

686. Wright, Anne. "An Ethnography of the Navajo Reproductive Cycle." *American Indian Quarterly* 6, 1-2 (Spring-Summer 1982): 52-70.

Wright records various Navajo attitudes toward menarche, children, and menopause. Navajo women differed from the Anglo women in their attitude toward menopause, approaching that time in their lives with far more acceptance.

687. Wright, Mary C. "Economic Development and Native American Women in the Early Nineteenth Century." *American Quarterly* 33, 5 (1981): 525-36.

In spite of their pivotal role in the development of the Northwest fur trade, Indian women eventually experienced a loss in economic and social standing. As the white market economy came to dominate the Native economic system, women were limited to domestic endeavors that restricted their opportunity to play public roles.

688. Yazzie, Ethelou. "Special Problems of Indian Women in Education." In *Contemporary Native American Addresses*. John R. Maestas, ed. Provo, UT: Brigham Young University, 1976, 360-72.

Yazzie discusses the deficiencies in the education available to Native American girls and the requisites for improving opportunities in a 1975 address to the Southwest Indian Women's Conference.

Visual and Performing Arts

VISUAL AND PERFORMING ARTS

689. "Buffy." *Talking Leaf* 41, 7 (August 1976): 8-9.

Interview with Buffy St. Marie, Cree folk singer.

690. *Conceptual Art: Four Native American Women Artists*. Anadarko, SD: Southern Plains Indian Museum and Crafts Center, 1980.

Exhibit brochure. Includes Jaune Quick-to-See Smith, Kay WalkingStick, Emmi Whitehorse.

691. "Dat-So-La-Lee. Greatest of the Basketmakers." *Nevada Highways and Parks* 17 (1957): 18-19.

Brief article on Dat-So-La-Lee and her baskets, with photograph.

692. "Film: *No Address*." *Canadian Woman Studies* 10, 2 & 3 (Summer/Fall 1989): 165-66.

Alanis Obomsawin's film *No Address* focuses on the homeless in Montreal and the organizations serving the homeless.

693. "Moon-Maidens: Five Part Indian Ballerinas." *Newsweek* 70 (November 6, 1967): 101-02.

Of the few American ballerinas who have gained international recognition, five are Oklahoma Indian women: Maria Tallchief, Marjorie Tallchief, Yvonne Chouteau, Rosella Hightower, and Moscelyne Larkin. At the sixty-year celebration of the state of Oklahoma these ballerinas were saluted.

694. "Sacheen." *Playboy* 20, 10 (October 1973): 93-95.

       Profile of actress Sacheen Littlefeather who came to attention
       when she made an appearance at the 1975 Academy Awards
       ceremony to announce Marlon Brando's rejection of an Oscar for
       best actor. She has appeared in two films.

695. *Teionkwahontasen: Basketmakers of Akwesasne.* Hogansburg, NY:
       Akwesasne Museum, 1983.

       Catalog of northeastern baskets.

696. "The Basketry of Dat-So-La-Lee." *Nevada Magazine* 3 (1948): 8-9.

       Brief description of the basketmaker and her work.

697. "The Most Beautiful Basket." *Masterkey* 25 (1951): 68.

       Contains brief note about Washoe basketmaker Dat-So-La-
       Lee and photograph.

698. "Washoe Baskets." *Papoose* 1, 4 (February 1903): 15-16.

       Discusses the work of basketmaker Dat-So-La-Lee.

699. "Women Artists and Writers of the Southwest." *New America: A
       Journal of American and Southwestern Culture* 4, 3 (1982).

       Special issue which includes "Navajo Matriarchs," a photo
       essay by Abigail Adler, and "Spider Woman's Art: A Brief
       History of Navajo Weaving" by Marian Rodee.

700. Albers, Patricia and William James. "Illusions and Illumination:
       Visual Images of Women in the West." In *The Women's West*.
       Susan Armitage and Elizabeth Jameson, eds. Norman:
       University of Oklahoma Press, 1987, 35-50.

       This article analyzes the changing stereotypes of Indian
       women on postcards, a popular medium of popular culture, from
       the late nineteenth century to the present. While portrayals of

women are less prevalent than those of men, they are significant in the projection of a romantic, anachronistic view of Indian women who are usually shown engaged in crafts. The women are always anonymous, usually youthful, and dressed in "Indian princess" costumes.

701. Allen, Elsie. *Pomo Basketmaking: A Supreme Art for the Weaver*. Healdsburg, CA: Naturegraph Publishers, 1972.

Chapter One, "The Life of Elsie Allen, Pomo Basketweaver," tells of Elsie's life and experiences. She was born on September 22, 1899, but didn't begin basketweaving in earnest until she was sixty-two years old. Most of the book describes the art of gathering materials and making baskets.

702. Ashton, Robert, Jr. "Nampeyo and Lesou." *American Indian Art Magazine* 1, 3 (Summer 1976): 24-33.

Nampeyo and her husband Lesou are credited with copying old designs and continuing the Hopi pottery traditions. Nampeyo was born around 1860 and learned to make pots from her grandmother in the village of Walpi.

703. Babcock, Barbara A. "At Home, No Women are Storytellers: Potteries, Stories and Politics in Cochiti Pueblo." *Journal of the Southwest* 30, 3 (Autumn 1988): 356-89.

Helen Cordero, a Cochiti Pueblo woman, made her first storyteller doll in 1964 and caused a revolution in Pueblo pottery. Babcock analyzes the influences on Cordero's life and the impact of her success. Cordero insists that the storytellers are male even though she herself tells stories.

704. Babcock, Barbara A. "Clay Changes: Helen Cordero and the Pueblo Storyteller." *American Indian Art Magazine* 8, 2 (Spring 1983): 30-39.

Helen Cordero made her first storyteller doll in 1964, reinventing a tradition of Cochiti figurative pottery which is now carried on by at least 160 artists in the Rio Grande Pueblos.

705.   Babcock, Barbara, Guy Monthan, and Doris Monthan. *The Pueblo Storyteller: Development of a Figurative Ceramic Tradition*. Tucson: University of Arizona Press, 1986.

Biographies of major artists, color photos of figures, and a text which traces the development of the ceramic genre and analyzes the works of outstanding artists makes up this study.

706.   Bates, Craig D. "Lucy Telles, A Supreme Weaver of the Yosemite Miwok Paiute." *American Indian Basketry* 2, 4 (1982): 23-29.

Discusses the innovations of Lucy Telles and their effects upon Yosemite Miwok/Paiute basketry.

707.   Bates, Craig D. "Lucy Telles, Outstanding Weaver of the Yosemite Miwok-Paiute." *Pacific Historian* 24, 4 (1980): 396-403.

A brief biographical sketch of Lucy Telles, with discussion of her basket weaving techniques, materials and designs.

708.   Bates, Craig D. "Tabuce: A Mono Lake Paiute Woman." *Moccasin Tracks* 9, 6 (February 1984): 4-8.

Discusses the basketmaking skills of Maggie "Tabuce" Howard, a Paiute woman from Northern California, who for more than twenty years demonstrated traditional Paiute crafts and activities to visitors at Yosemite National Park's Yosemite Indian village.

709.   Bates, Craig D. and Brian Bibby. "Amanda Wilson: Maidu Weaver." *American Indian Art Magazine* 9, 3 (Summer 1984): 38-43, 69.

Wilson was born in the 1860s in Chico, California, and lived at the Maidu village of Mikchopdo. She was a leader among her people and a master basket weaver.

710. Bates, Craig D. and Brian Bibby. "Collecting Among the Chico Maidu: The Stewart Culin Collection at the Brooklyn Museum." *American Indian Art Magazine* 8, 4 (1983): 46-53.

A catalog of approximately 150 items collected by Stewart Culin, curator of the Brooklyn Museum, from the Chico Maidu.

711. Bender, Roberta. "Ramona Sakiestewa: Beyond Limits." *Native Peoples* 2, 4 (Summer 1989): 30-34.

Sakiestewa is a Hopi weaver who combines traditional techniques with contemporary styles. She is influenced by American Indian patterns as well as African Kuba cloth and Chinese designs.

712. Blummer, Thomas J. "Rebecca Young Bird: An Independent Cherokee Potter." *Journal of Cherokee Studies* 5, 1 (1980): 41-49.

Discusses the works of the self-taught Cherokee potter, her techniques, and the southwestern tribal influences upon it.

713. Bol, Marsha Clift. "Lakota Women's Artistic Strategies in Support of the Social System." *American Indian Culture and Research Journal* 9, 1 (1985): 33-51.

The artistic support system maintained by Lakota women became even more important when the traditional society was threatened during the last half of the nineteenth century. During the reservation period the women's art supported and maintained the traditional value system.

714. Braudy, Susan. "Buffy Sainte-Marie: 'Native North American Me.'" *MS* 4 (March 1975): 14-18.

Braudy writes about the Cree singer and entertainer who has also been an activist for Indian people.

715. Bunzel, Ruth. *The Pueblo Potter.* New York: Columbia University Press, 1974.

An examination of Zuni, Acoma, Hopi and San Ildefonso pottery, this study analyzes how Pueblo women design and execute their pots, discussing design sources, instruction techniques, and the history and religious significance of pottery in the Southwest.

716.   Cohen, Ronny. "Jaune Quick-to-See Smith at Kornblee." *Art in America* 68, 3 (March 1980): 116-17.

The work of this Cree/Shoshone artist is characterized as a bold synthesis of American Indian art and twentieth century modernism. She combines dual currents in Plains art--narrative pictography and decorative abstraction--and an imagist quality to effect multiple layers of meaning.

717.   Cohodas, Marvin. "Dat-So-La-Lee and the 'Degikup.'" *Halcyon: a Journal of the Humanities* 4 (1982): 119-40.

Discusses the marketing of Dat-So-La-Lee's baskets by Abe Cohn's Emporium Company in Carson City, Nevada. Although Cohn advertised the baskets as part of a long preserved Washoe tradition, they were actually a blend of Washoe and Pomo designs.

718.   Cohodas, Marvin. "Dat-So-La-Lee's Basketry Designs." *American Indian Art Magazine* 1, 4 (Autumn 1976): 22-31.

Discusses the two approaches to compositional unity that the basketmaker took during her career: an open, checkerboard-like arrangement on the surface of the basket, used during her classical period, and the grouping of simpler, more solid motifs into bands using background space, which characterized her late period.

719.   Cohodas, Marvin. "Lena Frank Dick: An Outstanding Washoe Basket Weaver." *American Indian Art Magazine* 4, 4 (Autumn 1979): 32-41, 90.

A biographical sketch of Lena Frank Dick (1889-1965), a talented but little known Washoe basket weaver from Coleville, California, who learned basket weaving from her mother.

720. Cohodas, Marvin. "Sarah Mayo and her Contemporaries: Representational Designs in Washoe Basketry." *American Indian Art Magazine* 6, 4 (Autumn 1981): 52-59, 80.

Explores Sarah Mayo's use of representational designs in Washoe basketry, which she introduced in 1905, and which was in keeping with the spirit of the Washoe basketry style. Also discusses Mayo's contemporaries Maggie James and Lillie James.

721. Cohodas, Marvin, "Washoe Basketry." *American Indian Basketry* 3, 4 (1983): 4-30.

A history of Washoe basket making which discusses techniques, styles, important basketmakers, and the economics of basketmaking, with emphasis on the peak of Washoe basketmaking between 1895 and 1935.

722. Cohodas, Marvin. "Washoe Innovators and Their Patrons." In *The Arts of the North American Indian: Native Traditions in Evolution*. Edwin L. Wade, ed. New York: Hudson Hills Press, 1986, 203-20.

Cohodas shows that the stylistic differences among such noted Washoe basketmakers as Dat-So-La-Lee, Sarah Mayo, Maggie James, Tootsie Dick, and Lena Frank Dick were due to differences in their personal lifestyles and patronage. Their work was not heavily influenced by traditional designs or techniques, but rather by basket collectors and Indian craft dealers.

723. Collings, Jerold L. "Profile of a Chemehuevi Weaver." *American Indian Art Magazine* 4 (1979): 60-67.

A discussion of the basket making of Chemehuevi weaver Maggie Painter (1900-1963) from the Colorado River Indian Reservation, Arizona.

724. Collins, John. *Nampeyo, Hopi Potter: Her Artistry and Her Legacy*. Fullerton, CA: Muckenthaler Cultural Center, 1974.

An exhibition catalogue with a lengthy introduction discusses the seminal role of Nampeyo in the revival of Sikyatki style pottery and its commercial success. Though blind in the last five years of her life, she continued to make exceptionally fine pots.

725. Collins, John. *A Tribute to Lucy M. Lewis, Acoma Potter*. Fullerton, CA: Museum of North Orange County, 1975.

Exhibit catalog of the Lewis family's pottery. Includes a list of exhibits and shows.

726. Colton, Mary-Russell F. and Harold S. Colton. "An Appreciation of the Art of Nampeyo and her Influence on Hopi Pottery." *Plateau* 15, 3 (January 1944): 43-45.

Nampeyo's fame as a Hopi artist rests on the quality of her work and the fact that she was the first Indian to initiate an art movement among her own people. Her work is distinguished by a fluid quality of design and bold rhythmic forms which influenced her contemporaries to practice greater artistic freedom.

727. Cortright, Barbara. "Jody Folwell, Potter." *Art Space* 6, 3 (Summer 1982): 33-35.

Folwell, daughter of potter Rose Naranjo, uses ancient open fire methods and traditional patterns to produce her pottery but also invented pebble pots, "harmoniously shaped to echo the round lines of weatherized pebbles" and inset with pebbles, and has made other innovations in style and technique.

728. Culley, Lou Ann. "Helen Hardin: A Retrospective." *American Indian Art Magazine* 4, 3 (Summer 1979): 68-75.

Helen Hardin, daughter of Pablita Velarde, had her first show in 1963 when she was nineteen years old. Her contemporary paintings in a variety of media emphasize Indian traditions and motifs.

729. De Laurer, Marjel. "Helen Hardin." *Arizona Highways* 52, 8 (August 1976): 28-29, 44-45.

Santa Clara Pueblo artist Helen Hardin uses tradition as a point of departure for her own contemporary images. Daughter of famous Pablita Velarde, Hardin is recognized internationally for her work. Brief biography, a poem by Hardin, and illustrations of five of her works.

730. Duncan, Kate C. "American Indian Lace Making." *American Indian Art Magazine* 5, 3, (1980): 28-35, 80.

Article traces the history of lace making among Ojibwa women between 1890 and the 1930s, when it was introduced by Episcopal missionaries as an occupation for Native women.

731. Dunn, Dorothy. "Pablita Velarde, Painter of Pueblo Life." *El Palacio* 59 (1952): 335-41.

Pablita Velarde continues in the traditional two-dimensional style of Pueblo painting.

732. Dyler, Harry. "Mabel Taylor--West Coast Basket Weaver." *American Indian Basketry* 1, 4 (1981): 12-23.

A discussion of the techniques, materials and designs used by Mabel Taylor, an Indian from the Sheshaht Band of Vancouver Island's West Coast Indians.

733. Ewers, John C. "Climate, Acculturation, and Costume: A History of Women's Clothing Among the Indians of the Southern Plains." *Plains Anthropologist* 25, 87 (1980): 63-82.

Discusses the variation in traditional Plains Indian clothing as related to climate, economics and white contact.

734. Finney, Frank F., Sr. "Maria Tallchief in History: Oklahoma's
      Own Ballerina." *Chronicles of Oklahoma* 38 (Spring 1960): 8-
      11.

      This is a brief biographical account of ballerina Maria
      Tallchief with historical references to her family.

735. Fox, Nancy. "Rose Gonzales." *American Indian Art Magazine* 2, 4
      (Autumn 1977): 52-57.

      San Ildefonso potter Gonzales was born at San Juan Pueblo
      and went to San Ildefonso in 1920. She produces carved pots in
      both black and red.

736. Freeman-Witthoft, Bonnie. "Cherokee Indian Craftswoman and
      the Economy of Basketry." *Expedition: the Magazine of
      Archaeology/Anthropology* 19 (1977): 17-27.

      Identifies three different Cherokee basket traditions: cane
      split basketry, used in the distant past; the rib or melon basket,
      considered to be of European origin; and baskets made of broad
      oak splints, thought to be aboriginal. Also discusses the impact of
      tourist trade on the manufacture and selling of baskets and other
      Cherokee crafts.

737. Frisbie, Theodore R. "The Influence of J. Walter Fewkes on
      Nampeyo: Fact or Fancy?" In *The Changing Ways of
      Southwestern Indians: A Historic Perspective*. Albert H.
      Schroeder, ed. Glorieta, NM: Rio Grande Press, 1973, 231-44.

      Anthropologist J. Walter Fewkes is credited with substantially
      influencing Nampeyo's revival of the Sikyatki style in Hopi pottery
      in 1895, when she visited his excavation sites and made pencil
      copies of designs on mortuary bowls; his own autobiography fails
      to mention any relationship to Nampeyo and her art.

738. Gigli, Jane Green. "Dat-So-La-Lee, Queen of the Washoe Basket
      Makers." *Nevada State Museum Anthropological Papers* 16
      (March 1974): 1-27.

Born around 1835, in a village near Sheridan, Nevada, Debuda, known as Dat-So-La-Lee and Louise Keyser, began making baskets in her sixties, in a period when basket making and selling was no longer a vital necessity for Indian women. She achieved considerable regional fame and became the subject of many anecdotes about her flamboyant personality. Photos of her baskets are included in the analysis of her basketmaking techniques.

739. Gogol, John M. "Elsie Thomas Shows How to Make a Traditional Klickitat Indian Basket." *American Indian Basketry* 1, 1 (1979): 18-29.

The manufacture of a traditional Klickitat basket is demonstrated by Elsie Thomas, mother-in-law of Klickitat weaver Nettie Kuneki.

740. Hammond, Harmony and Jaune Quick-to-See Smith. *Women of Sweetgrass, Cedar and Sage*. New York: Gallery of the American Indian Community House, 1985.

"My Mother's Daughter: A History of Native American Women in Art," by Erin Younger features Karita Caffey, Georgia Masayesva, Jaune Quick-to-See Smith. "Women of Sweetgrass, Cedar and Sage"--Jaune Quick-to-See Smith. "Double Vision"--Lucy Lippard. Catalog quotes and describes each artist in the show. Brief autobiographical statements and a bibliography on women artists.

741. Herold, Joyce. "The Basketry of Tanzanita Peseta." *American Indian Art Magazine* 3, 2 (Spring 1978): 26-31, 94.

Analysis of a Jicarilla Apache basket maker's work including descriptions of photographs of her baskets in terms of techniques, shapes, dyes, and designs. Her unique designs act as her signature on her work which is recognized by her tribe as exceptional.

742. Hilger, Sister M. Inez. "Indian Women Preparing Bullrush Mats." *Indians at Work* 2, 2 (July 1, 1935): 41.

Description of the process of making bullrush mats by Indian women at the Red Lake Reservation in Minnesota. Traditionally these mats were used as "tables" around which families "squatted" during meals.

743. Hudson, J. W. "Pomo Basket Makers." *Overland Monthly* n.s. 21, 126 (June 1893): 561-78.

A brief history of Pomo culture focuses on the basketmaking skills as a symbol of the artistic, economic, and cultural values of the tribe. Also discusses basket weaving techniques in detail.

744. Hurst, Tricia. "Crossing Bridges: Jaune Quick-to-See Smith, Helen Hardin, Jean Bales." *Southwest Art* 10, 11 (April 1981): 82-91.

This illustrated article features three Indian women commenting on their artistic training, the artists and schools which have influenced their work, the spiritual aspects of their art, and their identities as both Indian and women artists.

745. Jones, Suzi, ed. *The Artists Behind the Work*. Fairbanks: University of Alaska Museum, 1986.

A museum catalog containing the biographies of Inupiaq skin sewer Lena Sours, bead worker Frances Demientieff, and Chilkat blanket weaver Jennie Thlunaut.

746. Katz, Jane B. *This Song Remembers: Self-Portraits of Native Americans in the Arts*. Boston: Houghton Mifflin, 1980.

In part biography and in part personal narrative, Katz relates the lives of several American Indian women who are active in the visual or performing arts: Pitseolak, Pearl Sunrise, Mary Morez, Grace Medicine Flower, Helen Hardin, Cecilia White, and Leslie Silko.

747. Knoll, John. "Fashion Designer Cuts from a Different Cloth." *New Mexico Magazine* 67, 8 (August 1989): 34-36, 38, 41.

Wendy Ponca is a contemporary Osage weaver who incorporates jet plane designs into her traditional art. She is a fashion designer whose works appear in both gallery shows and fashion boutiques.

748. Knudtson, Peter M. "Weavers of Wood: A Small Number of Haida Indian Women Help Keep the Fine Art of Northwest Coast Basketry Alive." *Natural History* 91, 5 (March 1982): 40-47.

A discussion of Haida basketry, focusing on those woven from the roots of Sitka spruce trees.

749. Kramer, Barbara. "Nampeyo, Hopi House and the Chicago Land Show." *American Indian Art* 14, 1 (Winter 1988): 46.

Biographical article about Hopi-Tewa potter Nampeyo that corrects the misinformation about how often she left the reservation to publicize the Fred Harvey Company.

750. LaDuke, Betty. "Winona: In Celebration of a Rite of Passage." *Women of Power* 13 (Spring 1989): 32-34.

In nine reproductions of her art, LaDuke pays homage to women and especially to her daughter, Winona.

751. Langley, Edna. *Coushatta Indian Crafts*. New Orleans: The Cabildo, 1974.

Catalog of exhibition of Coushatta Indian crafts assembled by Edna Langley as part of an effort to preserve the cultural heritage of her tribe.

752. Lannihan, Mark. "Original Style Benefits Artists." *The Indian Trader* 12, 10 (October 1981): 10-12.

Discussion of jewelers Gail Bird and Yazzie Johnson.

753. Lebrecht, Sue. "Angelique Merasty: Birch Bark Artist." *Canadian Woman Studies* 10, 2 & 3 (Summer/Fall 1989): 65-68.

Sixty-one year old Angelique Merasty continues the tradition of birch bark biting to create designs; she is the last one to continue this tradition.

754. Lichtenstein, Grace. "The Evolution of a Craft Tradition." *MS* 11, 10 (April 1983): 58-60, 92.

The Naranjo family women of Santa Clara Pueblo represent a significant trend among Indian artists--several generations, including young educated Indians participating in ceremonies and arts of their cultures. These women include traditional potters, contemporary stoneware potters, and sculptors, but all of them link their art to clay as a symbol of the nurturing quality of the earth and of women.

755. Little, Molly. "Mary Leaf, Mohawk Basketmaker." *Artifacts* 13, 3 (Summer 1985): 14.

Discussion of basketmaking of Mary Leaf.

756. Manewal, Ernest. "Buttons and Beads: Esther Littlefield: Tlingit Artist." *Alaska Journal* 8, 4 (1978): 338-41.

Discusses Littlefield's Tlingit background and art in button and beadwork, which she teaches at the Alaska Native Brotherhood Indian Cultural Center.

757. Marriott, Alice. "Maria of San Ildefonso, the Great Lady of the Pueblos." *Indian Life: The Magazine of the Inter-Tribal Indian Ceremonial* 40, 1 (May 1961): 1.

Marriott credits Maria Martinez's reintroduction of black-on-black pottery with revitalizing the San Ildefonso Pueblo when it was in a state of poverty. A brief biography is given.

758. Matthews, Washington. "Navajo Weavers." *Bureau of American Ethnology, 1881-82*. Washington, DC: US Government Printing Office, 1884, 371-91.

Study of Navajo weaving in the context of a longer report on archaeology and culture of the Navajo. Biographical profiles of several weavers are included.

759. McAnulty, Sarah. "Angel DeCora: American Indian Artist and Educator." *Nebraska History* 57 (1976): 143-99.

Born in 1871 on the Winnebago reservation in Nebraska, DeCora attended Hampton Institute and later Miss Burnham's school at Northampton, Massachusetts, to study music. In 1892 she entered the art department at Smith College, graduating in 1896. Going on to Drexel Institute, DeCora began producing art and became a part of eastern art circles. She did the illustrations for Zitkala Sa's *Old Indian Legends* and continued to use Indian material in her art. The article provides extensive biographical information as well as analysis of her art.

760. McCane-O'Connor, Mallory. "The Squaw as Artist: A Reevaluation." *The Southern Quarterly* 17, 2 (Winter 1979): 8-15.

McCane-O'Connor criticizes the catalog for the Indian art exhibition *Sacred Circles* for its insistent use of the masculine pronoun to discuss the production of Indian artists. The author points out the many contributions of Indian women to the artistic traditions of their tribes.

761. McCoy, Ronald. "Nampeyo: Giving the Indian Artist a Name." In *Indian Lives: Essays on Nineteenth and Twentieth-Century Native American Leaders*. L. G. Moses and Raymond Wilson, eds. Albuquerque: University of New Mexico Press, 1985.

Nampeyo (1860-1942) was a Hopi-Tewa potter who "rediscovered" Hopi techniques and created an atmosphere in which Indian artists were recognized by name and their work valued as art.

762. McGrew, Kate. "Partners in Art and Life: Gail Bird and Yazzie Johnson: Master Jewelers." *New Mexico Magazine* 67, 8 (August 1989): 60-65.

Bird (Laguna-Santa Domingo Pueblo) and Johnson (Navajo) work together to produce large contemporary pieces of jewelry. Bird is the designer.

763. McLaren, George. "The Arts of the Micmac of Nova Scotia." *Nova Scotia Historical Quarterly* 4, 2 (June 1974): 167-77.

Discusses the types of decoration used by Micmac women for domestic and clothing purposes, such as beadwork, quillwork, and dyes.

764. Monthan, Guy and Doris Monthan. "Dextra Quotskuyva Nampeyo." *American Indian Art Magazine* 2, 4 (Autumn 1977): 58-63.

The granddaughter of the Hopi potter Nampeyo, Dextra has only been producing pots seriously since 1972, but she has experimented with miniature pots, double-tiered jars, and seed jars.

765. Monthan, Guy and Doris Monthan. "Helen Cordero." *American Indian Art Magazine* 2, 4 (Autumn 1977): 72-76.

In 1964 Helen Cordero of Cochiti Pueblo introduced her storyteller dolls, pottery figurines of adults with tiny children clambering over them.

766. Nelson, Mary Carroll. "Pablita Velarde." *American Indian Art Magazine* 3, 2 (Spring 1978): 50-57, 90.

Born in 1918 in Santa Clara Pueblo, Velarde attended the BIA school in Santa Fe where Dorothy Dunn was teaching. She developed her talents there and continued to paint detailed and accurate works portraying Pueblo life.

767. Nequatewa, Edmund. "Nampeyo, Famous Hopi Potter." *Plateau* 15, 3 (January 1943): 40-42.

Brief biography of Nampeyo is followed by a discussion of her use of ancient Sikyatki Ruins designs and the jealousy this effected among the potters of Hano village who soon began to copy her work. Nampeyo continued to work as a potter even after losing her sight.

768. Nicholas, Ellen, ed. *Northwest Originals: Oregon Women and Their Art*. Portland: InUNISON Publishers, 1989.

This collection includes an article on Warm Springs artist Lillian Pitt who creates clay masks, and Lakota-Sioux/Comanche silversmith BlackStar White Woolf, who is also a storyteller.

769. Nichols, Phebe Jewell. "Weavers of Grass: Indian Women of the Woodlands." *Wisconsin Magazine of History* 36 (1952-1953): 130-33.

Describes the woven grass rugs of a Menominee woman known as Grandma Dutchman. Also describes wall and roof matting, sweet grass baskets, and basswood fiber bags.

770. Oleman, Minnie. "Lucy Lewis: Acoma's Versatile Potter." *El Palacio* 75, 2 (1968): 10-12.

Brief biographical information and a photo of Lucy Lewis.

771. Parezo, Nancy J. "Navajo Sandpainting: The Importance of Sex Roles in Craft Production." *American Indian Quarterly* 6, 1-2 (Spring-Summer 1982): 125-48.

Parezo looks at the blurring of sexual distinctions as Indian arts become of increasing economic importance. She details the role of women in preparing commercial sandpaintings.

772. Patterson, Edna B. "Mary Hall: Western Shoshone Basketmaker." *Quarterly, Northeastern Nevada Historical Society* 85, 4 (1985): 102-15.

A biographical sketch of Hall, including discussion of her craft and the work of her daughters.

773. Perlman, Barbara. "Courage: Her Greatest Asset." *Arizona Arts and Lifestyle* 2, 2 (Summer 1980): 20-21.

A Santa Clara potter from New Mexico, Jody Folwell discusses her rejection of the limitations of ceramic technique and her invention of experimental designs within traditional forms. Influences on her work from her grandmother and mother are also described.

774. Peterson, Susan. *The Living Tradition of Maria Martinez.* Tokyo: Koshanda International, 1977.

Picture and text document the life and pottery of Maria Martinez including a record of her designs and discussion of her molding and firing techniques. Includes historic and contemporary photos of Maria, her family, and her pottery as well as a history of pottery at San Ildefonso Pueblo.

775. Peterson, Susan. *Lucy M. Lewis: American Indian Potter.* Tokyo: Koshanda International, 1984.

Beautifully illustrated work about the Acoma potter who was born in the 1890s.

776. Peterson, Susan. *Maria Martinez: Five Generations of Potters.* Washington, DC: Renwick Galleries, 1978.

Presents brief biographical information about Maria Martinez and specific information about the pottery. Illustrated.

777. Peterson, Susan. *Master Pueblo Potters.* New York: ACA Gallery Catalog, 1980.

Includes Maria and Santana Martinez, Lucy Lewis, Fanny and Priscilla Nampeyo. Photographs.

778. Peterson, Susan. "Matriarchs of Pueblo Pottery." *Portfolio* (November/December 1980): 50-55.

Includes Maria Martinez, Lucy M. Lewis, Margaret Tafoya, and Fanny Nampeyo. Illustrated.

779. Phelps, Marion L. "An Ojibwa Chieftan's Granddaughter Once Lived in Potton." *Quebec-Histoire* 2, 2 (Winter 1973): 90-91.

This brief article discusses the handiwork of Charlotte Mono-nonco Katawebeday, a nineteenth century Ojibwa woman, and her creation of Ojibwa women's clothing.

780. Reynolds, Terry R. "Women, Pottery and Economics at Acoma Pueblo." In *New Mexico Women: Intercultural Perspectives*. Joan M. Jensen and Darlis A. Miller, eds. Albuquerque: University of New Mexico Press, 1986, 279-300.

At Acoma, a high mesa sixty miles west of Albuquerque, women shared equally in economic development before Spanish contact. But a shrinking land base and increasing population made life difficult and people depended more upon a cash economy. Because it was easier for men to enter the work system, women entered the market through pottery making.

781. Ross, George. "Lucy Telles, Basket Maker." *Yosemite Nature Notes* 26, 4 (1948): 67-68.

A brief look at the basketmaking of Miwok Indian Lucy Telles.

782. Rubinstein, Charlotte Streifer. *American Women Artists from Early Indian Times to the Present*. Boston: G. K. Hall, 1982.

Chapter 1 focuses on "Native Americans: The First American Women Artists." Traditional arts as well as twentieth century painting and sculpture are discussed.

783. Sainte-Marie, Buffy. *The Buffy Sainte-Marie Songbook*. New York: Grosset and Dunlap, 1971.

This collection includes a brief account by Sainte-Marie on song writing in addition to the words and music to her songs.

Illustrated. Specific introductions to some songs explain the background.

784. Schneider, Mary Jane. "The Production of Indian-Use and Souvenir Beadwork by Contemporary Indian Women." *Plains Anthropologist* 28, 101 (1983): 235-345.

    Production of beadwork among the Kiowa has been differentiated into two groups--one which makes items for sale to non-Indians, and one which makes items for Indian use. There is a disparity in knowledge and training between the two groups.

785. Schneider, Mary Jane. "Women's Work: An Examination of Women's Roles in Plains Arts and Crafts." *Plainswoman* 2 (1979): 8-11.

    The erroneous view that Plains men produced items of social and religious importance while women produced only mundane, secular items has perpetuated a misrepresentation of sexual roles and neglected the power, prestige, and wealth Plains women acquired through specialization in craft production.

786. Scott, Jay. *Changing Woman: The Life and Art of Helen Hardin*. Flagstaff: Northland Publishers, 1989.

    Lavishly illustrated biography of Helen Hardin (1943-1984), Santa Clara Pueblo artist.

787. Spivey, Richard L. "Signed in Clay." *El Palacio* 86, 4 (Winter 1980-81): 8-9.

    Spivey traces three eras of Maria Martinez's pottery career through her signatures on pots from 1907-1943, 1943-1956, and 1956-1970.

788. Stone, Margaret. "Craftsman of the Pahutes." *Desert Magazine* 6 (1943): 5-8.

A discussion of Paiute basketmaker Mary Pepo and government efforts to encourage the manufacture and sale of Indian crafts for the economic benefit of the craftspeople.

789. Tantaquidgeon, Gladys. "Newly Discovered Straw Basketry of the Wampanaog Indians of Massachusetts." *Indian Notes, Museum of the American Indian Heye Foundation* 7, 4 (1930): 475-84.

Description of the straw baskets made by Wampanoag Indian Emma Stafford, which were made from rye straw soaked in water and then split. Compares these baskets to similar type made by the Delaware Indians of Oklahoma.

790. Titus, Dorothy and Matt Titus. *This is the Way We Make Our Baskets*. Fairbanks: University of Alaska Press, 1979.

Dorothy and Matthew Titus of Minto, Alaska, give a step-by-step description of the process of collecting materials for and the making of willow, birch, and spruce root baskets. Bilingual text is accompanied by photographs. No tribal or language designation is given.

791. Toulouse, Betty. "Maria: The Right Woman at the Right Time." *El Palacio* 86, 4 (Winter 1980-81): 3-7.

Maria Martinez, famed potter of San Ildefonso Pueblo, is seen as central to the generation of a ceramic tradition based on techniques recovered from ancient potters through archaeological research. She is seen as significantly improving the economic status of her tribe through the quality and techniques of her work and the recognition her pots brought to Pueblo pottery.

792. Traugott, Joseph. "Emmi Whitehorse: Kin' Nah' Zin'." *Artspace* 6, 3 (Summer 1982): 40-41.

Kin' Nah' Zin' refers to a series of paintings by Navajo artist Emmi Whitehorse. Illustrations demonstrate the contemporary evocation of the pattern, form, and color of traditional Navajo weaving.

793. Tschopik, Harry Jr. "Taboo as a Possible Factor Involved in the Obsolescence of Navaho Pottery and Basketry." *American Anthropologist* 40, 2 (April-June 1938): 257-62.

A complex array of taboos which must be accommodated by women making ceremonial pots and baskets has contributed significantly to the decline of these arts, particularly to design experimentation.

794. Vander, Judith. *Ghost Dance Songs and Religion of a Wind River Shoshone Woman.* Los Angeles: Program in Ethnomusicology, Department of Music, University of California, 1986.

Emily Hill's knowledge of seventeen Ghost Dance songs is supplemented with background information on the Shoshone and a scholarly analysis of the music.

795. Vander, Judith. *Song Prints: The Musical Experience of Five Shoshone Women.* Urbana: University of Illinois Press, 1988.

This presentation of the songs and musical experience of five Wind River Shoshone women--Emily Hill, Angelina Wagon, Alberta Roberts, Helen Furlong, and Lenore Shoyo--includes life histories, songs, and commentary by them about their musical perception and processes, and the meaning of their work. Extensive use of quoted material from the five women.

796. Vander, Judith. "The Song Repertoire of Four Shoshone Women: A Reflection of Cultural Movement and Sex Roles." *Ethnomusicology* 26 (1982): 73-83.

Four Wind River Shoshone women ranging in age from 21 to 71 document the changing roles of women in their song repertoires. Each singer--Emily Hill, Alberta Roberts, Lenore Shoyo, and Helene Bonatsie--is profiled and her music is used to trace recent tribal history, cultural beliefs, sex roles, and life patterns.

797. Vigil, Arnold. "Blue Corn; Colorful Potter Carries on Maria's Legacy." *New Mexico Magazine* 67, 8 (August 1989): 54-59.

San Ildefonso potter uses polychrome technique as well as the black-on-black style of Maria Martinez. Blue Corn continues to use natural materials to carry on the ancient traditions.

798. Walters, Anna Lee. *The Spirit of Native America: Beauty and Mysticism in American Indian Art*. San Francisco: Chronicle Books, 1989.

Walters explores "Indianness" through artistic expressions, both traditional and contemporary. This is a collection of photographs accompanied by the writer's lyrical voice.

799. Whitehead, Ruth Holmes. "Christina Morris: Micmac Artist and Artist's Model." *Material History Bulletin* 3, (1977): 1-14.

Discusses the quillwork of nineteenth-century Nova Scotia Micmac artist Christina Morris.

800. Williams, Alice. "The Spirit of My Quilts." *Canadian Woman Studies* 10, 2 & 3 (Summer/Fall 1989): 49-51.

Anishinabe woman explains the designs in her quilts and the relationship of the patterns to her spirituality.

801. Willoughby, Nona Christensen. "Division of Labor Among the Indians of California." *Reports of the University of California Archaeological Survey*, no. 60. Berkeley: University of California Archaeological Survey, 1963, 7-79.

Discusses how the manufacture of baskets and other utensils and implements was divided between men and women in the Indian tribes of California.

802. Withers, Josephine. "Inuit Women Artists: An Art Essay." *FS: Feminist Studies* 10, 1 (Spring 1984): 85-96.

Illustrated article which explains the imagery of contemporary art forms of Inuit women. The meanings of the illustrations are explained in the text.

803. Wright, Robin K. "The Depiction of Women in Nineteenth Century Haida Argillite Carving." *American Indian Art Magazine* 11, 4 (Autumn 1986): 36-45.

Northwest Coast art provides clues as to the position and role of Indian women. Changes in carving styles as well as cultural changes affecting the Haida can be determined from a study of argillite carvings.

804. Zastro, Leona M. "American Indian Women as Art Educators." *Journal of American Indian Education* 18 (October 1978): 6-10.

Zastro discusses Pima, Papago and Pueblo women as art educators teaching their children traditional arts.

805. Zastro, Leona M. "Two Native Americans Speak on Art Values and the Value of Arts." *Journal of American Indian Education* 16, 3 (May 1977): 25-30.

Zastro interviewed two southwestern artists about the place of art within their cultures. Joe Gift, a Pima, and Mary Lewis Garcia, Acoma, both responded that the traditional arts are still valued but acknowledged that arts are not as central to cultural life as they once were.

806. Zwinger, Susan. "Viewpoint: An Interview with Artist Jaune Quick-to-See Smith." *El Palacio* 92, 1 (Summer/Fall 1986): 51-54.

Jaune Quick-to-See Smith, a Cree/Shoshone artist, notes that contemporary art by Indians is a problem for anthropologists who tend to see all non-traditional arts as indications of abandonment of culture. She also discusses her history as a painter.

Literature and Criticism

LITERATURE AND CRITICISM

807. *Contact II: Special Issue on Women Poets* 15, 27 (Fall/Winter 1982/83).

Includes reviews of poetry by Mary TallMountain, Linda Hogan, Wendy Rose, reviews by Paula Gunn Allen, Diane Burns, Joy Harjo, and a poem by Elizabeth Woody.

808. *Fireweed; A Feminist Quarterly* 22 (Winter 1986).

Entire issue on Native women, includes Elizabeth Woody, Anita Endrezze-Danielson, Winona LaDuke, Beth Brant, Chrystos, Linda Hogan, and others.

809. *Plainswoman* 8, 4 (December 1984): "Indian Women." Special Issue.

Includes articles on Louise Erdrich and Margaret Hawk.

810. "Special Issue: "Native Women." *Canadian Woman Studies/Les Cahiers de la Femme* 10, 2 & 3 (Summer-Fall 1989).

This comprehensive special issue includes some poetry, language studies, and a transcription of an Anishinabe story.

811. Ackerman, Maria. *Tlingit Stories*. Anchorage: Alaska Methodist University Press, 1975.

Stories collected by a Tlingit woman born in Juneau in 1927. Ackerman is a resource Native artist for Indian education in Anchorage.

812.   Alexander, Jo, *et al. Women and Aging: An Anthology by Women*. Corvallis, OR: Calyx Books, 1986.

A multi-genre anthology which includes Mary TallMountain and Gail Tremblay.

813.   Allen, Minerva. *Like Spirits of the Past Trying to Break Out and Walk to the West*. Albuquerque: Wopai Books, 1974.

Poetry and a story on traditional Indian themes by an Assiniboine writer.

814.   Allen, Paula Gunn. "Answering the Deer: Genocide and Continuance in American Indian Women's Poetry." *American Indian Culture and Research Journal* 6, 3 (1982): 35-45. Rpt. in *Coming to Light: American Women Poets in the Twentieth Century*. Diane Wood and Marilyn Yalom, eds. Ann Arbor: University of Michigan Press, 1985, 223-232.

Luguna writer discusses love, death, and humor in the poetry of contemporary Indian women to explain how metaphors are used to address the dual perceptions and divergent realities of modern Indian experience. Allen quotes extensively from poems by American Indian women to emphasize the transformation and continuance of Indian cultures.

815.   Allen, Paula Gunn. *The Blind Lion*. Berkeley: Thorp Springs Press, 1974.

Poetry.

816.   Allen, Paula Gunn. "Bringing Home the Fact: Tradition and Continuity in the Imagination." In *Recovering the Word: Essays on Native American Literature*. Brian Swann and Arnold Krupat, eds. Berkeley: University of California Press, 1987, 563-79.

Allen interprets N. Scott Momaday's novel, *House Made of Dawn* as "an act of the imagination designed to heal," discussing its mythic structure, its simultaneity, its revelation of "the significances created by events," and its merging of the spiritual and the human.

817. Allen, Paula Gunn. *A Cannon Between My Knees*. New York: Strawberry Press, 1983.

Poetry.

818. Allen, Paula Gunn. *Coyote's Daylight Trip*. Albuquerque: La Confluencia, 1978.

Poetry.

819. Allen, Paula Gunn. "The Feminine Landscape of Leslie Silko's *Ceremony*." In *Studies in American Indian Literature: Critical Essays and Course Designs*. Paula Gunn Allen, ed. New York: Modern Language Association of America, 1983, 127-33.

Allen discusses two types of characters found in *Ceremony*: those who live in harmony with the earth spirit and those who seek to destroy it. She suggests that the protagonist experiences an "initiation into womanhood" in the course of the novel, which results in his growth into a spiritually whole person.

820. Allen, Paula Gunn. "The Grace That Remains: American Indian Women's Literature." *Book Forum* 5 (1981): 376-82.

Focus on the poetry of American Indian women and what the poetry reveals about Indian women's lives. Contrasts the power of poetry with the threats to the power of women in many societies.

821. Allen, Paula Gunn. "Kochinnenako in Academe: Three Approaches to Interpreting a Keres Indian Tale." *North Dakota Quarterly* 53, 2 (Spring 1985): 84-105.

In a first person essay, Allen argues the necessity for a feminist perspective in the teaching of American Indian literatures through analysis of the Keres "Yellow Woman" myth. She demonstrates that a feminist approach reveals "not only the exploitation and oppression of the tribes by whites . . . but also reveals areas of oppression within tribes" and reasserts the centrality of women to harmonious human society.

822.   Allen, Paula Gunn. "The Mythopoetic Vision in Native American Literature." *American Indian Culture and Research Journal* 1 (1974): 3-12.

According to Allen, the term *myth* has been misused and misunderstood. Used correctly, the term can be applied to mythic narratives and shown to be related to Native American religions. Black Elk's vision is cited as an example.

823.   Allen, Paula Gunn. "The Psychological Landscape of *Ceremony*." *American Indian Quarterly* 5, 1 (1979): 7-12.

Allen discusses the male/female principles of Leslie Silko's book *Ceremony* in relation to the characters and the reverence for the land.

824.   Allen, Paula Gunn. "The Sacred Hoop: A Contemporary Indian Perspective on American Indian Literature." In *Literature of the American Indians: Views and Interpretations*. Abraham Chapman, ed. New York: New American Library, 1975, 111-35.

This examination of Native American cultures helps explain the differences between Indian literature and western literature, particularly in the differing views of religion, nature, and language. Allen also discusses the importance of ceremony and its relationship to the literature.

825.   Allen, Paula Gunn. *Shadow Country*. Los Angeles: American Indian Studies Center Series, 1982.

Poetry.

826.   Allen, Paula Gunn. *Skins and Bones*. San Francisco: West End Press, 1988.

Poetry.

827.   Allen, Paula Gunn, ed. "Special Issue: Native Women of New Mexico." *A: A Journal of Contemporary Literature* 3, 2 (Fall 1978).

Laguna writer Allen is guest editor for this special issue which includes works by Leslie Silko, Marisa Crumbo, Sandie Nelson, Luci Tapahonso, Mary TallMountain, Jaune Quick-to-See Smith, Carol Lee Sanchez, Nora Lea Yazzie, and Emmi Whitehorse.

828.   Allen, Paula Gunn. *Spider Woman's Granddaughters: Traditional Tales and Contemporary Writing by Native American Women*. Boston: Beacon Press, 1989.

Collection of stories from the oral tradition and contemporary fiction which depicts Indian women's experiences. Introduction by Allen places the works in historical and cultural context.

829.   Allen, Paula Gunn. *Star Child*. Marvin, SD: Blue Cloud Quarterly 1982.

Poetry.

830.   Allen, Paula Gunn. "A Stranger in My Own Life: Alienation in Native American Prose and Poetry." *ASAIL Newsletter* 3 (Spring 1979): 16-23; reprint, *MELUS* 7 (1980) 3-19.

In this discussion of the mixed-blood in life and literature, Allen makes brief references to comments made by N. Scott Momaday and James Welch and discusses at length the role of Tayo in Leslie Silko's *Ceremony*.

831.   Allen, Paula Gunn. *Studies in American Indian Literature: Critical Essays and Course Designs*. New York: MLA, 1983.

A collection of essays, course plans and bibliographies designed to facilitate the teaching of courses in Indian literatures. Includes material on Indian oral tradition, fiction, poetry, personal narrative, criticism, and the Indian in American literature.

832.   Allen, Paula Gunn. "This Wilderness in My Blood: Spirituality in the Work of Five American Indian Women Poets." In *Coyote Was Here: Essays on Contemporary Native American Literature and Political Mobilization*. Bo Scholer, ed. Aarhus, Denmark: University of Aarhus, 1983, 95-114.

Allen distinguishes the poetry of Indian women from that of non-Indian writers on the basis of their bi-cultural vision, their involvement in tribal religion, the knowledge of the spirit world, their traditional and personal relationship to the earth, their vital sense of kinship, and their shared history of threatened extinction. She analyzes these elements in the poetry of Joy Harjo, Linda Hogan, Mary TallMountain, Wendy Rose, and Carol Lee Sanchez.

833.   Allen, Paula Gunn. "What I Do When I Write. . . ." *The Women's Review of Books* 4, 10-11 (July 1989): 23.

Allen discusses the patterns and processes of her writing, noting that her poetry, fiction, and essays each require a different approach. Consciousness of writing for both Native and non-Native audiences is also discussed as well as her sense of responsibility toward the truth and the difficult yet delightful work writing is for her.

834.   Allen, Paula Gunn. "Where I Came From is Like This." In *Rereading America: Cultural Contexts for Critical Thinking and Writing*. Gary Colombo, Robert Cullen, and Bonnie Lisle, eds. New York: St. Martin's Press, 1990, 273-81.

Allen analyzes ways in which images of women in traditional culture differ from images of women in mainstream American culture stressing the practicality, strength, reasonableness, intelligence, and competence of Indian women. She discusses her shock at discovering negative images of Indian women held by outsiders and how contrary to her experiences they were. She credits oral storytelling and strong female characters from myth with sustaining the pride and strength of Indian women.

835. Allen, Paula Gunn. "Whose Dream is This Anyway?: Remythologizing and Self-Redefinition of Contemporary American Indian Fiction." In *Literature and the Visual Arts in Contemporary Society, Number Two*. Suzanne Ferguson and Barbara Groseclose, eds. Columbus: Ohio State University Press, 1985, 95-122.

Discussion of American Indian novels and the similarities to Indian circular narratives as well as contemporary Western fiction. Allen analyzes early work by McNickle and Mourning Dove as well as Momaday, Welch, and Silko novels.

836. Allen, Paula Gunn. *The Woman Who Owned the Shadows*. San Francisco: Spinster's Inc., 1983.

In this novel, which incorporates oral tradition, the female protagonist searches for personal stability and tribal identity in a contemporary context; narrative is interiorized.

837. Allen, Paula Gunn. *WYRDS*. San Francisco: Taurean Horn Press, 1987.

Poetry.

838. Allen, T. D., ed. *Arrows Four: Prose and Poetry by Young American Indians*. New York: Pocket, 1974.

Young Indian writers in BIA schools participated in a creative writing project which culminated in this volume of the best writing by Indian students.

839. Allen, Terry and Mae Durham, eds. *The Whispering Wind: Poetry by Young American Indians*. Garden City: Doubleday, 1972.

This anthology includes poetry by Liz Sohappy, Janet Campbell, Ramona Carden, Donna Whitewing, Patricia Irving, and Agnes T. Pratt. All of the poets included in this collection were then students at the Institute of American Indian Arts in Santa Fe, New Mexico.

840. Anderson, Marilyn J. "The Best of Two Worlds: The Pocahontas Legend as Treated in Early American Drama." *The Indian Historian* 12, 2 (Summer 1979): 54-59.

Anderson traces the characterization of Pocahontas in drama as early as 1808, showing how Indian images changed depending on current political views. Most of the portrayals were romantic accounts of harmonious co-existence between Indians and whites.

841. Andrews, Lynn V. *Medicine Woman*. San Francisco: Harper & Row, 1981.

First of a series of pseudo-Indian narratives which purport to tell stories of powerful medicine women and the trials and terrors of female initiates into power. In the Casteneda tradition, it is fiction more closely akin to "new age" philosophy than any tribal way.

842. Antell, Judith. "Momaday, Welch and Silko: Expressing the Feminine Principle Through Male Alienation." *American Indian Quarterly* 12, 3 (1988): 213-20.

Discusses the use of the feminine principle in Momaday's *House Made of Dawn*, Welch's *The Death of Jim Loney* and Silko's *Ceremony* as a cause of the alienation of each novel's male protagonist.

843. Armstrong, Jeannette. *Slash*. Penticton, BC: Theytus Books, 1985.

Armstrong presents a fictionalized autobiographical narrative of an Indian activist Tommy Kelasket. Issues such as the Okanagon moratorium on uranium mining have emerged from the Okanagon response to colonization, but so have personal and communal self-destruction.

844. Ataile, Princess. *The Earth Speaks*. New York: Fleming H. Revell, 1940.

Tales and stories collected and illustrated by a Cherokee woman. There is no indication of sources, making it difficult to determine the authenticity of the material included.

845. Babcock, Barbara A. "Taking Liberties, Writing From the Margins, and Doing it With a Difference." *Journal of American Folklore* 100, 398 (October-December 1987): 390-411.

Discussion of feminist folklore using potter Helen Cordero and anthropologist Elsie Clews Parsons to illustrate the need to examine women's folklore and feminist contributions.

846. Bannan, Helen M. "Spider Woman's Web: Mothers and Daughters in Southwestern Native American Literature." In *The Lost Tradition: Mothers and Daughters in Literature*. Cathy Davidson and E. M. Broner, eds. New York: Ungar, 1980, 268-79.

Bannan cites several traditional tales that establish the mother-daughter relationship that is expected. She links traditional roles to the expression of female images in contemporary poetry by Silko, Allen, and others.

847. Barrett, S. M. *Hoistah: An Indian Girl*. New York: Duffield, 1913.

This is a fictionalized story of a Cheyenne woman born in the early 1800s.

848.   Bartlett, Mary Daughterty, ed. *The New Native American Novel: Works in Progress*. Albuquerque: University of New Mexico Press, 1986.

Selections include excerpts from *The Beet Queen* (Louise Erdrich), *The Grace of Wooden Birds* (Linda Hogan), *Raven's Road* (Paula Gunn Allen), and *A Report from the Proceedings* (Elizabeth Cook-Lynn). Only *The Beet Queen* has been published as a novel.

849.   Basso, Keith. "Stalking with Stories: Names, Places and Moral Narratives Among the Western Apache." In *Text, Play and Story: The Construction and Preconstruction of Self and Society*. Stuart Plattner, ed. Washington: Proceedings of the American Ethnological Society, 1984, 19-54.

This essay on types of Apache historical stories includes a narrative by Annie Peaches which explains the harmful consequences of overstepping traditional role boundaries. Story concerns a mother-in-law who interferes in her daughter and son-in-law's lives without being properly requested to do so and becomes an acute source of embarrassment even though the meddling seems to serve a useful purpose. Basso also discusses his interview with a young Apache woman targeted for untraditional behavior in a story told by her grandmother, demonstrating the power of stories as behavioral sanctions.

850.   Beavert, Virginia. *The Way It Was (Anaku Iwacha): Yakima Legends*. Yakima, WA: Consortium of Johnson O'Malley Committees of Region IV, 1974.

A collection of Yakima legends translated into English by a Yakima woman.

851.   Bell, Robert C. "Circular Design in *Ceremony*." *American Indian Quarterly* 5 (1979): 47-62.

Bell compares the hoop ritual in Silko's *Ceremony* with the ritual found in the Coyote Transformation rite in the Myth of Red Antway, Male Evilway.

852. Bennett, Kay. "Letter to the Editor." In *American Indian Speaks*. John R. Milton, ed. Vermillion: University of South Dakota Press, 1969, 171-72.

Navajo Bennett briefly discusses her reason for writing: "to preserve a part of our history and culture."

853. Blanche, Jerry D., ed. *Native American Reader: Stories, Speeches and Poems*. Juneau, AK: The Denali Press, 1990.

Though primarily a collection of male speeches and writing, a number of women orators and poets are included in this anthology.

854. Blicksilver, Edith. *The Ethnic American Woman: Problems, Protests, Life style*. Dubuque, IA: Kendall-Hunt Publishing, 1978; expanded printing, 1989.

This anthology contains works by several Native American women: Rose Mary (Shingobe) Barstow, Joy Harjo, nila northSun, Buffy Sainte-Marie, Leslie Silko, Virginia Driving Hawk Sneve, Liz Sohappy, and Anne Webster.

855. Blicksilver, Edith. "Literature as Social Criticism: The Ethnic Woman Writer." *Modern Language Studies* 5, 2 (Fall 1975): 46-54.

Blicksilver discusses ethnic women's writings as they deal with universal problems, social protest, conflicts between new immigrants and native-born ethnic women, and intergroup relations. American Indian writers are only briefly noted.

856. Blicksilver, Edith. "Traditionalism vs. Modernity: Leslie Silko on American Indian Women." *Southwest Review* 64 (Spring 1979): 149-60.

Silko is seen as a link from the past to the present in the way she blends traditionalism with contemporary experiences in her fiction and poetry. Discusses "Lullaby," "Yellow Woman,"

"The Man to Send Rain Clouds," and poetry from *Laguna Woman*.

857.   Bowman, John Clarke. *Powhatan's Daughter*. New York: Viking, 1973.

This historical novel is based on legendary accounts of Pocahontas and John Smith.

858.   Brant, Beth, ed. *A Gathering of Spirit: Writing and Art by Native American Indian Women*. Rockland, ME: Sinister Wisdom, 1984.

Collection of stories and poetry by both well-known and new voices in Indian women's contemporary writing, edited by Mohawk Beth Brant. Most comprehensive anthology of Indian women's writing in print, including over 80 entries by over 50 writers.

859.   Brant, Beth. *Mohawk Trail*. Ithaca, NY: Firebrand Books, 1985.

Part myth, part poetry, part autobiography and short story, this volume explores the author's relationship to her family, the lesbian community, and the urban working class community in which she lives.

860.   Brewington, Lillian, Normie Bullard, and R. W. Reising. "Writing in Love: An Annotated Bibliography of Critical Responses to the Poetry and Novels of Louise Erdrich and Michael Dorris." *American Indian Culture and Research Journal* 10, 4 (1986): 81-86.

The collaboration of the husband-wife team is discussed in a brief introduction to a bibliography on *Jacklight, Love Medicine, The Beet Queen*, and *A Yellow Raft in Blue Water*.

861.   Brigham, Besmilr. *Heaved from the Earth*. New York: Alfred A. Knopf, 1971.

Poetry by a part-Choctaw woman from Mississippi.

862. Brown, Alanna Kathleen. "Mourning Dove, an Indian Novelist." *Plainswoman* 11, 5 (1988): 3-4.

Mourning Dove (1888-1936) wrote a novel before she was thirty years old and published a collection of Okanogan stories. Recognizing the flaws in Mourning Dove's novel, Brown nevertheless praises the groundbreaking nature of this Indian woman's fiction.

863. Brown, Alanna Kathleen. "Mourning Dove's Canadian Recovery Years, 1917-1919." *Canadian Literature* 124-125 (Spring/Summer 1990): 113-23.

Brown provides biographical information on Mourning Dove, showing the effect of her own experiences on her novel *Cogewea*.

864. Brown, Alanna Kathleen. "Mourning Dove's Voice in *Cogewea*." *Wicazo Sa Review* 4, 2 (1988): 2-15.

The problem of L. V. McWhorter's co-writing and editing of the *Cogewea* text is examined and the novel is described as autobiographical and essentially the product of Mourning Dove's Indian experience and voice.

865. Brown, Alanna Kathleen. "Profile: Mourning Dove (Humishuma) 1888-1936." *Legacy: A Journal of Nineteenth Century American Women Writers* 6, 1 (Spring 1989): 51-58.

Brown provides a summary of the life and work of this early American Indian woman novelist.

866. Brown, Dee. *Creek Mary's Blood*. New York: Holt, Rinehart, and Winston, 1980.

Brown's book is a novel of four generations of American Indian life told through the life of one family. Creek Mary is the daughter of a Muskogee chief who first married a white trader and later a Cherokee. The novel is the story of Creek Mary and her descendants.

867.   Bruchac, Carol, Linda Hogan, and Judith McDaniel. *The Stories We Hold Secret: Tales of Women's Spiritual Development*. Greenfield Center, NY: Greenfield Review Press, 1986.

Anthology of essays by women who understand their connections to the spiritual and to themselves. Linda Hogan, Beth Brant, Karen Cooper, Kathleen Shaye Hill, Norma Jean Ross, Georgianna Valoyce Sanchez, and Flying Clouds are authors in the collection who identify as American Indians.

868.   Bruchac, Joesph, ed. *New Voices From the Long House: An Anthology of Contemporary Iroquois Writing*. Greenfield Center, NY: Greenfield Review Press, 1989.

This collection includes memories, stories and poetry by eleven women writers from Iroquoian tribes. A rare category of anthology, since it represents a very specific cultural and regional population.

869.   Bruchac, Joseph, ed. *The Next World: Poems by 32 Third World Americans*. Trumansburg, NY: The Crossing Press, 1978.

This anthology includes poetry by Janet Campbell Hale, Wendy Rose and Leslie Silko. Brief biographies precede selections from each of the authors.

870.   Bruchac, Joseph, ed. *Songs from this Earth on Turtle's Back: Contemporary American Indian Poetry*. Greenfield Center, NY: Greenfield Review Press, 1983.

This anthology includes poetry by Paula Gunn Allen (Laguna/Sioux), Beth Brant (Mohawk), Diane Burns (Anishinabe/Chemehuevi), Gladys Cardiff (Cherokee), Charlotte DeClue (Osage), Anita Endrezze-Danielson (Yaqui), Nia Francisco (Navajo), Diane Glancy (Cherokee), Mary Goose (Mesquakie), Janet Campbell Hale (Coeur d'Alene),

Joy Harjo (Creek), Linda Hogan (Chickasaw), Wendy Rose (Hopi/Miwok), Leslie Silko (Laguna), Mary TallMountain (Koyukon), Luci Tapahonso (Navajo), Laura Tohe (Navajo), Roberta Hill Whiteman (Oneida), Phyllis Wolf (Anishinabe), and Elizabeth Woody (Sahaptin-Dine).

871. Burns, Diane. *Riding the One-Eyed Ford*. Brooklyn: Strawberry Press, 1982.

Poetry by an Anishinabe/Chemehuevi woman.

872. Burton, Jimalee. *Indian Heritage, Indian Pride*. Norman: University of Oklahoma Press, 1974.

Comprised of personal recollections, traditional stories, history, poetry, essays, character sketches, and painting, this collection pays tribute to the endurance and culture of Indian people. This Cherokee writer has been active in publication and print media and was editor of the Indian newspaper *The Native Voice* for fifteen years.

873. Callahan, Sophia Alice. *Wynema: A Child of the Forest*. Chicago: H. J. Smith and Co., 1891.

Often identified as the first novel by a Native woman; Callahan was Creek.

874. Cameron, Anne. *Daughters of Copper Woman*. Vancouver: Press Gang Publishers, 1981.

A collection of stories told to the author by Native women of Vancouver Island. The women remain anonymous by choice. Includes creation tales, hero tales, and stories of the women's secret society. The book is influenced by a contemporary feminist perspective.

875. Cardiff, Gladys. *To Frighten a Storm*. Port Townsend, WA: Copper Canyon Press, 1976.

Poetry by a Cherokee writer.

876.   Carlson, Vada and Polingaysi Qoyawayma. *Broken Pattern: Sunlight and Shadows of Hopi History*. Happy Camp, CA: Naturegraph Publishers, 1985.

Historical fiction portraying the Hopi life as it was altered by the coming of the Spanish. The novel tells the story of the courtship and marriage of Sevansi and Hohtski.

877.   Castro, Michael. *Interpreting the Indian: Twentieth Century Poets and the Native American*. Albuquerque: University of New Mexico Press, 1983.

In this historical study of twentieth century poetry, Castro focuses on non-Indian interpretations from Austin to Rothenberg and Snyder. In the last chapter he briefly discusses Leslie Silko and Marnie Walsh.

878.   Chalmers, John W. "Tekahionwake." *Alberta Historical Review* (Summer 1974): 24-25.

A brief critical assessment of the Albertan Pauline Johnson (Tekahionwake) as poet and entertainer.

879.   Chapman, Abraham, ed. *Literature of the American Indians: Views and Interpretations*. New York: New American Library, 1975.

Anthology which includes Paula Gunn Allen's "The Sacred Hoop: A Contemporary Indian Perspective on American Indian Literature," and critical essays , narratives and critical essays on Indian literary genres.

880.   Chrystos. *Not Vanishing*. Vancouver: Press Gang Publishers, 1988.

A collection of poetry by a Menominee woman from San Francisco who now resides on Bainbridge Island in the Pacific Northwest.

881. Clark, Patricia and Paula Gunn Allen. "Earthly Relations, Carnal Knowledge." In *The Desert is No Lady*. Vera Norwood and Janice Monk, eds. New Haven: Yale University Press, 1987, 174-96.

The relationships between American Indian literature and ritual and how women and wilderness are connected to these are discussed in terms of both traditional and contemporary literature of the southwest. Works by Luci Tapahonso (Navajo), Leslie Silko (Laguna), and Joy Harjo (Creek) are examined.

882. Cochran, Jo *et al.*, eds. "Bearing Witness/Sobreviviendo: An Anthology of Native American/Latina Art and Literature." *Calyx: A Journal of Art and Literature by Women* 8, 2 (1984). Special issue.

Includes Wendy Rose, Sherry Sylvester, Paula Gunn Allen, Janice Gould, Vickie Sears, Dian Million, Charlotte DeClue, Charlene Lowry, Elizabeth Woody, Laura Tohe, Jo Ellen Shively, Saunie Kaye Wilson, Gail Tremblay, Elizabeth Cook-Lynn, Denise Helene Panek, Rochelle DuBois, Woesha Hampson, Jo Carillo, Jo Cochran, Phyllis Wolf, Beth Brant, Sue Redbird Cochran, Linda Hogan. Art by Lillian Pitt, Linda Lomah‌eftewa, Charleen Touchette.

883. Cochran, Jo, J. T. Stewart, and Mayumi Tsutakawa. *Gathering Ground: New Writing and Art by Northwest Women of Color*. Seattle: The Seal Press, 1984.

Includes: Jo Cochran (Lakota), Debra Cecille Earling (Salish/Kootenai), Kathleen Shaye Hill (Klamath), Edna Jackson (Tlingit), Vickie Sears (Cherokee).

884. Coltelli, Laura, ed. *Native American Literatures: Forum I, 1989*. Pisa: Serrizo Editoriale Universitario, 1989.

This collection of critical essays includes a tribute to Osage critic Carol Hunter, articles on works by Joy Harjo and Leslie

Silko, and a Papago woman's autobiography. A brief essay by Judith Mountain Leaf Volbroth is also included.

885.   Coltelli, Laura. "Native American Literature and Mainstream American Literature 1968-1988: A Bibliographical Evaluation." *Storia Nordamerica* 5, 1 (1988): 185-211. Special Issue: "The American Indian Today."

This essay is particularly useful for its analysis of the meager representation of Indian literatures in major American literature anthologies, particularly the absence of poetry by Indian women. The accompanying bibliography provides a good beginning research tool for the study of Indian literatures.

886.   Coltelli, Laura. "Re-enacting Myths and Stories: Tradition and Renewal in Leslie Marmon Silko's *Ceremony*." In *Native American Literatures: Forum I, 1989*. Laura Coltelli, ed. Pisa: Serrizo Editoriale Universitario, 1989, 173-83.

Silko uses myth recast in contemporary reality to link past and present and oral and written narrative forms in her novel, creating a mythopoetic renewal of tribal myth paralleled by the protagonist's regenerative process.

887.   Conlon, Faith, Rachel de Silva, and Barbara Wilson, eds. *The Things that Divide Us: Stories by Women*. Seattle: Seal Press, 1985.

Stories by Vickie L. Sears (Cherokee) and Linda Hogan (Chickasaw) are included.

888.   Cook, Elizabeth. "American Indian Literature in Servitude." *Indian Historian* 10 (1977): 3-6.

A Crow Creek Sioux woman's analysis of American Indian literature.

889. Cook, Elizabeth. "Propulsives in Native American Literature." *College Composition and Communication* 24, 3 (1973): 271-74.

Discusses the roots of contemporary literature in the traditional philosophies and literatures of American Indians.

890. Cook-Lynn, Elizabeth. *Abenaki Ghosts*. Marvin, SD: Blue Cloud Press, 1987.

Poetry.

891. Cook-Lynn, Elizabeth. *Seek the House of Relatives. Blue Cloud Quarterly* 29, 4 (1983).

Poetry and short story "A Visit from Reverend Tileston."

892. Cook-Lynn, Elizabeth. *Then Badger Said This*. New York: Vantage Press. 1977.

Cook-Lynn's prose and poetry focus on the traditions and experiences of this Sioux woman.

893. Copeland, M. W. "*Black Elk Speaks* and Leslie Silko's *Ceremony*: Two Visions of Horses." *Critique* 24 (Spring 1983): 158-72.

The horse is seen as a symbol of transition, the means of journey which reconnects Tayo in *Ceremony* to the natural world and effects his cure, and as a contrast to the world of dream and vision in Black Elk's narrative of warrior horses.

894. Cox, Jay. "Dangerous Definitions: Female Tricksters in Contemporary Native American Literature." *Wicazo Sa Review* 5, 2 (Fall 1989): 17-21.

In contemporary writing by Native Americans female trickster figures operate both within the community and in the liminal space outside the village. They tend to shake the status quo and function very similarly to male tricksters except in their ability to move between the center and fringes of the community.

895. Culleton, Beatrice. *In Search of April Raintree*. Winnipeg: Pemmican, 1983.

Culleton's novel of the lives of two Metis sisters is based on Culleton's experiences. Cheryl and April are rejected, abused in foster homes, and separated from each other. It is a novel of anger and frustration, but also of ultimate hope.

896. Currie, Noel Elizabeth. "Jeannette Armstrong and the Colonial Legacy." *Canadian Literature* 124-125 (Spring/Summer 1990): 138-155.

In *Slash,* Okanagon writer Jeannette Armstrong describes racism, sexism, and classism as the results of colonialism and uses fiction as a forum for political expression.

897. Danielson, Anita Endrezze. *Burning the Fields*. Lewiston, ID: Confluence Press, 1983.

Poetry by a Yaqui woman.

898. Danielson, Anita Endrezze. *Claiming Lives*. Lewiston, ID: Confluence Press.

Poetry.

899. Danielson, Anita Endrezze. *The North People*. Marvin, SD: Blue Cloud Quarterly, 1983.

Poetry.

900. Danielson, Linda L. "*Storyteller*: Grandmother Spider's Web." *Journal of the Southwest* 30, 3 (Autumn 1988): 324-55.

Danielson analyzes Leslie Silko's *Storyteller* using both a feminist approach and a Laguna interpretation. She interprets Silko's personal view of her tribe and her history as the "feminist" stance she must take to be consistent with her culture.

901.   Dauenhauer, Nora Marks. *The Droning Shaman*. Haines, AK: The Black Current Press, 1988.

Poetry by a Tlingit writer.

902.   Day, David and Marilyn Bowering, eds. *Many Voices: An Anthology of Contemporary Canadian Indian Poetry*. Vancouver: J.J. Douglas, 1977.

Collection of poetry which includes Mary Augusta Tappage, Mary Jacobson, Rose Fleury, Marcia Anderson, Cam Hubert, Pauline Doore, Eleanor Crowe, Shirley Daniels, Susan Landell, Skyros Bruce, Mireille Sioui, Jeannette Armstrong, Bonneau Loucheux, Sheila Erickson, and Lydia Yellowbird.

903.   Dearborn, Mary V. *Pocahontas's Daughters: Gender and Ethnicity in American Culture*. New York: Oxford University Press, 1986.

The author sees literature produced by American ethnic women as presenting in "dramatically high relief" aspects of American culture as well as gender and ethnic experience in America, and uses the Pocahontas legend as a focus of her analysis of literary works by ethnic women in America. First chapter focuses on fiction by American Indian women--"Pocahontas's Sisters"--and addresses the issue of establishing authoral authority and the frequent process of a white intermediary in both autobiography and fiction by Native women before the 1977 publication of Leslie Silko's *Ceremony*. The author also focuses two chapters on Pocahontas's marriage as symbolic of cultural merging.

904.   Defender, Adelina. "No Time for Tears." In *An American Indian Anthology*. Benet Tvedten, ed. Marvin, SD: Blue Cloud Abbey, 1971, 23-31.

Nine-year-old Moon Rainbow is aware of the religious conflicts at the Pueblo where Catholicism and Protestantism are in competition with traditional Pueblo beliefs.

905.   Deloria, Ella Cara. *Dakota Texts*. New York: G. E. Stechert, 1932. Rpt. New York: AMS Press, 1974.

This edition, a reprint of the 1932 publication, provides background on Ella Deloria, who was born in 1889 on the Yankton Sioux reservation. She had collected materials for Franz Boas between 1927 and 1942. Included in this book are Dakota narratives and translations of traditional stories of Iktomi, Double-Face, Iya, Stone-Boy, and Rolling Skull, in addition to more contemporary stories.

906.   Deloria, Ella Cara. *Speaking of Indians*. New York: Friendship Press, 1944; Rpt. Agnes Picotte and Paul Pavich, eds. Vermillion, SD: Dakota Press, 1979.

The introduction by Agnes Picotte and Paul Pavich provides information about Deloria, a Sioux woman whose text is influenced by tradition, by ethnology training at Columbia University, and by Christianity.

907.   Deloria, Ella Cara. *Waterlily*. Lincoln: University of Nebraska Press, 1988.

Deloria's novel, written nearly fifty years earlier, is the story of a Sioux woman who lived before white settlement disrupted traditional Dakota ways. While this is a novel, it is largely a vehicle for documentary presentation of a typical Teton Sioux woman's life. Characters are mostly based on personality types. The plot of the narrative traces the passage of the protagonist into womanhood, but while rich in ethnographic data, it falls short of creating convincing, individual characters and portrays the protagonist almost entirely in relationship to kinsmen, rather than as an individual.

908.   Deming, Caren J. "Miscegenation in Popular Western History and Fiction." In *Women in Western American Literature*.

Helen Winter Stauffer and Susan J. Rosowski, eds. Troy, NY: Whitson, 1982, 90-99.

Although the focus is on white women and their encounters with men of other races, Deming provides literary examples of relationships Indian women had with white men as well as the attitudes of white men toward women of color.

909.   Dodge, Robert K. and Joseph B. McCullough, eds. *Voices from Wah' Kon-Tah: Contemporary Poetry of Native Americans*. New York: International Publishers, 1974.

This collection of contemporary poetry is a broad selection of Indian writers. It was updated and revised in 1985 under the title *New and Old Voices of Wah'Kon-Tah*. Poems by fifteen women are included.

910.   Dorris, Michael. *A Yellow Raft in Blue Water*. New York: Henry Holt and Co., 1987.

This novel by a Modoc writer spans three generation of tribal women, focusing on a young girl's introduction into contemporary tribal life and the healing of family wounds as the events of the past and the alienation of her mother are clarified.

911.   Erdrich, Louise. *Baptism of Desire: Poems*. New York: Harper, 1989.

Poetry.

912.   Erdrich, Louise. *The Beet Queen*. New York: Henry Holt and Co., 1986.

This novel begins in the 1930s in an off-reservation town in North Dakota and explores the relationships and secrets of community members who live on the periphery of both American life and tribal life.

913.   Erdrich, Louise. *Jacklight*. New York: Holt, Rinehart and Winston, 1984.

       Poetry by a Chippewa writer.

914.   Erdrich, Louise. *Love Medicine*. New York: Holt, Rinehart and Winston, 1984.

       A multi-voiced narrative, *Love Medicine* explores the response of a Chippewa community to the death and memory of one of its central members, June Kashpaw, and traces family relationships and conflicts and the reassertion of solidarity among the characters. The narratives covers a period from 1934 to 1984.

915.   Erdrich, Louise. *Tracks*. New York: Henry Holt and Co., 1988.

       Chronologically the first of the three novels set in a Chippewa community, it is narrated by Nanapush, who embodies tribal tradition, and by Pauline Puyat, who represents the rejection of tribal wisdom and ways.

916.   Erdrich, Louise. "Where I Ought to Be: A Writer's Sense of Place." *New York Times Book Review* 90 (28 July 1985): 188.

       Erdrich sees landscape in the tribal world as enlivened by a sense of family and group history that is both mythic and contemporary; people and landscape are inseparable. She examines the use of landscape by such authors as Faulkner and Cather and sees the attention to setting as characteristic of American literature but more intensely significant in American Indian literature which recognizes the interdependency of language and place.

917.   Erickson, Sheila. *NOTICE: This is An Indian Reserve*. Kent Gooderham, ed. Toronto: Griffin House Publishers, 1972.

Photographs of Canadian Indian reserve and poetry by Erickson, a member of the Carrier tribe in northeastern British Columbia.

918. Evers, Larry. "Notes on Deer Woman." *Indiana Folklore* 11, 1 (1978): 35-46.

Evers explores modern variations of Deer Woman folktales.

919. Evers, Lawrence J. "The Killing of a New Mexico State Trooper: Ways of Telling an Historical Event." In *Critical Essays in American Indian Literature*. Boston: G. K. Hall and Co., 1985, 246-62.

Evers analyzes the records of the 1952 killing of New Mexico State policeman Nash Garcia and the trial of two Acoma men accused and convicted of the killing in order to examine how the series of events is transformed into the thematic core of short stories by Simon Ortiz and Leslie Marmon Silko and a novel by N. Scott Momaday.

920. Evers, Lawrence J. *South Corner of Time: Hopi, Navajo, Papago, Yaqui Tribal Literature*. Tucson: University of Arizona Press, 1981.

A collection of oral and written literature from Navajo, Hopi, Yaqui and Papago tribes. Includes general introductory material, photo-essays, pronunciation guides, many bi-lingual texts, maps, analytical information on many texts, and suggested reading lists. Several contributors are women.

921. Fee, Margery. "Upsetting Fake Ideas; Jeannette Armstrong's *Slash* and Beatrice Culleton's *April Raintree*." *Canadian Literature* 124-125 (Spring/Summer 1990): 168-82.

Fee discusses these two works by Native women writers as political statements exposing the struggle of women subjected to institutional racism and economic marginalization.

922. Felt, Margaret, ed. *Daughters of the Land*. Bend, OR: Maverick Publications, 1988.

Included in this anthology of short stories by and about western women are several works by American Indian writers. Each is based on a real woman, but they are marred by romanticism and stereotyping.

923. Fisher, Alice Poindexter, ed. *The Third Woman: Minority Women Writers of the United States*. Boston: Houghton Mifflin, 1980.

A collection of poetry and prose by minority women writers, including selections from Native Americans Gertrude Bonnin, Mourning Dove, Wendy Rose, Joy Harjo, Paula Gunn Allen, Anita Endrezze Probst [Danielson] and Roberta Hill.

924. Fisher, Dexter. "The Transformation of Tradition: A Study of Zitkala-Sa and Mourning Dove, Two Transitional American Indian Writers." In *Critical Essays on Native American Literature*. Andrew Wiget, ed. Boston: G. K. Hall, 1985, 202-11.

Mourning Dove, an Okanogan, and Zitkala-Sa, a Dakota Sioux woman, are discussed as the first Indian writers to publish oral stories from their cultures. They are also notable early twentieth century women writers, Mourning Dove as the first Indian woman to publish a novel, and Zitkala-Sa for autobiographical sketches which appeared in *Harper's* and *Atlantic Monthly*.

925. Fisher, Dexter. "Zitkala-Sa: The Evolution of a Writer." *American Indian Quarterly* 5, 3 (August 1979): 229-38.

Fisher provides biographical data on Zitkala-Sa (Gertrude Bonnin) and describes her as "a curious blend of civilized romanticism and aggressive individualism."

926. Foss, Phillip, ed. *The Clouds Threw This Light: Contemporary Native American Poetry*. Santa Fe: Institute of American Indian Arts Press, 1983.

Collection of American Indian poetry which includes over twenty-five women out of over 75 contributors. There is no introduction or biographical information on the contributors.

927. Francisco, Nia. *Blue Horses for Navajo Women*. Greenfield Center, NY: Greenfield Review Press, 1988.

Poetry by a Navajo woman.

928. Fry, Maggie Culver. *The Umbilical Cord*. Chicago: Windfall Press, 1971.

A collection of forty-seven poems by a Cherokee woman born in 1900 in Oklahoma.

929. Fry, Maggie Culver. *The Witch Deer: Poems of the Oklahoma Indian*. New York: Exposition Press, 1954.

This Cherokee woman from Oklahoma has transformed many Cherokee tales into poems. Brief notes are included to explain names and events.

930. Fuller, Iola. *The Loon Feather*. New York: Harcourt, Brace, 1941.

In this fictionalized account, Tecumseh's daughter is torn between her Indian heritage and the life of her French stepfather.

931. Gedalof, Robin, ed. *Paper Stays Put: A Collection of Inuit Writing*. Edmonton: Hurtig, 1980.

Collection of writings by Inuit people, some of which originally was written in Inuktitut. Songs, stories, and essays by several women are included. One contributor, Mary

Panegoosho, was the founder of the Eskimo language magazine *Inuktitut*.

932.   Glancy, Diane. *Brown Wolf Leaves the Res and other Poems*. Marvin, SD: Blue Cloud Quarterly Press, 1984.

Poetry by a Cherokee woman.

933.   Glancy, Diane. *Dry Stalks of the Moon*. Tulsa, OK: Hadassah, 1981.

Poetry.

934.   Glancy, Diane. *Offering: Aliscolidodi*. Duluth, MN: Holy Cow!, 1988.

Poetry and prose.

935.   Glancy, Diane. *One Age in a Dream*. Minneapolis: Milkweed Editions, 1986.

Poetry.

936.   Glancy, Diane. *Red Deer*. Tulsa, OK: Myrtlewood Press, 1982.

Poetry.

937.   Glancy, Diane. *Traveling On*. Tulsa, OK: Myrtlewood Press, 1982.

Poetry.

938.   Gleason, William. "'Her Laugh an Ace': The Function of Humor in Louise Erdrich's *Love Medicine*." *American Indian Culture and Research Journal* 11, 3 (1987): 51-74.

Gleason argues that *Love Medicine*, rather than portraying a painful picture of Indian life, is a novel about survival, love, and humor with a unifying vision of redemption.

939. Goddard, Barbara. "The Politics of Representation: Some Canadian Women Writers." *Canadian Literature* 124-125 (Spring/Summer 1990): 183-228.

Goddard discusses the racism and sexism of publishers, distributors, and reviewers and the impact of the negative attitudes on Canadian Native women writers. Native women writers are subject to critics' views which attempt to interpret their work according to inappropriate standards. She discusses *I Am Woman* by Lee Maracle and *Slash* by Jeannette Armstrong as political responses to the status quo.

940. Grant, Agnes. "Contemporary Native Women's Voices in Literature." *Canadian Literature* 124-125 (Spring/Summer 1990): 124-32.

Grant uses Maria Campbell's *Halfbreed*, Beatrice Culleton's *In Search of April Raintree* and Lee Maracle's *I Am Woman* to demonstrate the cultural point of view from which Native women write. All three writers use their own lives and experiences to explore the reality of Indian life in Canada.

941. Green, Rayna. "The Pocahontas Perplex: The Image of Indian Women in Popular Culture." *Massachusetts Review* 16 (Autumn 1975): 698-714.

Green discusses the princess and squaw images in literature and folklore. This is a particularly useful essay for tracing the paradoxical views of Indian women that permeate popular literature.

942. Green, Rayna, ed. *That's What She Said; Contemporary Poetry and Fiction by Native American Women*. Bloomington: Indiana University Press, 1984.

Anthology which includes sixteen Indian women and an introduction by Green which combines fiction and fact to explain the creative process of the authors. A glossary provides needed definitions to clarify some of the language of the fiction and poetry.

943.   Haberly, David T. "Women and Indians: *The Last of the Mohicans* and the Captivity Tradition." *American Quarterly* 28 (1976): 431-43.

Critical analysis of the *Last of the Mohicans* as a parallel to an Indian captivity narrative focuses on the "Indianization" of Cora as a character who loses her "whiteness," becomes a suitable object of Uncas's courtship, and receives an Indian burial when she becomes too intrusive in the male-centered fiction of Cooper.

944.   Haile, Father Bernard. *Women Versus Men: A Conflict of Navajo Emergence*. Lincoln: University of Nebraska Press, 1981.

This Navajo and English text is a part of the Navajo Creation story, focusing on the underworld separation of the sexes and the resulting birth of monsters and the flood that precede the emergence of the Navajo people onto the earth and the subsequent slaying of monsters and origins of various Navajo ceremonies. In this narration First Man is represented as a victim of woman's infidelity and is said to have arranged for the birth of Changing Woman and her marriage to the sun and for the birth of the monster slayers.

945.   Hale, Janet Campbell. *Custer Lives in Humboldt County and Other Poems*. Greenfield Center, NY: Greenfield Review Press, 1978.

Poetry by a Coeur d'Alene woman.

946.   Hale, Janet Campbell. *The Jailing of Cecilia Capture*. New York: Random House, 1985.

Cecilia Eagle Capture is a law student at Berkeley who at age 30 remembers her past on an Idaho reservation while sobering up in the Berkeley jail. The novel examines the dilemma of the modern tribal woman and suggests traditions as the key to identity.

947.   Hale, Janet Campbell. *The Owl's Song*. New York: Doubleday, 1974.

Hale's novel is about fourteen-year-old Billy who struggles with the white world and finds sustenance in his home environment.

948.   Halpern, A. M. "Sex Differences in Quechan Narrative." *Journal of California and Great Basin Anthropology* 2, 1 (1980): 51-59.

Presents two (male and female) examples of Quechan storytelling to illustrate the difference in style and content between storytelling by men and women in a Quechan community near Yuma, Arizona.

949.   Halsell, Grace. *Bessie Yellowhair*. New York: Warner Books, 1974.

This novel, with an Indian woman as the main character, tells of life both on and off the reservation.

950.   Hanson, Elizabeth I. *Forever There: Race and Gender in Contemporary Native American Fiction*. New York: Peter Lang, 1989.

Hanson includes chapters on Silko, Allen, and Erdrich along with McNickle, Momaday, Welch, and Dorris. Her discussions of gender in the works of these novelists adds little to previous criticism.

951.   Harjo, Joy. *In Mad Love and War*. Middletown, CT: Wesleyan University Press, 1990.

Poetry.

952.   Harjo, Joy. *The Last Song*. Las Cruces, NM: Puerto Del Sol Press, 1975.

Poetry.

953.   Harjo, Joy. *She Had Some Horses*. New York: Thunder's Mouth Press, 1982.

Poetry.

954.   Harjo, Joy. *What Moon Drove Me to This*. Berkeley: Reed and Cannon, 1979.

Poetry.

955.   Harjo, Joy and Stephen Strom. *Secrets From the Center of the World*. Tucson: University of Arizona Press, 1989.

A prose poem by Creek writer Harjo evokes a sense of the sacred landscape depicted in Strom's photographs.

956.   Hart, Hazel. *Daughters, I Love You*. Denver: Research Center on Women, 1981.

Poetry inspired by the Black Hills Survival Gathering, 1980.

957.   Hart, Hazel. "Ge Chi Maung Won: The Life Story of an Old Chippewa Woman." In *Arrows Four: Prose and Poetry by Young American Indians*. T. D. Allen, ed. New York: Pocket Books, 1974, 165-71.

In this short story of life and death, the grandmother tells the story of her grandmother and her mother, Gesis. She tells of being raised by her grandparents. The importance of the oral tradition and of relatives is stressed.

958.   Heath, Caroline, ed. *The Land Called Morning; Three Plays*. Saskatoon: Fifth House, 1986.

In this collection of three plays, *Teach Me the Ways of the Sacred Circle* by Valerie Dudoward explores Indian cultural values in an urban setting which is constantly challenging traditional ways. Vye Bouvier writes a brief introduction about theater in Canada. The other two plays are *Gabrielle* and *The Land Called Morning*.

959. Henry, Jeanette, ed. *The American Indian Reader: Literature*. San Francisco: Indian Historian, 1973.

This early study was prepared as a guide to American Indian literature. Translations of early songs, contemporary poetry and stories, and a critical article by Ronald Sanders are included. This is a limited study of the literature.

960. Herzog, Kristin. "Thinking Woman and Feeling Man: Gender in Silko's *Ceremony*." *MELUS* 12, 1 (1985): 25-36.

Silko's writing style is seen as feminine in that it is fragmented, emotive, circular and visionary. Her characterization of Tayo in *Ceremony* challenges the reader's idea of gender because he is portrayed in terms of female characteristics--instinct and sensuous perception--and her use of a mythic female character posits the importance of the female principle in achieving harmony.

961. Herzog, Kristin. *Women, Ethnics and Exotics: Images of Power in Mid-Nineteenth Century Fiction*. Knoxville: University of Tennessee Press, 1983.

In the final chapter of this book, "The Epic of Dekanawida: Aboriginal Strength in Native American Narrative," Herzog analyzes the central role of Iroquoian women to the governing systems, religion, and curing rituals which is imaged in the narrative as power, peace, and thanksgiving. The effect of colonization on women's roles is also discussed.

962. Hilbert, Vi, trans. and ed. *Haboo; Native American Stories from Puget Sound*. Seattle: University of Washington Press, 1985.

Hilbert is a Skagit Indian of the Northern Lushootseed of western Washington who has devoted her career to analyzing and archiving her language and stories. Many of the stories are related by women, and Hilbert provides biographical information; linguist Thomas Hess wrote the introduction.

963.   Hobson, Gary. *The Remembered Earth*. Albuquerque:
        University of New Mexico Press, 1980.

        An anthology of contemporary Indian fiction and poetry
        organized by region and including an introduction by the
        editor. This is a comprehensive collection of contemporary
        literature and includes short fiction, poetry, and literary
        criticism by major female literary figures as well as lesser
        known female writers.

964.   Hobson, Gerald. "Round Dance--Native American Writing at
        the University of New Mexico." *New America* 2, 3
        (Summer/Fall 1976): 4-16.

        Hobson begins with a review of literature from the 1930s
        about Indians and examines literature of the 1960s and 1970s
        by Indian authors, then moves on to discuss Leslie Silko's role
        as a faculty member in creative writing in encouraging work by
        young Indian men and women and the resulting collection
        which includes works by ten Indian women from the Navajo,
        Acoma, Isleta, and Kutchin tribes.

965.   Hodgson, Heather. *Seventh Generation: Contemporary Native
        Writing*. Penticton, BC: Theytus, 1989.

        In this collection, six of the contributors are women--Kateri
        Damm, Jeannette Armstrong, Lenore Keeshig-Tobias, Mary
        Sky Blue Morin, Annharte, and Tracey Bonneau. The
        collection is primarily poetry.

966.   Hogan, Linda. *Calling Myself Home*. Greenfield Center, NY:
        Greenfield Review Press, 1978.

        Poetry by a Chickasaw woman.

967.   Hogan, Linda. *Daughters, I Love You*. Denver: Loretto Heights
        College, 1981.

        Poetry.

968. Hogan, Linda. *Eclipse*. Los Angeles: University of California, Los Angeles, American Indian Studies Center, 1983.

   Poetry with a foreword by Kenneth Lincoln.

969. Hogan, Linda. *Mean Spirit*. New York: Athenaeum, 1990.

   Novel about Indians in Oklahoma in the 1920s based on historical facts of the discovery of oil on Indian land and the subsequent fraud, intimidation, and murder which deprived Indians of their rights and money.

970. Hogan, Linda. *Savings*. Minneapolis: Coffee House Press, 1988.

   Poetry by a Chickasaw writer.

971. Hogan, Linda. *Seeing Through the Sun*. Amherst: University of Massachusetts Press, 1985.

   Poetry.

972. Hogan, Linda. "The Transformation of Tribalism." *Book Forum* 5, 3 (1981): 403-09.

   Hogan stresses the importance of the combination of innovation and tradition in contemporary Indian communities, noting that survival and growth will depend on creating new traditions that combine Anglo and Native ways.

973. Hogan, Linda, ed. *Frontiers: Special Issue on Native American Women* 6, 3 (1981).

   Includes works by Anna Lee Walters, Paula Gunn Allen, Sandra LeBeau, Rayna Green, Joy Harjo, Wendy Rose, and Louise Erdrich.

974. Hogan, Linda and Charles Colbert Henderson. *That Horse*. Acoma, NM: Acoma Press, 1985.

   Short stories.

975. Hoilman, Dennis R. "A World Made of Stories: Silko's *Ceremony*." *South Dakota Review*, 17 (1979-80): 54-66.

Sees the novel as an attempt to inform the non-Indian about Keresan culture. Explains that *Ceremony* is difficult for non-Indians because of its structure and its use of Laguna mythology.

976. Hubbell, Jay. "The Smith-Pocahontas Story in Literature." *The Virginia Magazine of History and Biography* 65, 3 (July 1957): 275-300.

Hubbell describes Pocahontas as "guardian angel of the infant colony and the ancestress of distinguished families" as he traces the literary and often clearly fictionalized accounts of the lives of Captain John Smith and Pocahontas.

977. Hungry Wolf, Beverly. "The Ways of My Grandmothers." *Women of Power* 14 (Summer 1989): 60-61.

Excerpts from Hungry Wolf's book *The Ways of My Grandmothers* about the traditional life of Blackfoot women.

978. Irwin, Hadley. *We Are Mesquakie; We Are One*. Old Westbury, NY: Feminist Press, 1980.

This fictional account of a young Mesquakie woman tells of the return of the Mesquakie people from the reservation in Kansas to their home in Iowa. Although written for a high school audience, the book is a compelling and accurate record of Mesquakie history.

979. Isom, Joan Shaddox. *Fox Grapes: Cherokee Verse*. Palmer Lake, CO: The Felter Press, 1978.

Poetry with illustrations by the Cherokee author.

980. Isom, Joan Shaddox. *The Moon in Five Disguises*. Tahlequah, OK: Foxmoor Press, 1981.

Poetry.

981.   Jackson, Helen Hunt. *Ramona*. New York: Avon, 1970.

Originally published in 1884 by an important activist for Indian rights, this romantic novel of an Indian girl in California attained great popularity and became the basis of several films in the early twentieth century. It is important in shaping stereotypes of Indian women and for the sympathy for Indians it generated.

982.   Jahner, Elaine. "An Act of Attention: Event Structure in *Ceremony*." *American Indian Quarterly* 5, 1 (February 1979): 37-46. Rpt. in *Critical Essays in American Indian Literature*. Andrew Wiget, ed. Boston: G. K. Hall and Co., 1985, 238-245.

Jahner sees events in Leslie Marmon Silko's novel *Ceremony* as boundary experiences that mark stages of life in the protagonist, which when they converge, allow emergence to "new levels of comprehension" for both the protagonist and the reader.

983.   Jahner, Elaine, ed. *The American Indians Today: Thought, Literature and Art*. Special Issue of *Book Forum* 5, 3 (1981): 312-432.

Includes essays on stereotyping in film, American Indian women's literature, an interview with Leslie Silko, research guides on contemporary creative work, and small presses featuring literature by Native American writers.

984.   Jahner, Elaine. "A Laddered Rain-Bearing Rug: The Poetry of Paula Gunn Allen." In *Women and Western American Literature*. Helen Winter Stauffer and Susan J. Rosowski, eds. Troy, NY: Whitson Press, 1982, 311-26.

Allen has been publishing poetry since 1963 and is one of the most active critics of American Indian literature. In this discussion, Jahner provides biographical background and analysis of specific poems in *Coyote's Daylight Trip*.

985.   Jaskoski, Helen. "'My Heart Will Go Out': Healing Songs of Native American Women." *International Journal of Women's Studies* 4, 2 (March-April 1981): 118-34.

Demonstrates the use of poetry and song as a healing agent used by American Indian women in Papago, Crow, Tlingit, Comanche, Mandan, and Apache ceremonies and rites. Discusses the role of the woman healer in traditional societies.

986.   Joe, Rita. *Song of Eskasoni; More Poems of Rita Joe*. Charlottetown, Prince Edward Island: Ragweed Press, 1988.

Poetry by a Micmac writer.

987.   Johnson, E. Pauline [Tekahionwake]. *Canadian Born*. Toronto: George N. Morang and Co., 1903.

Poetry by a Mohawk woman.

988.   Johnson, E. Pauline [Tekahionwake]. *Flint and Feather*. Toronto: Musson Book Co., 1912.

A collection of poetry by a Mohawk woman born in 1862.

989.   Johnson, E. Pauline [Tekahionwake]. *The Legends of Vancouver*. Toronto: McClelland and Stewart, 1922.

Johnson retells legends she heard from Chief Joe Capilano of Vancouver. In spite of little education, Johnson published collections of poetry and stories and traveled widely to recite her poetry. This volume includes fifteen stories.

990.   Johnson, E. Pauline [Tekahionwake]. *The Moccasin Maker*. Toronto: William Briggs, 1913.

Johnson lived on the Canadian Iroquois Reserve for many years and was a poet and writer. She was part white but identified with her mother's life as she told it. Her mother, Lydia Bestman, had come from England and lived among the Indians in Canada, marrying the Mohawk George Mansion. The book also relates stories of Canadian Indian legends.

991. Johnson, E. Pauline [Tekahionwake]. *The Shagganappi.* Toronto: William Briggs, 1913.

This is a collection of short stories by the woman who preferred to be called Tekahionwake.

992. Johnson, E. Pauline [Tekahionwake]. *The White Wampum.* London: John Lane, 1895.

Poetry.

993. Jones, Louis Thomas. "Eloquent Indian Women." In *Aboriginal American Oratory.* Los Angeles: Southwest Museum, 1965, 113-20.

Jones gives examples from the writings of the Cupena orator Celsa Apapas and the Sioux women Warcaziwin and Gertrude Bonnin (Zitkala-Sa).

994. Josie, Edith. *Here Are the News.* Toronto: Charles Irwin, 1966.

Edith Josie is the Loucheaux correspondent for the *Whitehorse Star* living in Old Crow, a Yukon village eighty miles north of the Arctic Circle. Her column "News from Old Crow" appears regularly in several newspapers, and the book reproduces news from 1962 to 1966.

995. Kaczkurkin, Mini Walenquela. *Yoeme: Lore of the Arizona Yaqui People.* Tucson: Sun Tracks, 1977.

Stories heard from the author's grandmother, Mrs. Carmen Garcia, are printed to preserve the oral tradition for the children. They are in English because so many of the children have not learned the Yaqui language.

996.   Katz, Jane B. *I Am the Fire of Time: The Voices of Native American Women*. New York: E. P. Dutton, 1977.

This anthology of literature by American Indian women from various tribes includes ninety examples of autobiography, poetry, oral history, fiction, prayer, and essay. While there are no full-length personal narratives, the book generally provides a comprehensive picture of the roles of Indian women from traditional tribal times to contemporary. Variety of forms, experiences, and tribal and regional representation is good.

997.   Keiser, Albert. *The Indian in American Literature*. NY: Oxford University Press, 1953.

The Pocahontas legend is analyzed and challenged but seen as a central theme in American literature. Helen Hunt Jackson's novel *Ramona* is also discussed, primarily as a vehicle for relief of the plight of Mission Indians in California.

998.   Kenny, Maurice, ed. *Wounds Beneath the Flesh: 15 Native American Poets*. Marvin, SD: Blue Cloud Quarterly Press, 1983. Rpt. Fredonia, NY: White Pine Press, 1987.

Poets Paula Gunn Allen, Diane Burns, Gladys Cardiff, Elizabeth Cook-Lynn, Joy Harjo, Linda Hogan, Wendy Rose, Leslie Marmon Silko, and Roberta Hill Whiteman are included. The volume includes a preface by Karl Kroeber and brief biographical notes on the contributors.

999.   Kilpatrick, Jack F. and Anna G. Kilpatrick, eds. *Friends of Thunder: Folktales of the Oklahoma Cherokees*. Dallas: Southern Methodist University Press, 1964.

This collection of Cherokee tales recorded by two Cherokee scholars includes an exchange about witchcraft between a brother and sister as well as a record of a husband and wife discussing Cherokee economics. Four women were interviewed for the collection.

1000. King, Captain Charles. *An Apache Princess: A Tale of the Indian Frontier*. New York: Hobart Company, 1903.

A novel which explores the relationship of a genteel army lieutenant and a Pocahontas-like Indian "princess" who is devoted to him and saves his life but is left to marry a Chiricahua "brave" when the officer marries his eastern society bride.

1001. Knudson, Rozanne. *Fox Running*. New York: Harper & Row, 1975.

Story of two female runners, one of whom is a Mescalero Indian, who train for the Olympics. For junior high and high school level.

1002. Kopp, Karl and Jane Kopp, eds. *Southwest: A Contemporary Anthology*. Albuquerque: Red Earth, 1977.

This collection of poetry and fiction includes some Indian women: Paula Gunn Allen, Besmilr Brigham. Nia Francisco, Joy Harjo and Leslie Marmon Silko.

1003. Kroeber, Karl, ed. "ASAIL Bibliography No. 2; Wendy Rose." *Studies in American Indian Literatures* 6, 2 (Spring 1982): 19-23.

Bibliography without annotations of Rose's books of poetry and contributions to anthologies.

1004. Kroeber, Karl, ed. "Linda Hogan." *Studies in American Indian Literatures* 8, 1 (Spring 1984): 1-18.

The majority of the issue is devoted to criticism and reviews of Linda Hogan's poetry. Contributors include Geoffrey Gardner, Kathleen Cain, Susan Fraiman, and Mabel Anderson.

1005. Kroeber, Karl, ed. "Louise Erdrich: *Love Medicine*." *Studies in American Indian Literatures* 9, 1 (Winter 1985): 1-41.

This issue is devoted to the study of Louise Erdrich, particularly her novel *Love Medicine*. Contributors include Dee Brown, Ursula K. LeGuin, Scott Sanders, Kathleen M. Sands, Linda Ainsworth, and Elaine Jahner. A bibliography of Erdrich's work is included.

1006. Kroeber, Karl, ed. "Paula Gunn Allen." *Studies in American Indian Literatures* 7, 3 (Fall 1983): 55-80.

This special issue on Paula Gunn Allen's poetry and fiction includes a bibliography and articles by John Lowe, A. LaVonne Brown Ruoff, Mary TallMountain, and Elaine Jahner.

1007. Krupat, Arnold. "The Dialogue of Silko's *Storyteller*." In *Narrative Chance: Postmodern Discourse on Native American Indian Literatures*. Gerald Vizenor, ed. Albuquerque: University of New Mexico Press, 1989, 55-68.

Using elements of Bakhtin's theory on language as polyvocal, Krupat analyzes Silko's *Storyteller*, a collection of poems, stories, and photos, as a uniquely Native form of autobiographical dialogism grounded in "Pueblo ways as a reference point."

1008. Larson, Charles R. *American Indian Fiction*. Albuquerque: University of New Mexico Press, 1978.

After an introductory discussion of the development of American Indian fiction and the problems of identifying authentic Indian authors, Larson analyzes representations of Pocahontas in American fiction, early fiction by Indian writers, and novels since the 1930s, including Mourning Dove's *Cogewea, The Half Blood* and Leslie Marmon Silko's *Ceremony*.

1009. Lerner, Andrea, ed. *Dancing on the Rim of the World: An Anthology of Contemporary Northwest Native American Writing*. Tucson: University of Arizona Press, 1990.

Anthology of thirty-four writers from the Pacific Northwest with biographical and bibliographical information on each. Women included are Gloria Bird, Gladys Cardiff, Chrystos, Jo Whitehorse Cochran. Debra Earling. Anita Endrezze, Maxine Franklin, Janet Campbell Hale, June McGlashan, Dian Million, Nancy Neal, nila northSun, Sandra Oswan, Agnes Pratt, Vickie Sears, Mary TallMountain, Gail Tremblay, Ramona Wilson, and Elizabeth Woody.

1010. Levitas, Gloria, Frank Robert Vivelo, and Jacqueline J. Vivelo, eds. *American Indian Prose and Poetry: We Wait in the Darkness*. New York: Putnam's, 1974.

Basically a collection of traditional stories and songs, the last section includes contemporary poetry by Dolly Bird, Julie Wilson, Mary McDaniels, Susan Edwards, and Bertha Francisco. Many of the poems were previously published in *Akwesasne Notes*.

1011. Lincoln, Kenneth. *Native American Renaissance*. Berkeley: University of California Press, 1983.

Detailed critical study of contemporary authors such as Leslie Silko, Louise Erdrich, James Welch, and N. Scott Momaday. Lincoln introduces the term Renaissance for the surge of writing by American Indians since the late 1960s.

1012. Lourie, Dick, ed. *Come to Power: Eleven Contemporary American Indian Poets*. Trumansburg, NY: The Crossing Press, 1974.

In this early collection of eleven contemporary Indian poets, Suzan Shown, Minerva Allen, and Leslie Silko are included.

1013. Lowenfels, Walter, ed. *From the Belly of the Shark: A New Anthology of Native Americans*. New York: Vintage Books, 1973.

This is one of the earliest multi-cultural anthologies of poetry. A lengthy section features American Indian poets, many of whom are women.

1014.   Luckert, Karl W. ed. *Women Versus Men: A Conflict of Navajo Emergence/The Curly to Aheedliinii Version*. Recorded by Bernard Haile; Navajo orthography by Irvy M. Goosen. Lincoln: University of Nebraska Press, 1981.

Recorded in 1932 when Father Bernard was a research associate in anthropology at the University of Chicago. The text is part of the Navajo origin which describes the separation of the sexes and the consequences of wrong behavior-- monsters and the need for monster slayer. Both English and Navajo text.

1015.   MacShane, Frank. "American Indians, Peruvian Jews." *New York Times Book Review* 43, 604 (12 June 1977): 15.

Leslie Marmon Silko's *Ceremony* is viewed as a curing process; Tayo, the protagonist, is seen in search of psychic wholeness. The author praises Silko's unsentimental description of Indian life and says her perspective as a woman is a key factor in her ability to write movingly of a male character.

1016.   Markoosie. "Strange Happenings: Two Sisters/The Woman Who Could See the Future." *North/Nord* 18, 1 (1971): 23-27.

The first Inuit story describes women of power who transform themselves into wolves. The second, a historical account, narrates the experiences of a woman who has the power to foretell future events and see events happening in distant locales.

1017.   Marriott, Alice. *The Ten Grandmothers*. Norman: University of Oklahoma Press, 1945.

Legends of ten medicine bundles of the Kiowa are included. The bundles were called the Ten Grandmothers.

Spear Woman and Eagle Plume are the two principal women informants for Marriott about Kiowa history and experience.

1018. McClellan, Catharine. *The Girl Who Married the Bear*. Ottawa: National Museum Publications in Ethnology, 2, 1970.

This analysis of one of the most popular stories of the southern Yukon Indians includes eleven versions of the tale, four of them narrated by women. Brief description of each narrator is given. The tale is seen as the basis for ceremonies, and each version is analyzed in terms of the circumstances under which it was narrated and the narrator's style.

1019. McCullough, Ken. "*Star Quilt* as Mandala: An Assessment of the Poetry of Roberta Hill Whiteman." *North Dakota Quarterly* 53, 2 (Spring 1985): 194-203.

Poet Richard Hugo is seen as an important influence on Whiteman's poetry, The author discusses Whiteman's work in the context of literature by nineteenth and twentieth century Indian women, particularly contemporary poets.

1020. McDaniel, Wilma. *I Killed a Bee for You*. Marvin, SD: Blue Cloud Quarterly Press, 1987.

Poems by a Creek woman.

1021. McDaniel, Wilma Elizabeth. *Toll Bridge*. New York: Contact II, 1980.

Poetry.

1022. McDaniel, Wilma Elizabeth. *Who Is San Andreas: Poems to Survive Earthquakes*. Marvin, SD: Blue Cloud Quarterly Press, 1984.

Poetry.

1023. McDowell, Leonora Hayden. *Moccasin Meanderings*. New York: Gusto Press, 1979.

Poetry by a Cree woman.

1024. McFarland, Ronald E. "Leslie Silko's Story of Stories." *A: A Journal of Contemporary Literature*. 4, 2 (Fall 1979): 18-23.

Discusses traditional Pueblo storytelling and analyzes the narrative structure of Leslie Marmon Silko's *Ceremony*. McFarland finds three major narrative strands in the novel: the Pueblo tale of curing and pacification, the story of the Indian in post-World War II United States, and Tayo's story.

1025. McFarland, Ronald E. "Women's Roles in Contemporary Native American Writing and in Welch's *The Death of Jim Loney*." In *James Welch*. Ronald E. McFarland, ed. Lewiston, ID: Confluence Press, 1986.

McFarland discusses a pattern of absent or dislocated women in Welch's novel and other works of Indian fiction, suggesting that women have been as debased as Indian men by modern experience.

1026. McKenzie, James. "Lipsha's Good Road Home: The Revival of Chippewa Culture in *Love Medicine*." *American Indian Culture and Research Journal* 10, 3 (1986): 53-64.

As a central character, Lipsha is analyzed as a sign of renewal in the fragmented Chippewa culture represented in *Love Medicine*. The novel is also seen as challenging stereotypes of Indians through its multiplicity of characters and narrative voices.

1027. McLaughlin, Marie L. *Myths and Legends of the Sioux*. Bismarck: Bismarck Tribune Co., 1916.

The author is one-quarter Sioux. She was born in 1842 in Wabasha, Minnesota, married an Indian agent, and lived on reservations for forty years. In this collection she repeats stories told to her by older Indians.

1028. Meese, Elizabeth A. *(Ex)Tensions: Re-Figuring Feminist Criticism*. Champaign: University of Illinois Press, 1990.

Included in Meese's study of the racial, social, and cultural differences within feminist literary criticism is a reading of Leslie Silko's work. The focus of her literary interpretation is exploring constructive ways in which women can bring about social change and transform institutional structures.

1029. Miller, Jay. "Mourning Dove: The Author as Cultural Mediator." In *Being and Becoming an Indian: Biographical Studies of North American Frontiers*. James A. Clifton, ed. Chicago: Dorsey Press, 1989, 160-82.

Mourning Dove, Christine Quintasket, was a Salish from the Pacific Northwest, who published a novel, *Cogewea* in 1927 and later a collection of legends, *Coyote Stories*. During her life she was active in reservation politics, but after her death there was little note made of her contributions.

1030. Milton, John R., ed. *Four Indian Poets*. Vermillion, SD: Dakota Press, 1974.

Milton includes a biographical sketch of Paula Gunn Allen and ten of her poems; Allen is Laguna.

1031. Mitchell, Carol. "*Ceremony* as Ritual." *American Indian Quarterly* 5, 1 (1979): 27-35.

Leslie Silko's novel *Ceremony* is structured on three planes--individual, socio-cultural, mythic--all of which must be understood in order to comprehend the protagonist's movement from disharmony to personal balance within his Pueblo culture.

1032. Mourning Dove [Humishuma]. *Cogewea, the Half-Blood*. Boston: Four Seas, 1927; Rpt., Lincoln: University of Nebraska Press, 1981.

Mourning Dove was among the first of Indian women to write fiction. This novel is based on her life as an Okanogan and the Indian experience on the cattle ranges. Cogewea, a mixed-blood girl, ultimately chooses her Indian identity over her white heritage.

1033. Mourning Dove [Humishuma]. *Coyote Stories*. Heister Dean Guie, ed. Caldwell, ID: Caxton Printers, 1933. Rpt. Lincoln: University of Nebraska Press, 1990.

Foreword by Chief Standing Bear and notes by Mourning Dove's collaborator L. V. McWhorter. In the Preface, Mourning Dove tells of her family and the storytelling tradition among her people. The book includes twenty-seven stories. The Nebraska edition includes an introduction by Jay Miller.

1034. Mourning Dove [Humishuma]. *Tales of the Okanogans*. Donald M. Hines, ed. Fairfield, WA: Ye Galleon Press, 1976.

Mourning Dove retells thirty-eight traditional tales of the Okanogan Indians who live on the border area of Washington State and Canada. Mourning Dove had collected the tales from her parents, friends, and relatives and translated them into English. The tales come from the Kettle Falls area near the confluence of the Colville, Columbia, and Kettle Rivers in Eastern Washington. The preface is personal narrative.

1035. Mullett, G. M. *Spider Woman Stories*. Tucson: University of Arizona Press, 1979.

Hopi stories collected by Mullett who worked with Walter Fewkes of the Smithsonian in the late 1880s and early 1890s. Mullett reworked many of the stories for children. This collection is introduced by anthropologist Fred Eggan.

1036. Niatum, Duane, ed. *Carriers of the Dream Wheel*. New York: Harper & Row, 1975.

Collection of poetry which includes Liz Sohappy Bahe, Gladys Cardiff, Roberta Hill, Dana Naone, Anita Endrezze Probst [Danielson], Wendy Rose, and Leslie Silko.

1037.   Niatum, Duane, ed. *Harper's Anthology of 20th Century Native American Poetry*. San Francisco: Harper & Row, 1988.

A lengthy introduction by Brian Swann precedes a comprehensive collection of contemporary poets. Fifteen women are included, among them Paula Gunn Allen, Joy Harjo, and Louise Erdrich. Brief biographies of all the contributors complete the volume.

1038.   northSun, nila. *Diet Pepsi and Nacho Cheese*. Fallon, NE: Duck Down Press, 1977.

Poetry by a Shoshone/Chippewa woman.

1039.   northSun, nila and Jim Sagel. *Small Bones, Little Eyes*. Fallon, NE: Duck Down Press, 1981.

A two-part collection of poetry, northSun's is "Small Bones."

1040.   Norwood, Vera. "Thank you for My Bones: Connections Between Contemporary Women Artists and the Traditional Art of Their Foremothers." *New Mexico Historical Review* 58 (January 1983): 57-78.

Leslie Silko's novel *Ceremony* is discussed in terms of the nature of women's power in daily life as it is connected to myth making and the woman power that provides resolution to the novel. Poetry by Paula Gunn Allen is used to demonstrate the connection of women to tradition and ritual. Both writers retrieve the past to give substance and force to contemporary women's lives.

1041.   Olsen, Sarah Keesic. "The Story of the Rabbitskin Blanket." *Canadian Woman Studies* 10, 2 & 3 (Summer/Fall 1989): 85-86.

A story told in Anishinaabe by Sarah Keesic Olsen is presented in the Native language and brief comments point out how much is lost when oral stories are written down.

1042. Oman, Lela Kiana. *Eskimo Legends*. Anchorage: Alaska Methodist University Press, 1975.

This is a collection of stories retold in English by an Eskimo woman who was born in 1915. One selection is the narrative of Susie Lockhart, an Eskimo woman from Katzebue, Alaska, who was born in 1876. The introduction and Susie's story reveal a great deal about the lives of Eskimo women.

1043. Ortiz, Simon H., ed. *Earth Power Coming: Short Fiction in Native American Literature*. Tsaile: Navajo Community College Press, 1983.

This anthology of short stories includes work by twelve women writers including Louise Erdrich, Leslie Silko, Anna Lee Walters, Paula Gunn Allen, Linda Hogan, and Elizabeth Cook-Lynn; represents tribal experience from all regions of the country.

1044. Oswalt, Wendall H. "Traditional Story Knife Tales of the Yuk Girls." *Proceedings of the American Philosophical Society* 108 (1964): 310-36.

Oswalt analyzes forty-one stories, most of which feature the grandmother or granddaughter as the central character.

1045. Pacosz, Christina V. and Susan Oliver, eds. *Digging for Roots: Dalmo'ma 5; Works by Women of the North Olympic Peninsula*. Port Townsend, WA: Empty Bowl, 1985.

Contributions from American Indian women include fiction from Frances McEvers (Cherokee), poetry from Fostine Bright Talltree, and autobiography from Helma Swan Ward (Makah) as recorded by Linda J. Goodman.

1046.   Paul, Frances Lackey. *Kahtahah*. Anchorage, AK: Alaska Northwest Publishing, 1976.

Stories that recreate the life of a nineteenth century Tlingit Indian girl.

1047.   Pearlman, Mickey, ed. *American Women Writing Fiction: Memory, Identity, Family, Space*. Lexington: University Press of Kentucky, 1989.

Focusing on women writers' awareness of changes in the lives of contemporary women, this collection of essays by ten critics includes an analysis of Louise Erdrich's fiction. Includes bibliography of Erdrich's work.

1048.   Petrone, Penny, ed. *Northern Voices: Inuit Writing in English*. Toronto: University of Toronto Press, 1988.

Collection of legends, folk histories, personal statements and autobiographical accounts as well as poetry and fiction by Inuit people of the Arctic. Many women are included.

1049.   Peyer, Bernd, ed. *The Elders Wrote: An Anthology of Early Prose by North American Indians, 1768-1931*. Berlin: Deitrich Reimer Verlag, 1982.

This collection of very early writing by American Indians includes Sarah Winnemucca ("The Pah-Utes") and Gertrude Bonnin ("Why I Am a Pagan"). Although the majority of the selections are by Indian men, many of the authors provide the only early statements about the social and cultural conditions of Indians in the eighteenth and nineteenth centuries.

1050.   Ramsey, Jarold. "The Teacher of Modern American Indian Writing as Ethnographer and Critic." *College English* 41, 2 (October 1979): 163-69.

Using Leslie Silko's novel *Ceremony* and other works by contemporary Indian authors, Ramsey argues the need for teachers of American Indian literature to avoid presenting

Indian literary works as simply ethnographic fiction or Indian authors merely as spokespersons for their people. He recommends giving their work the aesthetic presentation given to mainstream authors.

1051.   Rice, Julian. "Why the Lakota Still Have Their Own: Ella Deloria's *Dakota Texts*." *Western American Literature* 19, 3 (November 1984): 205-17.

Though Ella Deloria's collection of Dakota texts must be interpreted in the light of 1930s reservation outlooks and context, the stories still provide a synchronic view of the world that offers restoring wisdom to initiate growth and fulfillment within the tribe.

1052.   Ronnow, Gretchen. "Tayo, Death and Desire: A Lacanian Reading of *Ceremony*." In *Narrative Chance: Postmodern Discourse on Native American Literatures*. Gerald Vizenor, ed. Albuquerque: University of New Mexico Press, 1989, 69-90.

A Lacanian analysis of Silko's novel argues that the protagonist Tayo is a continually emerging character whose existence is an interconnected series of stories that reveal how his desire for death results in "a desire to go on living in order to perpetuate the possibilities of presence."

1053.   Rose, Wendy. *Academic Squaw: Reports to the World from the Ivory Tower*. Marvin, SD: Blue Cloud Quarterly, 1977.

Poetry by a Hopi woman.

1054.   Rose, Wendy. "American Indian Poets--and Publishing." *Book Forum* 5, 3 (1981): 400-02.

Critical of publishers and editors who never go beyond the "Indian" label in dealing with American Indian writers, which leads to miscategorizing most Indian literature as anthropology.

1055. Rose, Wendy. *Builder Kachina: A Home-Going Cycle*. Marvin, SD: Blue Cloud Press, 1979.

Poetry.

1056. Rose, Wendy. *The Halfbreed Chronicles and Other Poems*. Los Angeles: West End Press, 1985.

Poetry.

1057. Rose, Wendy. *Hopi Roadrunner Dancing*. Greenfield Center, NY: Greenfield Review Press, 1973.

Poetry.

1058. Rose, Wendy. "Just What's All This Fuss About White Shamanism Anyway?" In *Coyote Was Here: Essays on Contemporary Native American Literary and Political Mobilization*. Bo Scholer, ed. Aarhus, Denmark: University of Aarhus, 1984, 13-24.

Rose sees the problem of white shamanism as one of "integrity and intent, not topic, style or experimentation," and notes that non-Native poets cannot produce Indian perspective, nor can they assume the role of cultural interpreters.

1059. Rose, Wendy. *Long Division: A Tribal History*. New York: Strawberry Press, 1976.

Poetry.

1060. Rose, Wendy. *Lost Copper*. Morongo Indian Reservation, CA: Malki Museum Press, 1980.

Poetry.

1061. Rose, Wendy. *Poetry of the American Indian: Wendy Rose*. Sacramento: American Visual Communication Bank, 1978.

Poetry.

1062.   Rose, Wendy. *What Happened When the Hopi Hit New York*. New York: Contact II Publications, 1982.

Poetry.

1063.   Rosen, Kenneth, ed. *The Man to Send Rain Clouds: Contemporary Stories by American Indians*. New York: Viking, 1974.

The first and very influential collection of short fiction by American Indian authors. Includes several stories by Leslie Silko and one by Anna Lee Walters.

1064.   Rosen, Kenneth. *Voices of the Rainbow: Contemporary Poetry by American Indians*. New York: Viking, 1978.

Collection of poetry which includes Roberta Hill, Leslie Marmon Silko, Janet Campbell Hale, Anna Walters, Anita Endrezze-Probst, Ramona Wilson, and Patty L. Harjo.

1065.   Ruoff, A. LaVonne Brown. "Alienation and the Female Principle in *Winter in the Blood*." *American Indian Quarterly* 4, 2 (May 1978): 107-22.

Ruoff discusses women in Welch's book. The grandmother, the Cree girlfriend, and the narrator's mother are important in his "healing."

1066.   Ruoff, A. LaVonne Brown. "American Indian Authors, 1774-1899." In *Critical Essays on Native American Literature*. Andrew Wiget, ed. Boston: G. K. Hall and Co., 1985, 191-201.

Using the "narrative technique of mixing personal experience and tribal ethnology," Sarah Winnemucca makes Indian-white relations the central focus of her autobiographical narrative which dramatically depicts important episodes in Paiute culture and in her powerful role in her tribe. Her narrative is seen as a transition from conversion narratives to the use of personal narrative to gain recognition and redress for tribal people.

1067. Ruoff, A. LaVonne Brown. *American Indian Literature: An Introduction, Bibliographic Review, and Selected Bibliography*. New York: Modern Language Association, 1990.

An important source of information on traditional and contemporary American Indian literature with extensive bibliographies on general references as well as specific authors.

1068. Ruoff, A. LaVonne Brown. "American Indian Literatures: Introduction and Bibliography." *American Studies International* 14 (October 1986): 2-52.

The essay, intended to serve as a guide to oral and written literatures and scholarship on the Indian literary tradition, addresses major genres of Indian literature and is followed by an extensive bibliography organized by genre and including sections on anthologies and criticism. Many women writers are cited and scholarship on women's writing is included.

1069. Ruoff, A. LaVonne Brown. "Nineteenth-Century American Indian Autobiographers: William Apes, George Copway and Sarah Winnemucca." In *Redefining American Literary History*. A. LaVonne Brown Ruoff and Jerry W. Ward, Jr., eds. New York: Modern Language Association, 1990.

In this essay which traces the evolution of nineteenth century autobiography written by Indian authors, Ruoff discusses Sarah Winnemucca's *Life Among the Paiutes* as the most personalized and dramatized narrative and the least concerned with the theme of spiritual journey usually dominant in this period. She notes that Winnemucca is also more critical of white hypocrisy than are her contemporaries.

1070.   Ruoff, A. LaVonne Brown. "Ritual and Renewal: Keres Traditions in the Short Fiction of Leslie Silko." *MELUS* 5 (1978): 2-17.

Ruoff discusses the relationship between oral tradition and Silko's fiction.

1071.   Ruoff, A. LaVonne Brown. "The Survival of Tradition: American Indian Oral and Written Narratives." *Ethnicity and Literature*. Special issue of *Massachusetts Review* 28, 2 (Summer 1986): 274-92.

In this general survey of traditional and contemporary narratives, Ruoff analyzes Leslie Silko's novel *Ceremony* in terms of its thematic use of traditional emergence, migration and culture figures as well as the healing power of stories.

1072.   Ruoff, A. LaVonne Brown. [essay on *No Turning Back*] *Studies in American Indian Literatures*, n.s., 1, 2 supplement, (Fall 1977): 22-24.

In this review essay of the autobiography of Polingaysi Qoyawayma (Elizabeth Q. White), Ruoff summarizes the life story and provides a critical assessment of the narrative.

1073.   Ruppert, James. "Patterns of Life." *Wicazo Sa Review* 2, 1 (Spring 1986): 47-49.

Lengthy analysis of Louise Erdrich's *Love Medicine* (1984); Ruppert praises the novel and Erdrich's creation of characters.

1074.   Ruppert, James. "Paula Gunn Allen and Joy Harjo: Closing the Distance between Personal and Mythic Space." *American Indian Quarterly* 7, 1 (1983): 27-40.

Compares Allen's and Harjo's poetry as it reveals mythic space and personal space. Quotes extensively from their poetry.

1075.   Salerno, Nan F. and Rosamond M. Vanderburgh. *Shaman's Daughter*. Englewood Cliffs, NJ: Prentice-Hall, 1980.

Written by a woman who claims Indian ancestry and an anthropologist, this novel traces the life of an Ojibwa woman who became a healer during the transition from traditional to reservation life.

1076. Sanchez, Carol Lee. *Conversations from the Nightmare*. Berkeley: Casa Editorial Publications, 1975.

Poetry by a Laguna-Sioux woman.

1077. Sanchez, Carol Lee. *Coyote's Journal*. Berkeley: Wingbow Press, 1981.

Poetry.

1078. Sanchez, Carol Lee. *Excerpts From a Mountain Climber's Handbook*. San Francisco: Taurean Horn and Out West Limited, 1985.

Collection of poems (1971-1985) with an introduction by Bill Vartnaw.

1079. Sanchez, Carol Lee. *Message Bringer Woman*. San Francisco: Taurean Horn, n.d.

Poetry.

1080. Sanchez, Carol Lee. *Morning Prayer*. Brooklyn: Strawberry Press, 1977.

Poetry.

1081. Sanchez, Carol Lee. *Time Warps*. San Francisco: Taurean Horn Press, 1976.

Poetry.

1082. Sands, Kathleen Mullen, ed. *Circle of Motion: Arizona Anthology of Contemporary American Indian Literature*. Tempe: Arizona Historical Foundation, 1990.

This anthology of poetry, fiction and essays includes sixteen American Indian women with Arizona connections. Well-published writers such as Joy Harjo and Mary TallMountain are included as are many young writers publishing for the first time.

1083.   Sands, Kathleen Mullen. "Ethnography, Autobiography and Fiction: Narrative Strategies in Cultural Analysis." *Native American Literatures: Forum I, 1989*. Laura Coltelli, ed. Pisa: Serrizo Editoriale Universitario, 1989, 39-52.

An analysis of the collaborative work of anthropologist Ruth M. Underhill and Papago Maria Chona in the construction of the *Papago Woman* text. Emphasizes the manipulation of field data to develop a literary text and compares Underhill's use of material in personal narrative text and her novel *Hawk Over Whirlpools*.

1084.   Sands, Kathleen Mullen. "Indian Women's Personal Narratives: Voices Past and Present." *Fea(s)ts of Memory*. Margo Culley, ed. Madison: University of Wisconsin Press, 1991.

This essay analyzes the literary strategies used by Sarah Winnemucca, Maria Chona, Leslie Silko, and Paula Gunn Allen in their autobiographical writing to trace the development of Indian women's personal narrative from the nineteenth century to the present.

1085.   Sands, Kathleen Mullen. "*Love Medicine*: Voices and Margins." *Studies in American Indian Literatures* 9, 1 (Spring 1984): 12-24.

This essay addresses the multiple narrative technique of Louise Erdrich's novel as reflecting the fragmentary nature of rumor and gossip in the community and the fact that no individual ever knows the whole story.

1086.   Sands, Kathleen Mullen, ed. "Special Symposium Issue on Leslie Marmon Silko's *Ceremony*." *American Indian Quarterly* 5, 1 (1979).

Six essays analyze various themes and narrative strategies in *Ceremony* including: event structure, elements of ritual healing, the significance of animals in the protagonist's cure, and the centrality of the female principle in the success of the novel. Includes an introduction which surveys reviews and current criticism.

1087. Sands, Kathleen Mullen and Allison Sekaquaptewa Lewis. "Seeing With a Native Eye: A Hopi Film on Hopi." *American Indian Quarterly* 15, 1 (October 1990): 387-97.

Hopi scholar Allison Lewis and critic Kathleen Sands analyze the filming techniques that make Victor Masayesva's first film uniquely Hopi in character. Part of the film focuses on Hopi women.

1088. Sands, Kathleen Mullen and Emory Sekequaptewa. "Four Hopi Lullabies." *American Indian Quarterly* 4, 3 (1978): 195-210.

Analysis of texts and cultural context of Helen Sekequaptewa's versions of traditional lullabies. Emphasis is on this genre of songs as cultural primer.

1089. Sapir, Edward, ed. *Yana Texts*. New York: Kraus Reprint, 1964.

Yana woman Betty Brown narrates traditional texts in her Native language which are presented with both literal and literary English translations. Several of the narratives focus on women, marriage, and childbirth, and one concerns the dream of the narrator about a visit to her deceased mother in a land of flowers.

1090. Saucerman, James R. "Wendy Rose: Searching Through Shards, Creating Life." *Wicazo Sa Review* 5, 2 (Fall 1989): 26-29.

In her poetry, Wendy Rose brings order and healing to counter the fragmentation and depersonalization of her work in Anglo society. She applies the medicine of art to the disruption of technology.

1091.   Scarberry, Susan J. "Memory as Medicine: The Power of Recollection in *Ceremony*." *American Indian Quarterly* 5, 1 (1979): 19-26.

The loss of memory of the protagonist of Leslie Silko's novel is analyzed as the cause of his psychological alienation and regaining memory is seen as a healing force in his recovery of tribal identity.

1092.   Scholer, Bo, ed. *Coyote Was Here: Essays on Contemporary Native American Literary and Political Mobilization*. Aarhus, Denmark: University of Aarhus, 1984.

This collection includes essays by or about eleven American Indian women writers, all of which address the relationship of literature and politics as they affect Indian writers and cultures.

1093.   Sears, Vickie. *Simple Songs*. Ithaca, NY: Firebrand Books, 1990.

Fourteen stories about the lives of Native children, women, and elders, all of which celebrate Indian survival.

1094.   Seyersted, Per. *Leslie Marmon Silko*. Boise: Boise State University Western Writers Series, no. 45, 1980.

History of Laguna Pueblo, biographical notes and background, description and evaluations of Silko's *Ceremony*, her short stories, and poetry.

1095.   Shaw, Anna Moore. *Pima Legends*. Tucson: University of Arizona Press, 1968.

A collection of traditional stories based on the recollections of tales she heard in her youth on the Gila River Reservation in central Arizona.

1096.   Shrive, Norman. "What Happened to Pauline?" *Canadian Literature* 12 (Summer 1962): 25-38.

        Shrive looks at critical reactions to Mohawk poet Pauline Johnson and her place in Canadian literature.

1097.   Sidney, Angela, Kitty Smith, and Rachel Dawson. *My Stories are My Wealth*. Recorded by Julie Cruikshank. Whitehorse: Council for Yukon Indians and Government of Yukon, 1977.

        Cruikshank recorded the stories of three Yukon women between 1974 and 1976. The stories were told in English and are unedited in this collection

1098.   Silberman, Robert. "Opening the Text: *Love Medicine* and the Return of the Native American Woman." In *Narrative Chance: Postmodern Discourse on Native American Indian Literatures*. Gerald Vizenor, ed. Albuquerque: University of New Mexico Press, 1989, 101-20.

        Love Medicine by Louise Erdrich is seen as a departure from the established patterns of American Indian novels in that the central character is a woman and her attempt at return "does not lead to a prolonged series of encounters." Her death raises issues in those around her and becomes the central problem of the multiple narrator/narratives strategy of the novel.

1099.   Silko, Leslie Marmon. *Ceremony*. New York: Viking Press, 1977.

        In this novel, Tayo, a World War II veteran, returns to Laguna and must find the right "way" to live there again; he must complete a ceremony which will bring him back into harmony with himself, his tribe, and the natural world.

1100.   Silko, Leslie Marmon. *Laguna Woman*. Greenfield Center, NY: Greenfield Review Press, 1974.

Poetry by a Laguna woman.

1101.	Silko, Leslie Marmon. "Landscape, History and the Pueblo Imagination." *Antaeus* 57 (Autumn 1986): 83-94.

Silko discusses death, emergence motifs in pottery and petroglyph designs, storytelling and landscape in relationship to survival with particular attention to Laguna Pueblo migration stories in order to comment on the history and cultural views of Pueblo peoples of Arizona and New Mexico.

1102.	Silko, Leslie Marmon. "Language and Literature from a Pueblo Indian Perspective." In *English Literature: Opening Up the Canon; Selected Papers from the English Institute.* Leslie Fiedler and Houston A. Baker, Jr., eds. Baltimore: Johns Hopkins University Press, 1981, 54-72.

This is an edited transcript of Silko's oral presentation about language from a Pueblo perspective. She relates a Pueblo creation story, linking the narrative to history and personal identity. She relates stories told by Aunt Suzie and Simon Ortiz, discusses humor and clowning, and the capacity of language to forge culture.

1103.	Silko, Leslie Marmon. "An Old-Time Indian Attack Conducted in Two Parts." *Yardbird Reader* 5 (1976): 77-84.

Silko discusses the failure of white novelists and poets to effectively represent Indian "beliefs, values, and emotions" in their attempts to write literature about American Indians. She attacks the arrogance of such writers as Oliver LaFarge, and particularly the poet Gary Snyder, for their racist assumption that they have the right to imitate Native literary forms and viewpoints and she defines such imitation as cultural theft.

1104.	Silko, Leslie Marmon. *Storyteller.* New York: Richard Seaver, Random House and Grove Books, 1981.

Using a mixed format of family photographs, traditional stories, short fiction, and poetry, Silko structures this work and unifies it with autobiographical fragments that point to the interplay of remembrance and creative writing. The work includes all of the author's short stories and most of her poetry.

1105.   Slipperjack, Ruby. *Honour the Sun*. Winnipeg: Pemmican Publications, 1987.

Slipperjack, an Ojibway from northern Ontario, is the author of this novel which reads like an autobiography. The child Owl records her perceptions of events as she matures and decides to leave her community. The despair of the adults is reflected in Owl's descriptions of her environment.

1106.   Smith, Barbara. *Renewal; The Prophecy of Manu, Book One*. Penticton, BC: Theytus, 1985.

This novel is the story of Teoni, an Indian girl who is abducted and taken to live under the sea with the Anishoni. Smith combines American Indian mythology with fantasy to create a fictional world set in British Columbia and Alaska.

1107.   Smith, Barbara. *Renewal; Teoni's Giveaway, Book Two*. Penticton, BC: Theytus, 1986.

This is the sequel to *The Prophecy of Manu*. Teoni leaves the sea world to return to the land. Smith uses her characters and fiction to present a vision of survival from the contemporary disasters through reliance on Native American philosophy.

1108.   Smith, Dana Margaret [Mrs. White Mountain Smith]. *Hopi Girl*. Palo Alto: Stanford University Press, 1931.

This fictional account tells of Po-la-ma-na, Butterfly Girl of Hopi Land, who was sent away to government schools and came back to live with her people.

1109.   Smith, Patricia Clark. "Coyote's Sons, Spider's Daughters: Western American Indian Poetry, 1968-1983." In *A Literary*

History of the American West. J. Golden Taylor, ed. Fort Worth: Texas Christian University Press, 1987, 1067-1078.

Smith discusses several Indian poets, among them Mary TallMountain, Leslie Silko, nila northSun, Joy Harjo, Luci Tapahonso, and Paula Gunn Allen.

1110.   Stout, Mary. "Zitkala Sa: The Literature of Politics." In *Coyote Was Here: Essays on Contemporary Native American Literary and Political Mobilization*. Bo Scholer, ed. Aarhus, Denmark: University of Aarhus, 1984, 70-78.

Zitkala Sa (Gertrude Bonnin) is seen as a key figure in the emergence of written American Indian literature. Her satirical poems and essays protested the injustices toward Indians, and she worked consistently toward progressive reform. The author notes that Zitkala Sa's life closely paralleled those of characters in contemporary Indian fiction. An annotated bibliography of her work follows the essay.

1111.   Sullivan, Elizabeth. *Indian Legends of the Trail of Tears and Other Creek Stories*. Tulsa, OK: Giant Services, 1974.

Legends and stories told to the author by her great-grandmother and other elders are collected in this volume.

1112.   Sundquist, Asebruit. *Pocahontas & Co.; The Fictional American Indian Woman in Nineteenth Century Literature: A Study of Method*. Atlantic Highlands, NJ: Humanities Press International, 1987.

Analysis of 126 Indian women as characters in the works of 56 authors. Sundquist studies character traits and stereotypes and finds that the three most prevalent themes are love, sex, and the death of the Indian woman. This is a quantitative analysis.

1113. Swann, Brian and Arnold Krupat, ed. *Recovering the Word: Essays on Native American Literature.* Los Angeles: University of California Press, 1987.

This collection of essays on critical theory and methodology as applied to oral and written texts by Native Americans includes an analysis of coyote tales performed by Hopi Eagle Clan matriarch Helen Sekaquaptewa and an interpretation of N. Scott Momaday's *House Made of Dawn* by Laguna writer and critic Paula Gunn Allen.

1114. TallMountain, Mary. *Green March Moons.* Berkeley: New Seed Press, 1987.

Fiction by a Koyukons woman.

1115. TallMountain, Mary. *Nine Poems.* San Francisco: Friars, 1977.

Chapbook of poems.

1116. TallMountain, Mary. "Paula Gunn Allen's 'The One Who Skins Cats': An Enquiry into Spiritedness." *Studies in American Indian Literature* 7, 3 (Fall 1983): 69-75.

Discussion of Allen's article "This Wilderness in my Blood" and other critical reviews of American Indian women and poetry.

1117. TallMountain, Mary. *There Is No Word for Goodbye.* Marvin, SD: Blue Cloud Quarterly, 1982.

Poetry.

1118. Tapahonso, Luci. *A Breeze Swept Through.* Albuquerque: West End Press, 1987.

Poetry by a Navajo woman.

1119. Tapahonso, Luci. *One More Shiprock Night.* San Antonio: Tejas Art Press, 1981.

Poetry by a Navajo woman with illustrations by Acoma artist Earl P. Ortiz.

1120.   Tapahonso, Luci. *Seasonal Woman*. Santa Fe: Tooth of Time Press, 1982.

Collection of poetry with brief introduction by John Nichols and illustrations by R. C. Gorman.

1121.   Theisz, R. D., ed. *Buckskin Tokens: Contemporary Oral Narratives of the Lakota*. Aberdeen, SD: Sinte Gleska College/North Plains Press, 1975.

Brief interviews with four Lakota storytellers precede their versions of traditional tales. Three narrators are women: Kate Blue Thunder, Irene Clairmont, and Christine Dunham.

1122.   Thompson, Joan. "Yellow Woman, Old and New: Oral Tradition and Leslie Marmon Silko's *Storyteller*." *Wicazo Sa Review* 5, 2 (Fall 1989): 22-25.

Thompson sees the multiple versions of the Yellow Woman story as the cohesive device in Leslie Silko's *Storyteller*. She sees the variations in the versions as indicating the importance of change and adaptability for maintaining the oral tradition and as demonstrating the link between past and present storytelling.

1123.   Tremblay, Gail. *Indian Singing in 20th Century America*. Corvallis, Oregon: Calyx Books, 1989.

Poetry by Onondaga/Micmac woman.

1124.   Tsosie, Rebecca. "Changing Women: The Cross-Currents of American Indian Feminine Identity." *American Indian Culture and Research Journal* 12, 1 (1988): 1-38.

A review of the literature about American Indian women which analyzes literary image as well as autobiographical accounts and contemporary fiction and poetry.

1125.   Van Steen, Marcus, ed. *Pauline Johnson: Her Life and Work*. Toronto: Hodder and Stroughton, 1965.

Sparked by a revival of interest in the work of Mohawk poet and fiction writer Pauline Johnson, this collection of material provides biographical background as well as analysis of her written work.

1126.   Vangen, Kate Shanley. "The Devil's Domain: Leslie Silko's 'Storyteller.'" In *Coyote Was Here: Essays on Contemporary Native American Literary and Political Mobilization*. Bo Scholer, ed. Aarhus, Denmark: University of Aarhus, 1984, 116-23.

Silko's story is seen as a form of discourse which demands that the reader envision political and linguistic alternatives, since unlike many works of Indian fiction, it does not provide much culturally specific information, but rather demands "movement away from what is exotic" toward "what is unintelligible" and therefore threatening.

1127.   Vizenor, Gerald, ed. *Narrative Chance: Postmodern Discourse on Native American Indian Literatures*. Albuquerque: University of New Mexico Press, 1989.

This collection of essays focusing primarily on Native American fiction includes applications of critical theories to Leslie Silko's *Ceremony* and *Storyteller* and to Louise Erdrich's *Love Medicine*.

1128.   Volborth, Judith Ivaloo. *Thunder Root: Traditional and Contemporary Native American Verse*. Los Angeles: UCLA American Indian Culture and Research Center, 1978.

Poetry by an Apache/Comanche woman; introduction by Kenneth Lincoln.

1129.   Volborth, Judith Mountain Leaf. "Pollen Beneath the Tongue." In *Native American Literatures: Forum 1, 1989*. Laura

Coltelli, ed. Pisa: Serrizo Editoriale Universitario, 1989, 67-70.

Volborth discusses the importance of sound and language and the power of the word in Native American oral and written literatures, quoting from poems by Joy Harjo, Paula Gunn Allen, and Leslie Marmon Silko.

1130. Waldie, Jean H. "The Iroquois Poetess, Pauline Johnson." *Ontario History* 60 (1948): 65-76.

Discusses the phases and characteristics of Johnson's career, as well as giving some biographical background.

1131. Walsh, Marnie. *A Taste of the Knife*. Boise, ID: Ahsahta Press, 1976.

Poetry by a Sioux woman.

1132. Walters, Anna Lee. "American Indian Thought and Identity in American Fiction." In *Coyote Was Here: Essays on Contemporary Native American Literary and Political Mobilization*. Bo Scholer, ed. Aarhus, Denmark: University of Aarhus, 1984, 35-39.

Walters, a fiction writer, discusses the publication problems facing Indian writers and calls for more active involvement by both whites and Indians in the publication of all forms of Indian literatures.

1133. Walters, Anna Lee. *Ghost Singer*. Menomonie, WI: Northland Publishing, 1988.

Navajo life in the 1830s is linked with Washington, D.C., in the 1960s and 1970s and contemporary reservation life through the exploration of the perspectives of Smithsonian Museum personnel, Anglo historians, and Navajo people who understand their own history. Walters weaves together a story of mysterious deaths, a seven-foot Indian "ghost" and the ultimate healing of tribal people who remain true to their own history.

1134. Walters, Anna Lee. "Odyssey of Indian Time." *Book Forum* 5, 3 (1981): 396-99.

This Pawnee/Otoe writer draws on her experience living in the Navajo tribe to discuss survival and change in Indian cultures as they are shaped by the long tenure of Native peoples on the land and their sense of time as associated with cycle rather than the clock.

1135. Walters, Anna Lee. *The Sun is Not Merciful*. Ithaca: Firebrand Books, 1985.

Eight short stories by a Pawnee/Otoe woman about contemporary tribal life.

1136. Warner, N. O. "Images of Drinking in 'Woman Singing,' *Ceremony* and *House Made of Dawn*." *MELUS* 11 (Winter 1984): 15-30.

Alcohol abuse is analyzed as a barrier between Indian characters and their traditions and seen as a major source of alienation and cultural disintegration in the works of three Native writers. Only by rejecting drinking and returning to cultural values does the protagonist in each story attain some sense of meaningful identity.

1137. Washburne, Heluiz and Anauta. *Children of the Blizzard*. London: Dennis Dobson, 1960.

This collection of stories recorded by Washburne is based on the experiences of Anauta, an Eskimo woman from Baffin Island. The stories tell primarily of the life of Eskimo children.

1138. Wasserman, Nancy. "Beyond the Pocahontas Perplex." *Indian Truth: Special Issue on Native Women*. Marg Emery and Ann Laquer, eds. 239 (May-June): 12.

Rayna Green's discussion of the princess and squaw stereotypes of Indian women is examined and the author traces how this dual misconception is challenged in contemporary literature about Indian women.

1139.   Watson, Virginia. *The Princess Pocahontas*. Philadelphia: Penn Publishing, 1916.

This is a fictional account of the life of Pocahontas from the forests of Virginia to the courts of England.

1140.   Weigle, Marta. "Creation and Procreation, Cosmogony and Childbirth; Reflections on *Ex Nihilo*; Earth Diver and Emergence Mythology." *Journal of American Folklore* 100, 398 (October-December 1987): 426-35.

Native American myths are analyzed to determine the value placed on aspects which relate particularly to female images and actions.

1141.   Weigle, Marta. *Spiders and Spinsters: Women and Mythology*. Albuquerque: University of New Mexico Press, 1982.

This sourcebook focuses on American and European myths, including many Native American myths of Spider Woman. A good comparative study of women in mythology.

1142.   Weigle, Marta and Peter White. *The Lore of New Mexico*. Albuquerque: University of New Mexico Press, 1988.

Deals in general with Indian, Hispanic and Anglo folk traditions in New Mexico, but includes many illustrations and quotations from Native American women.

1143.   Whiteman, Roberta Hill. *Star Quilt*. Minneapolis: Holy Cow! Press, 1984.

Poetry by an Oneida woman.

1144.   Wiget, Andrew. *Critical Essays on Native American Literature*. Boston: G. K. Hall, 1985.

Essays on traditional and contemporary Indian literatures include analysis of Sarah Winnemucca's autobiography, Zitkala Sa and Mourning Dove as transitional writers, and a source study of Leslie Marmon Silko's short story "Tony's Story."

1145.   Wiget, Andrew. "Nightriding with Noni Daylight! The Many Horse Songs of Joy Harjo." In *Native American Literatures: Forum 1, 1989*. Laura Coltelli, ed. Pisa: Serrizo Editoriale Universitario, 1989, 185-96.

An assessment of the "nature, powers, and direction" of Creek poet Joy Harjo's voice and poetic vision, this essay analyzes the themes and poetic strategies used by the poet to move beyond observation and reflection to self-realization.

1146.   Wiget, Andrew. "Singing the Indian Blues: Louise Erdrich and the Love that Hurts So Good." *Puerto del Sol* 21, 2 (1986): 166-75.

Wiget sees Erdrich walking "a fine line between character and caricature" in her novel *Love Medicine* and discusses her book of poetry *Jacklight* as being grounded in the use of double signs. Both books are seen as works exalting desperate energies.

1147.   Wiget, Andrew. "Telling the Tale: A Performance Analysis of a Hopi Coyote Story." In *Recovering the Word: Essays on Native American Literature*. Brian Swann and Arnold Krupat, eds. Los Angeles: University of California Press, 1987, 297-336.

Performance theory is applied to a Hopi coyote tale as told by Helen Sekaquaptewa in a videotaped performance in 1976. Hopi text and translation are given; analysis discusses audience, style, and form in the performance, including paralinguistic elements.

1148.   Witt, Shirley Hill and Stan Steiner, eds. *The Way: An Anthology of American Indian Literature*. New York: Vintage Books, 1972.

Anthology of orations, songs, essays, narratives, poetry and prophecies by American Indians which includes work by Anna Hainois (Cherokee), Frances Kisto (Papago), and Bertha Desidero (Navajo).

1149.   Woody, Elizabeth. *Hand Into Stone*. New York: Contact II, 1988.

Poetry by a Warm Springs woman.

1150.   Wright, Anne, ed. *The Delicacy and Strength of Lace: Letters Between Leslie Marmon Silko and James Wright*. St. Paul: Graywolf Press, 1986.

Anne Wright edited the letters exchanged between her late husband and Silko from 1978 until James Wright's death in 1980. The letters demonstrate the progression of the friendship which developed between the two poets.

1151.   Yazzie, Ethelou, ed. *Navajo History*. Many Farms, AZ: Navajo Community College Press, 1971.

This collection includes previously unrecorded history of the Navajos with photographs and illustrations. It includes certain myths, tales of monsters, the story of Changing Woman, and stories of the twins and Spider Woman. The stories are recorded from those obtained from Navajo storytellers.

1152.   Young, Philip. "The Mother of Us All: Pocahontas Reconsidered." *The Kenyon Review* 24 (Summer 1962): 391-415.

In this discussion of what "facts" are known about Pocahontas, Young points out how she has become a "goddess" and "myth" of literature.

1153.   Zak, Nancy C. "Sacred and Legendary Women of Native America." *Wildfire* 1, 1 (Winter 1984): 12-16; *Wildfire* 2, 1&2 (1986): 59-61.

Among the Sioux, White Buffalo Calf Woman is a culture hero who brought the tribe the sacred pipe. She is a life-giving figure who represents cosmic knowledge and energy. Another figure of importance is Bad Lands Woman who is characterized in legend as staving off universal destruction of creation. A third in the triad of central Sioux female mythic spirit-women is Maya Owichapaha who judges souls and determines their fate in the after-life. The second article discusses numerous sacred and legendary women from a number of different Native tribes.

1154.   Zepata, Ofelia, ed. *When It Rains, Papago and Pima Poetry.* *Sun Tracks* 7. Tucson: University of Arizona Press, 1982.

A bilingual collection of poetry introduced by a Papago linguist and writer.

1155.   Zitkala-Sa [Gertrude Bonnin]. "Address by Mrs. Gertrude Bonnin." *The American Indian Magazine* 7 (Fall 1919): 153-57.

An address by the Dakota Sioux author to the eighth annual convention of the Society of American Indians, urging its membership to organize itself and include women.

1156.   Zitkala-Sa [Gertrude Bonnin]. *American Indian Stories.* 1921; Rpt., Glorieta, NM: Rio Grande Press, 1976; Lincoln: University of Nebraska Press, 1985.

This collection includes reprints from the *Atlantic Monthly*, *Harper's Magazine*, and *Everybody's Magazine*. There are ten stories of Indian life that are laced with the resentment toward the Bureau of Indian Affairs that characterized Bonnin's lectures and writing.

1157. Zitkala-Sa [Gertrude Bonnin]. "The Indian's Awakening." *American Indian Magazine* 4 (January-March 1916): 57-59.

Poem which tells of the cutting of her hair and loss of traditional clothing but reaffirms that her heart was left unchanged.

1158. Zitkala-Sa [Gertrude Bonnin]. *Old Indian Legends*. Boston: Ginn, 1901.

Collection of Sioux legends.

1159. Zitkala-Sa [Gertrude Bonnin]. "A Sioux Woman's Love for Her Grandchild." *American Indian Magazine* 4 (October-December 1917): 230.

Poem reflecting about Custer and the Battle of the Little Big Horn.

1160. Zitkala-Sa [Gertrude Bonnin]. "The Soft-Hearted Sioux." *Harper's Magazine* 102 (March 1902): 505-8.

This story is told in the first person about a young boy who was sent to the mission school, learned to be a Christian, and returned home to find his father dying. His attempt to secure meat for his starving parents ended in the murder of a white man and his eventual imprisonment.

1161. Zitkala-Sa [Gertrude Bonnin]. "The Trial Path." *Harper's Magazine* 103 (October 1901): 741-44.

In this story of two Dakota women, a grandmother is telling a story to a young woman about the tribal history and the death of the young woman's grandfather.

Autobiography, Biography, and Interviews

AUTOBIOGRAPHY, BIOGRAPHY, AND INTERVIEWS

1162.   "A Woman's Ways: An Interview with Judy Swamp: Maintaining Traditional Values in the Context of Contemporary Conflict." *Parabola* 5, 4 (Fall 1980): 52-61.

Judy Swamp lives on the Mohawk reservation, part in New York and part in Canada. She discusses her role as a woman among the Mohawk, particularly the power women have as Council members and members of the Women's Council. She expresses her concern for the environment and for maintaining tradition.

1163.   "An Indian Woman Physician." *Indian's Friend* 1, 7 (1899): 2.

Brief recognition to Susan LaFlesche upon her graduation from Hampton Institute as a medical student.

1164.   "Buffy." *Talking Leaf* 41, 7 (August 1976): 8-9.

Interview with Cree singer and songwriter Buffy Sainte-Marie.

1165.   "Diana." In *Breasts: Women Speak About Their Breasts and Their Lives*. Daphna Ayalah and Isaac J. Weinstock, eds. New York: Summit Books, 1979, 268-75.

In this collection of women's accounts of how they view their breasts and womanhood, Diana, a Native American great-grandmother, speaks of puberty, childbirth, nursing, menopause, and the natural way she views her body.

1166.   "Leaders of their People: Native Women Working for the Future." *Indian Truth: Special Issue on Native Women.* Marg Emery and Ann Laqner, eds. 239 (May-June): 9-10.

Indian women active in health care, government, the arts, and law are very briefly profiled.

1167.   "Miss Ann Padlo." *Canadian Indians and Eskimos of Today* 3 (April 1966).

This bulletin features a Baffin Island woman born in 1935 who became an announcer for CBC in Montreal, Encouraged by her own success, she has urged others to attain an education and serve their people.

1168.   "Nellie Shaw Harner." *Indian Historian* 2, 8 (October 1965): 17.

Nellie Shaw Harner was a Paiute schoolteacher whose thirty-two year teaching career and academic achievements are celebrated in a brief tribute to her.

1169.   "Pioneer Medical Woman: Dr. Susan LaFlesche Picotte." *Medical Women's Journal* 37 (1930): 20.

A brief family history and biography of LaFlesche, the first Indian woman to practice medicine; depicts her as a leader of the Omaha people.

1170.   "Roberta Jamieson: A Profile." *Canadian Woman Studies* 10, 2&3 (Summer/Fall 1989): 37.

This Mohawk woman was the first Native woman to receive a law degree in Ontario. She was also the first Native to serve as Indian Commissioner in Ontario.

1171.   *Speaking Together: Canada's Native Women.* Ottawa: Secretary of State, 1975.

Published in conjunction with the celebration of International Women's Year. Includes brief biographical sketches, personal statements, and photographs of twenty-nine Canadian Indian women.

1172. "The Life of a Chief: An Interview with Nora Bothwell." *Canadian Woman Studies* 10, 2&3 (Summer/Fall 1989): 33-35.

Nora Bothwell is chief of the Alderville First Nation in Southeastern Ontario. In this interview she discusses her personal life and community activism.

1173. Adams, Winona, ed. "An Indian Girl's Story of a Trading Expedition to the Southwest about 1841." *Frontier* 10 (May 1930): 338-51, 367.

Told by Catherine, daughter of a Nez Perce woman and a Mohawk and white father. The story of her trip to the mouth of the Colorado River was copied down about 1875 by her husband.

1174. Alilkatuktuk, Jeela. "Canada: Stranger in My Own Land." *MS* 3, (February 1974): 8-10.

A Native woman of Canada comments about the role of an educated Indian women in her country.

1175. Allen, Paula Gunn. "Autobiography of a Confluence." *I Tell You Now: Autobiographical Essays by Native American Writers*. Brian Swann and Arnold Krupat, eds. Lincoln: University of Nebraska Press, 1987, 141-54.

Allen uses the metaphor of a road to develop a journey theme in her narrative, connecting her deep sense of place to her identity and sense of memory, emphasizing the importance of Cubero, New Mexico, as the central place that is connected to all her movement.

1176. Anahareo [Gertrude Motte]. *Devil in Deerskins: My Life with Grey Owl*. Toronto: New Press, 1972.

Grey Owl was Archie Belamey, an Englishman who passed as an Indian and worked actively for wildlife conservation projects. The story is told by the Mohawk woman who influenced him and shared much of her life with him.

1177.   Anauta. *Land of Good Shadows: The Life Story of Anauta, an Eskimo Woman.* Heluiz Chandler Washburne, ed. New York: John Day Co., 1940.

Anauta is also the author of *Children of the Blizzard*, stories about Eskimo children, and *Wild Like the Foxes*, a narrative based on her mother's childhood. This autobiography of a Baffin Island Eskimo relates her experiences through youth, marriage, and widowhood, focusing primarily on her relationship to white society and her regret at the loss of traditional lifeways. Text includes an Eskimo alphabet and glossary.

1178.   Anauta. *Wild Like the Foxes: The True Story of an Eskimo Girl.* New York: John Day, 1956.

Based on the childhood life of Anauta's mother Alea, up to her marriage to Yorgki. The book tells of hunting, trapping, and hardships. Alea was sent to school in England by her father, a change from her traditional ways.

1179.   Anderson, Irving W. "Probing the Riddle of the Bird Woman." *Montana: The Magazine of Western History* 23, 4 (1973): 2-17.

Sacajawea, the Shoshone woman who accompanied Lewis and Clark, has been romanticized by countless writers because the facts of her life are obscure. Anderson argues that he has proof of the death of her son Baptiste in 1866 and further evidence which will resolve the historical contradictions about Sacajawea's life.

1180.   Anderson, Owanah. *Ohoyo One Thousand: A Resource Guide of American Indian/Alaska Native Women, 1982.* Wichita Falls, TX: Ohoyo Resource Center, 1982.

Biographical sketches of 1,004 American Indian/Alaska Native women indexed according to area of expertise.

1181. Anderson, Rufus. *Memoir of Catherine Brown: A Christian Indian of the Cherokee Nation.* Philadelphia: American Sunday School Union, 1931.

Anderson relates the story of an Indian woman born about 1800 in Alabama who attended missionary school at Brainerd, was converted to Christianity, and then worked to convert other Indians. Excerpts from the diary are included.

1182. Antonides, John. "Siba's Last Stand." *MS* 7, 3 (September 1978): 22.

Account of Siba Baum, Sikiska Blackfoot from Long Island, who quit school to protest racist attitudes.

1183. Apes, William. *The Experiences of Five Christian Indians of the Pequod Tribe.* Boston: James B. Dow, 1933.

This religious tract by Apes includes personal religious testimonies of four Indian women who converted to Christianity and preached among their people.

1184. Arnaktauyak, Germaine, illustrator. *Stories from Pangnirtung.* Edmonton: Hurtig Publishers, 1976.

Although this collection includes several stories by men, there are two pieces by women who tell stories and their childhood experiences. Katsoo Eevic and Koodloo Pitsualak tell of the changes in the Baffin Island area.

1185. Ashley, Yvonne. "'That's the Way We Were Raised': An Oral Interview with Ada Damon." *Frontiers: A Journal of Women Studies* 2, 21 (Summer 1977): 59-62.

Ada Damon is the interviewer's great aunt who was born in 1900 south of Shiprock, New Mexico. She tells of weaving, trading on the reservation, and her experiences attending boarding school and raising her adopted children.

1186. Axford, Roger W. *Native Americans: Twenty-three Indian Biographies*. Indiana, PA: A. G. Halldin Publishing, 1980.

Although the format for these biographical sketches is mixed, Axford provides information on a number of American Indian women: Ida Carnnen, Betsy Kellas, Clara Sue Kidwell, Veronica L. Murdock, Joanne Linder, Vivian Ayoungman, Yvonne Talachy, Gay Lawrence, Carol Allen Weston, and Roxie Woods.

1187. Badger, Julia. "Autobiographical Material and Commentary." In *Acculturation and Personality among the Wisconsin Chippewa*. Victor Barnouw, ed. *Memoirs of the American Anthropological Association* 72 (1950): 112-44.

Barnouw introduces Julia Badger as an unreliable narrator, often given to fancy and exaggeration in her personal narration. He includes her brief (25 page) autobiography in his ethnography of Wisconsin Chippewa as a study in deviant personality. In her narrative Badger describes her interest in and growing acculturation to Anglo society during her time off reservation as cut short by ill health and gives details of traditional curing rituals applied to her chronic illnesses. She uses daydream and fantasy and occasional train trips away from the reservation to cope with an unsuccessful marriage.

1188. Bagnell, Kenneth. "Interview with Gloria Webster." *United Church Observer* 25, 17 (1963): 21.

A Canadian Indian anthropologist, Webster urges young Indians not to attempt going back to reservation life once they have become urbanized and criticizes government and church programs directed at Indians.

1189. Balassi, William, John F. Crawford, and Annie O. Eysturoy, eds. *This is About Vision: Interviews With Southwestern*

Writers. Albuquerque: University of New Mexico Press, 1990.

This collection of sixteen interviews includes Paula Gunn Allen, Linda Hogan, Joy Harjo, and Luci Tapahonso. A useful introduction places these writers' comments within the context of the environment of the desert and mountains of the Southwest. Photographs and bibliographies accompany each interview.

1190. Ball, Eve. *Indeh: An Apache Odyssey*. With Nora Henn and Lynda Sanchez. Provo, UT: Brigham Young University Press, 1980.

A three-part work containing transcribed interviews with Mescalero Apaches, concerning Apache history and culture.

1191. Ballinger, Franchot and Brian Swann. "A MELUS Interview: Paula Gunn Allen." *MELUS* 10, 2 (Summer 1983): 3-25.

Allen received her Ph.D. from the University of New Mexico in 1975 and has published criticism, poetry and a novel. Interview includes biographical information and touches other topics, such as Indian writing styles, women's consciousness, publishers, bi-culturalism and her own writing.

1192. Barnes, Kim. "A Leslie Marmon Silko Interview." *Journal of Ethnic Studies* 13, 4 (Winter 1986): 83-105.

Silko discusses her sense of audience, her relationship to traditional storytelling, the roles of women in Pueblo societies, her development of a male protagonist in *Ceremony*, her poetry, and the significance of the word "almanac" in her novel-in-progress.

1193. Barnett, Franklin. *Viola Jimulla: The Indian Chieftess*. Prescott, AZ: Yavapai-Prescott Indian Tribe, 1968.

Biography of Viola Jimulla who served as tribal leader of the Prescott Yavapai tribe for 26 years. She was born in 1878, died in 1966, and was responsible for bringing the Presbyterian Church to Prescott.

1194. Barnouw, Victor. "The Phantasy World of the Chippewa Woman." *Psychiatry: Journal for the Study of Interpersonal Relations* 12 (February 1949): 67-76.

This comparison of the life histories of Tom Badger and his wife, Julia, emphasizes the fantasies of Julia, especially those with the guardian spirit Beoukowe and her visions.

1195. Bataille, Gretchen M. "An Interview With Geraldine Keams." *Explorations in Ethnic Studies* 10, 1 (January 1987): 1-8.

Geraldine Keams, Navajo actor and poet, discusses her childhood on the Navajo Reservation in Arizona and her aspirations in Hollywood.

1196. Bataille, Gretchen M. "Transformation of Tradition: Autobiographical Works by American Indian Women." In *Studies in American Indian Literature: Critical Essays and Course Designs*. Paula Gunn Allen, ed. New York: MLA, 1983, 85-99.

A brief summary of the evolution of Indian women's autobiographies followed by a reading list including autobiographies and resource material on Indian women.

1197. Bataille, Gretchen M. and Kathleen Mullen Sands. *American Indian Women: Telling Their Lives*. Lincoln: University of Nebraska Press, 1984.

This book examines American Indian women's personal narratives and the centrality of women in tribal cultures, challenging common stereotypes of Indian women. A study of the antecedents of, influences on, and the characteristics and processes of Native women's personal narratives, this work analyzes eight autobiography texts and speculates on emerging forms of autobiography by American Indian women. A substantial annotated bibliography of works by and about

American Indian women including sections on autobiography, biography, ethnography and history, and literature and criticism.

1198. Bates, Craig D. "Dorothy Stanley, 1924-1990." *News From Native California* 5, 1 (November/January 1990-91): 6-8.

This is a transcript of the eulogy delivered by Bates at the memorial service for Dorothy Stanley, a Northern Mewuk woman who became active in cultural activities late in life. She was a cultural liaison for the Department of the Interior as well as tribal chair for the Tuolumne Mewuk Tribal Council.

1199. Beauregard, Margaret. "An Indian Girl On Wifehood." *Indian's Friend* 23, 2 (October 1910): 11.

An unidentified Indian woman writes to encourage other Native women to master the domestic arts and to take responsibility for childrearing, praising the influence of Christian women on her during her stay at Chilocco.

1200. Beckwourth, James P. "Indian Amazon: Story of Pine Leaf." *Golden Book Magazine* 1 (February 1925): 301-304.

This account by famed trapper James Beckwourth praises a young Crow woman whom he finds to be exceptionally intelligent and articulate, an outstanding warrior, and an important influence in the council. When she consents to marry him, she gives up her role as a warrior woman.

1201. Bedford, Denton R. "First Thunder of the Rocky Boys." *Indian Historian* 10, 1 (1977): 37-41.

The life story of Mary Rego, a Chippewa-Cree woman. The account tells of the early twentieth century life on the reservation from the point of view of this leader of a large family.

1202. Bennett, Kay. *Kaibah: Recollections of a Navajo Girlhood*. Los Angeles: Western Lore Press, 1964.

Covering the period 1928 to 1935, this narrative details the New Mexico childhood and girlhood of the author, including family relationships, work and play experiences, and ceremonial life. The work is a loosely connected series of vignettes with illustrations by the author.

1203.   Bennett, Kay and Ross Bennett. *A Navajo Saga*. San Antonio: The Naylor Co., 1969.

The text is a Navajo family chronicle from 1845 to 1868 using fictional form with dialogue, incorporating family events with emphasis on hardships and the resiliency and loyalty of family members. The central figure in the narrative is Shebah, who is based on the author's grandmother. The focus is on the Bosque Redondo experience and "The Long Walk" back.

1204.   Benson, Bjorn, Elizabeth Hampsten, and Kathryn Sweeny, eds. *Day in Day Out: Women's Lives in North Dakota*. Grand Forks: University of North Dakota, 1988.

Sponsored by the Committee for the North Dakota History of Women Project, this collection includes "Conversions," a youthful reminiscence by Louise Erdrich. "Metis Women at Turtle Mountain," a series of interviews with women on the Turtle Mountain Reservation, and "Working at Wahpeton Indian School," a contemporary view of Indian education by Angie Erdrich.

1205.   Bighead, Kate. "She Watched Custer's Last Battle: The Story of Kate Bighead." Interpreted by Thomas Bailey Marquis. Hardin, MT: Custer Battlefield Museum, 1933.

As a girl, Kate Bighead witnessed the battle of the Washita, and, later in her young adulthood, witnessed the Battle of the Little Bighorn, where Custer died, the ensuing separation of the tribes taking part in the battle, and the final surrender of the Cheyenne people a year later. Her first-person account of the Little Bighorn battle focuses on the Cheyenne tribe as the heroes of the encounter with the Custer forces, giving details of soldiers killing themselves, which she interprets as a form of madness brought on by their attack on a peaceful tribal gathering. She captures in detail the chaos, heat, dust, smoke, and noise of the battle. Little of her personal life is revealed in the short narrative, and no interpretive material is supplied.

1206. Bighorse, Tiana. *Bighorse, the Warrior*. Noel Bennett, ed. Tucson: University of Arizona Press, 1990.

Tiana's father Gus Bighorse died in 1939. In this book Tiana recalls the stories of The Long Walk which she heard from her father. After a brief introduction, Tiana's voice becomes the voice of her father, telling the events as they happened.

1207. Blackman, Margaret B., ed. *During My Time: Florence Edenshaw Davidson, a Haida Woman*. Seattle: University of Washington Press, 1982.

Biography of Davidson, a Haida woman born in 1896. Davidson represents women in cultures undergoing rapid change. Blackman places biography in both literary and anthropological contexts, recounting for the reader the process of obtaining the life story.

1208. Blackman, Margaret B., ed. *Sadie Bower Neakok: An Inupiaq Woman*. Seattle: University of Washington Press, 1989.

The life history of the daughter of an Eskimo woman and her Anglo husband, this personal narrative depicts a woman who blends her two cultures effectively. Educated in modern schools, she returns to her Native culture first as a teacher, then as a health and welfare worker, and then as a magistrate and advocate for her people. Blackman is skillful in meshing cultural context with Neakok's narrative, and she provides analysis of the process of the life history and community, and on the theory and methodology of collecting and editing oral narrative.

1209. Boissiere, Robert. *Po Pai Mo: The Search for White Buffalo Woman*. Santa Fe: Sunstone Press, 1983.

A memoir of a French man who married a woman from Taos Pueblo who became his partner and spiritual guide until her death. The text is a tribute to her and the aid she gave him in his search for understanding of the Sioux Buffalo woman. Combines Native American spiritualism, Asian philosophy, Aztec materials, and astrology in a highly romanticized biography/memoir.

1210.   Boudinot, Elias. *Poor Sarah*. Park Hill, Indian Territory: Mission Press, 1843.

Published in the Cherokee language and orthography, this narrative purports to be a story of an Indian woman connected to Christianity but is actually the translation of a New England missionary tract.

1211.   Bourguignon, Erika. "A Life History of an Ojibwa Young Woman." *Primary Records in Culture and Personality*, 1, 10 Madison, WI: Microcard Foundation, 1956.

Bourguignon records the life story, collected in 1946, of a Lac de Flambeau woman. This is a literal transcription of conversations in which the personal names have been changed.

1212.   Brand, Johanna. *The Life and Death of Anna Mae Aquash*. Toronto: James Lorimer, 1978.

This is a thorough study of Anna Mae Aquash, AIM organizer and activist, and her death near Wamblee on the Pine Ridge Reservation in South Dakota. Includes reports published by the FBI related to AIM and Wounded Knee.

1213.   Brant, Beth. "Grandmothers of a New World." *Women of Power* 16 (Spring 1990): 40-47.

Delivered as an address during Women's History Month in 1987 at the University of Illinois by Quinte Mohawk editor and author Beth Brant, this analysis of the lives of Pocahontas and Nancy Ward challenges the stereotypes and legends which have risen around them. She sees both women as misinterpreted by white historians and presents them as powerful, visionary women who shaped their tribal histories and led fulfilling personal lives.

1214. Brimlow, George F. "The Life of Sarah Winnemucca: The Formative Years." *Oregon Historical Quarterly* 53 (June 1952): 103-34.

In this account of Thoc-me-to-ny (Sarah Winnemucca) Brimlow writes of her childhood, school years, marriage to Lieutenant Barlett, and her struggles to aid her people.

1215. Broker, Ignatia. *Night Flying Woman: An Ojibway Narrative*. St. Paul: Minnesota Historical Society Press, 1983.

Broker recounts the life story of her great-great grandmother, Night Flying Woman, who lived during the changes to the Ojibway way of life in the nineteenth century when her family was removed to the White Earth Reservation.

1216. Bronson, Ruth Muskrat. *Indians are People Too*. New York: Friendship Press, 1944.

Discussion of reservation life, values, family, education and Indian leadership in the first half of the twentieth century by a Cherokee woman.

1217. Bruchac, Joseph, ed. *Survival This Way: Interviews with Native American Poets*. Tucson: University of Arizona Press, 1987.

This is a collection of interviews focused on the influences on and content and form elements of the work of 20 contemporary American Indian poets, nine of them women writers: Paula Gunn Allen, Linda Hogan, Joy Harjo, Louise Erdrich, Diane Burns, Luci Tapahonso, and Elizabeth Cook-Lynn.

1218. Bruchac, Joseph. "As a Dakotah Woman: An Interview with Elizabeth Cook-Lynn." In *Survival This Way: Interviews with*

Native American Poets. Joseph Bruchac, ed. Tucson: University of Arizona Press, 1987, 57-71.

Cook-Lynn discusses her early work as a writer, her personal background and family, her concentration on narrative in her poetry, Momaday's influence on her work, and tribal gender roles.

1219.   Bruchac, Joseph. "The Bones are Alive: An Interview with Wendy Rose." In *Survival This Way: Interviews with Native American Poets*. Joseph Bruchac, ed. Tucson: University of Arizona Press, 1987, 249-269.

Rose discusses her childhood away from tribal tradition, her mixed ancestry, the attitude of anthropology toward Indian people, slurs in language describing ethnic minorities, her works as an artist, and the body metaphors that she uses in her poems.

1220.   Bruchac, Joseph. "For What It Is: An Interview With Luci Tapahonso." In *Survival This Way: Interviews with Native American Poets*. Joseph Bruchac, ed. Tucson: University of Arizona Press, 1987, 251-85.

Tapahonso discusses her use of memories--her own and others--in her work, the importance of community as a theme, recurring characters in her poems, humor, conflict with whites in the narratives of her poetry, and her sense of "birthing" poems.

1221.   Bruchac, Joseph. "I Climb the Mesas in My Dreams: An Interview with Paula Gunn Allen." In *Survival This Way: Interviews With Native American Poets*. Joseph Bruchac, ed. Tucson: University of Arizona Press, 1987, 1-22.

Allen discusses the influences on her poetry, the song structure she favors, her mixed blood ancestry, Indian women, and important experiences and authors who have influenced her.

1222. Bruchac, Joseph. "Interview with Joy Harjo." *North Dakota Quarterly* 53, 2 (Spring 1985): 220-34.

Harjo discusses her poetry including an analysis of the recurring character of Noni Daylight, the development of her interest in writing, and the women who have influenced her writing.

1223. Bruchac, Joseph. "An Interview with Wendy Rose." *Greenfield Review* 12, 1-2 (Summer/Fall 1984): 43-75. Rpt. *Survival This Way*. Joseph Bruchac, ed. Tucson: University of Arizona Press, 1987, 87-104.

Rose discusses the themes and meanings of several poems, female imagery, and the place of ethnic writers in American literature. Seven poems follow the interview.

1224. Bruchac, Joseph. "Massaging the Earth: An Interview with Roberta Hill Whiteman." In *Survival This Way: Interviews with Native American Poets*. Joseph Bruchac, ed. Tucson: University of Arizona Press, 1987, 323-35.

Whiteman discusses making a book in terms of making a quilt, her difficult childhood which she's beginning to write about, the influence of Richard Hugo in her work, the problem of alienation, and the changing conception of reality.

1225. Bruchac, Joseph. "A *MELUS* Interview: Luci Tapahonso." *MELUS* 11 (Spring 1984): 88-91.

Tapahonso was born in Shiprock, New Mexico, and graduated from the University of New Mexico in 1980. A poet influenced by Leslie Silko, Tapahonso talks about her own work, the importance of the Navajo language to her, and her relationship with other Indian writers.

1226. Bruchac, Joseph. "The Story of All Our Survival: An Interview with Joy Harjo." In *Survival This Way: Interviews with Native American Poets*. Joseph Bruchac, ed. Tucson: University of Arizona Press, 1987, 87-103.

Harjo discusses her reliance on contemporary storytelling in her work, the importance of movement balanced by connection to a home place, the connection of Indian life and writing to global tribalism, her use of horse imagery, and the strength of women's writing in the U.S.

1227.   Bruchac, Joseph. "That Beat, That Pulse: An Interview with Diane Burns." In *Survival This Way: Interviews with Native American Poets*. Joseph Bruchac, ed. Tucson: University of Arizona Press, 1987, 43-56.

Burns discusses the difficulties of city living and their influences on her work, popular culture, women's capacity for self-expression, and the pulse of Indian music in her poetry rhythms.

1228.   Bruchac, Joseph. "To Take Care of Life: An Interview with Linda Hogan." In *Survival This Way: Interviews With Native American Poets*. Joseph Bruchac, ed. Tucson: University of Arizona Press, 1987, 119-34.

Hogan discusses her growing identity as a writer, her mixed blood ancestry, estrangement from white culture, her grandmother's influence on her life, and her sense of the political and spiritual nature of writing.

1229.   Bruchac, Joseph. "Whatever is Really Yours: An Interview with Louise Erdrich." In *Survival This Way: Interviews with Native American Poets*. Joseph Bruchac, ed. Tucson: University of Arizona Press, 1987, 73-86.

Erdrich discusses her boarding school experiences, her mixed background, her collaboration with her husband Michael Dorris, stereotyping of Indians, her sense of place, how women realize their power, and the storytelling tradition in her family.

1230.   Brumble, H. David III. *American Indian Autobiography*. Los Angeles: UCLA Press, 1988.

Critical study of American Indian first person narratives is the first attempt at a comprehensive analysis of Indian autobiography forms and dominant themes. A very small proportion of the book addresses women's narratives.

1231. Buehrle, Marie Cecilia. *Kateri of the Mohawks*. Milwaukee: Bruce Publishing, 1954.

Biography of a Mohawk woman who was scarred by smallpox, never married, was converted by the Jesuits, and ministered to her people.

1232. Burt, Olive. *Sacajawea*. New York: Franklin Watts, 1978.

Brief biography of Sacajawea illustrated with authentic prints and documents. The account relies on the journals of Lewis and Clark as well as other published accounts of Sacajawea's life.

1233. Butterfield, Nancy. "Roleen Hargrove." *Pacific Northwest* 24, 12 (December 1990): 42-43.

A brief profile of Puyallup tribal chairwoman Roleen Hargrove who guided the $162 million Puyallup lands claim settlement. A 1970s grass-roots leader, she fought to obtain basic services for tribal members. Hargrove is also a successful business woman, was instrumental in the Puyallup participation in the 1990 Goodwill Games Trade Exhibition, and is spearheading negotiations for business ties with Pacific Rim countries and the tribe's port facilities. She credits her grandmother with opening the door for her entrepreneurship with a trust-fund she invested in property.

1234. Callihoo, Victoria. "Our Buffalo Hunts." *Alberta Historical Review* 8, 1 (1960): 24-25.

Callihoo, a Cree/Iroquois, recalls going on her first hunt at thirteen and gives a detailed account of the series of events from the onset of the journey through the making of pemmican from the dried meat.

1235.   Cameron, Barbara. "Gee, You Don't Seem Like an Indian
         from the Reservation." In *This Bridge Called My Back:*
         Writings by Radical Women of Color. Gloria Anzaldua and
         Cherrie Moraga, eds. New York: Kitchen Table; Women of
         Color Press, 1981, 46-52.

         Brief personal account by a Lakota woman who explores
         the issue of identity for herself and for other Indians
         confronted with racism.

1236.   Campbell, Maria. *Halfbreed*. Toronto, Canada: McClelland and
         Stewart, 1973; Rpt. Lincoln: University of Nebraska Press,
         1982.

         A contemporary autobiography of a Metis woman, this
         narrative includes historical background on Metis in central
         Canada but concentrates primarily on the history of the
         author's family. Extreme poverty and a sense of isolation from
         both Indians and whites are detailed through anecdotes that
         range from serious to comic to bitter. The general theme is
         one of breakdown in government, community, schools, family
         and personal life. The narrative is confessional in tone as the
         author describes her bad marriage, drug addiction and
         prostitution, and drinking problems, but there is a tenacious
         sense of hope in the reuniting of her family and her success in
         returning to a normal life.

1237.   Canfield, Gae Whitney. *Sarah Winnemucca of the Northern*
         Paiutes. Norman: University of Oklahoma Press, 1983.

         A biography of Sarah Winnemucca that fills in areas of her
         life not covered in her autobiography and presents her as a
         woman of intense personal commitment to her tribe and an
         heroic figure in Indian-white relations.

1238.   Carius, Helen Slwooko. *Sevukakmet: Ways of Life on St.*
         Lawrence Island. Anchorage: Alaska Pacific University
         Press, 1979.

In this short book, which is divided into three sections, an Eskimo woman who was born on St. Lawrence Island writes about the history and traditions of her people, how those lifeways were changed by the missionaries and the traders, and how her own life was shaped by her heritage. As a child she had polio and had to learn to deal with the crippling effects of the disease. After twenty years of living in the Lower 48, Carius returned to St. Lawrence Island to live and work as a resource person for the Anchorage schools.

1239.   Carlo, Poldine. *Nulato: An Indian Life on the Yukon*. Caldwell, ID: Caxton Publishers, 1978.

Personal account by an Athabascan woman who grew up in the 1920s and 1930s along the Yukon River. Her grandparents were medicine people and from them she learned about the history and ways of her people. Illustrated with photographs of the author and her family.

1240.   Carlson, Bob. "Grace Lambert." *North Dakota History: Journal of the Northern Plains* 44, 4 (Fall 1977): 8-10.

Part of the North Dakota Oral History Project. Lambert tells of growing up on the Fort Totter reservation in North Dakota.

1241.   Carr, Helen. "In Other Words: Native American Women's Autobiography." In *Life/Lines: Theorizing Women's Autobiography*. Bella Brodzski and Celeste Schenck, eds. Ithaca: Cornell University Press, 1988, 131-53.

Carr discusses Indian women's personal narrative in terms of "interpreting a text in which a marginalized subject speaks a dominant discourse," and sees this genre of writing divided into early works written by Christianized women, anthropological texts, and contemporary texts written by Indian women. She argues and illustrates a case for feminist criticism of Native women's narratives focusing primarily on anthropological works collected and textualized by Truman

Michelson and Ruth Underhill, analyzing them as colonial texts.

1242. Cash, Joseph H. and Herbert T. Hoover, eds. *To Be an Indian: An Oral History*. New York: Holt, Rinehart and Winston, 1971.

Eight Sioux women are included: Celina Goolsby, Neola Walker, Henrietta Chief, Mildred Stinson, Dorothy Lunderman, Mabel Trudell, Meri Pat Cuney, and Lucille Childs.

1243. Castellano, Marlene Brant. "In Loving Memory." *Canadian Woman Studies* 10, 2 & 3 (Summer/Fall 1989): 25-26.

Tribute to Pearl Brant by her daughter. Brant died at age eighty-two and was buried at the Tyendinaga Indian Reserve.

1244. Chalmers, John W. "Tekahionwake." *Alberta Historical Review* 22 (1974): 24-25.

Mohawk poet Pauline Johnson is described as a popular entertainer who read her works in halls and saloons across Canada and was highly praised for her work. Though her poetry is viewed as naive and sentimental today, her tribal pride and haunting rhythms make her Victorian style verses deserving of respect.

1245. Chandler, Milford G. "Sidelights on Sacajawea." *Masterkey* 43 (1969): 58-66.

Account of the Lewis and Clark expedition with special reference to Sacajawea and the historical research which has been done to substantiate her identity and role in the experience.

1246. Chona, Maria. *Papago Woman*. Ruth M. Underhill, ed. 1936; Rpt. New York: Holt, Rinehart, and Winston, 1979.

Lyrically narrated, with detailed descriptions, dialogue and interpretation, this full life story of a Papago woman, born in 1845, incorporates song, ceremony, and curing rituals as well as day-to-day events. As the daughter of a chief, Chona is privy to, and carefully observant of, all aspects of tribal life in her youth. Married to a medicine man who takes her to tribal fiestas and ceremonies, she is constantly in the center of tribal activity. Although she was not untouched by tragedy--the deaths of most of her children, in particular--she is basically positive in her narrative. She is aware of the influence of white presence in Papago territory in her later life, but is minimally affected by it. Chona is a self-conscious narrator, aware of her role as a trusted woman to whom men can speak of serious matters, and of her own special powers in curing. The editor describes Chona as an "executive" woman in her informative discussion of their friendship and work together and of Papago culture.

1247. Chuinard, E. G. "The Actual Role of Bird Woman." *Montana: Magazine of Western History* 26 (1976): 18-29.

Sacajawea's contribution to the Lewis and Clark expedition as a guide was probably minimal, but she was useful as an interpreter and gained services from her own Shoshone tribe for the expedition.

1248. Clark, Ella E. and Margot Edmonds. *Sacagawea of the Lewis and Clark Expedition*. Berkeley: University of California Press, 1979.

The role of Sacajawea in the expedition is traced and an historical perspective on the controversies concerning her part in the journey and her later life and death is developed in order to separate fact from legend.

1249. Clark, Jerry C. and Martha Ellen Webb. "Susette and Susan LaFlesche: Reformer and Missionary." In *Being and Becoming Indian: Biographical Studies of North American Frontiers*. James A. Clifton, ed. Chicago: Dorsey Press, 1989, 137-59.

Susette LaFlesche (1854-1903) and Susan LaFlesche (1865-1915), daughters of Joseph LaFlesche, received formal education and used their training to serve the Omaha. Susette was involved in public reform activities and Susan was a medical missionary.

1250.   Clough, Wilson D. "Mini-Aku, Daughter of Spotted Tail." *Annals of Wyoming* 39 (1967): 187-216.

Biography of a young Indian woman who died in 1866 at the age of seventeen. Her story was popularized in Wyoming as the story of Falling Leaf.

1251.   Coles, Robert and Jane Hallowell Coles. "Climbing the Mesas." In *Women of Crisis II: Lives of Work and Dreams*. New York: Delacorte Press/Seymour Lawrence, 1980, 151-92.

Maria, a young "Pueblo" woman resists marriage and motherhood until she meets a Pueblo man working for the Forest Service. They raise their children off reservation but return frequently to the mesa. Her youth is complicated by identity questions that are solved by combining Anglo and Pueblo ways. Though based on taped interviews, this biography is very generalized and the tribe and woman's last names are never identified.

1252.   Coles, Robert and Jane Hallowell Coles. *Women of Crisis: Lives of Struggle and Hope*. New York: Delacorte, 1978.

Includes a biography of an Eskimo known only as Lorna who claims the Arctic wind takes possession of her and puts her in a shamanist state of spirit travel. Her "dream travel" is seen as a response to her dissatisfaction with the constraints of village life. The biography ends with her traveling, literally, in a small plane.

1253.   Coles, Robert and Jane Hallowell Coles. "'Women of Crisis'--Lorna Free Spirit of the North." *MS* 7, 1 (July 1978): 54-55, 76-80.

Excerpt from Coles' book about an Eskimo woman who became a force for change in her Native village.

1254. Colson, Elizabeth, ed. *Autobiographies of Three Pomo Women*. Berkeley: Archaeological Research Facility, Department of Anthropology, University of California, 1974.

Intended to supplement ethnographic work on Pomo culture, these three narratives are concerned primarily with conflicts of traditional and white ways in the lives of women growing up in the early twentieth century. Collected in the 1940s, the accounts reveal regret at the passing of the old ways and recognize the inevitability of the effects of white culture.

1255. Coltelli, Laura, ed. *Winged Words: Native American Writers Speak*. Lincoln: University of Nebraska Press, 1990.

A series of interviews with ten prominent Indian writers including Paula Gunn Allen, Louise Erdrich, Linda Hogan, Joy Harjo, Wendy Rose, and Leslie Marmon Silko. Authors focus their discussion on their work. Includes a substantial bibliography of primary and critical sources on the authors included in the volume.

1256. Colwell, Kristin, Carmen Loie, and Nootura. "Three Inuit Women Speak: Surviving is What Counts." *Canadian Woman Studies* 10, 2 & 3 (Summer/Fall 1989): 58-60.

Three Inuit women discuss their lives, families, and traditions.

1257. Comer, Nancy Axelrad. "Hohake! A Look at the Younger Indian Women." *Mademoiselle* 71, 6 (October 1970): 158-159, 195-98.

The author has interviewed several young Indian women who are activists in their tribes or pursuing academic goals. They all articulately express the frustrations and aspirations facing American Indians in the 1970s.

1258.   Cook-Lynn, Elizabeth. "You May Consider Speaking About Your Art. . .." In *I Tell You Now: Autobiographical Essays by Native American Writers*. Brian Swann and Arnold Krupat, eds. Lincoln: University of Nebraska Press, 1987, 55-63.

This Crow Creek-Sioux woman discusses her childhood desire to be a writer and how writing functions as a means of survival for her and as a means of expressing history and events and the legacy of her ancestors to the modern world.

1259.   Cornelius, Melissa. "Reminiscences of an American Indian." In *We Were Children Then*. Vol. 2, Clarice Dunn and Gen Lewis, eds. Madison: Stanton and Lee, 1982, 64-66.

Cornelius, an Oneida, attended Carlisle Indian School and in this brief article tells of learning English, getting tuberculosis, living with a Quaker family, and returning home before graduation because of her mother's illness.

1260.   Coulter, E. Merton. "Mary Musgrove, 'Queen of the Creeks': A Chapter of Early Georgia Troubles." *Georgia Historical Quarterly* 1 (March 1927): 1-30.

Cousaponakeesa, daughter of a white trader, married John Musgrove, ran a trading house, and served as an interpreter in the 1700s.

1261.   Cowan, Susan, ed. *We Don't Live in Snow Houses Now: Reflections of Arctic Bay*. Ottawa: Canadian Arctic Producers, 1976.

This book includes a series of interviews with Arctic Bay residents, several of whom are women. There are photographs, English translations, and Inuktitut text. The interviews chronicle the changes in means of subsistence, housing, education, and society in general. One informant comments, "I still remember it all clearly and if I were to go back to that life I could do it all exactly as I was taught. It's just that we don't live in snow houses now."

1262. Crary, Margaret. *Susette LaFlesche: Voice of the Omaha Indians*. New York: Hawthorn Books, 1973.

Life story of an Omaha woman who was an activist on behalf of her tribe. LaFlesche was born in 1854, the daughter of chief Iron Eyes.

1263. Crosby, Louise. "She Hasn't Changed Her Tune: An Indian Profile." *Plainswoman* 5, 8 (1982): 8-9.

This profile of Elsena Rose Belgarde (Turtle Mountain Chippewa), written by her daughter, praises her for her hard work and her development of a jam and jelly processing plant in Dunseith, North Dakota, as well as for her role as an exemplary mother.

1264. Crow Dog, Mary and Richard Erdoes. *Lakota Woman*. New York: Grove Weidenfeld, 1990.

Mary Crow Dog, wife of American Indian Movement leader Leonard Crow Dog, tells the story of her life before, during, and after the 1973 siege at Wounded Knee. She was thirty-four when she collaborated with Erdoes to present her narrative of the life of a Sioux woman activist in South Dakota.

1265. Cruikshank, Julie. *Athapaskan Women: Lives and Legends*. Canadian Ethnology Service Paper No. 57. Ottawa: National Museums of Canada, 1979.

Report of a project of interviewing and recording biographies of Athapaskan women between the ages of 40 and 85 in the Yukon Territory. Includes excerpts from the biographies and versions of some Athapaskan legends.

1266. Cruikshank, Julie. *Life Lived Like a Story: Life Stories of Three Yukon Native Elders*. Lincoln, NE: University of Nebraska Press, 1991.

Presentation of life stories by three women of Southern Yukon Territory with analysis of narrative strategies and techniques. Includes Angela Sidney, Kitty Smith, and Annie Ned.

1267. Cruikshank, Julie. *The Stolen Woman: Female Journeys in Tagish and Tutchone*. National Museum of Man Mercury Series, Paper No. 87. Ottawa: National Museums of Canada, 1983.

Cruikshank uses narratives from Tagish and Tutchone women in the central and southern Yukon to provide a conceptual framework for understanding the changing roles of women in northern Canada. Two women, Angela Sidney and Kitty Smith, provide the bulk of the Athapaskan myths.

1268. Crying Wind. *Crying Wind*. Chicago: Moody Press, 1977.

Kickapoo artist, short-story writer, and poet, Crying Wind is active in missionary work among American Indian people. Her autobiography, written in a rather fictional style, traces her childhood and youth in a traditional household racked by poverty and dissension. Disillusioned with her life, she seeks solace in peyote ritual but quickly rejects that for conventional Christianity. Her personal narrative incorporates dramatic incidents and dialogue but places emphasis on analysis of her spiritual and emotional responses to the events in her life.

1269. Cuero, Delfina. *The Autobiography of Delfina Cuero: A Diegueno Indian*. Florence Shipek, ed. Los Angeles: Dawson's Book Shop, 1968.

The narrator, now living in Mexico, with no way to reenter the United States, records the destruction of her tribe's self-sufficiency, its culture, and religion when they were forced from their Southern California home by farmers. Because they were never given a reservation, they became nomads and squatters. The narrative includes recollections, the puberty ceremony (defunct by her time), and other remembrances passed down from her grandparents concerning childbirth, healing, and storytelling. The tone is optimistic and uncomplaining despite the concentration of the narrative on the disintegration of old ways and the focus on the tragic effects of poverty and family disintegration experienced in her three marriages. She consistently rejects government help and holds a tenacious hope for reuniting her family and returning to California. Her narration is thoughtful and interpretive and is preceded by an historical introduction.

1270. Daniels, Mary. "Indian Women." *Akwesasne Notes* 3, 5 (1971): 34-35.

Stereotypes of Indian women are attacked by means of contemporary examples of women in leadership and community service roles. Included are Josephine Kelly Pomer, chair of the Standing Rock Sioux tribe; Carol Warrington, a Winnebago activist; Rose Bobidash, secretary of a Chicago Indian service program; Charlene Cooper, an Oneida beauty shop owner; Ann Marr, a lab technician; and Minnie Bacon, an Assiniboine activist.

1271. DeCora, Angel. "Gray Wolf's Daughter." *Harper's New Monthly Magazine* 99 (1899): 860-62.

This brief third person narrative by a Winnebago woman describes the conflict a young school girl feels when she decides to go to boarding school to learn the knowledge of the white man. The author describes the girl's last ceremonial dance and the give-away of her ceremonial clothing and possessions before she departs for school.

1272. DeCora, Angel. "The Sick Child." *Harper's New Monthly Magazine* 98 (1899): 446-48.

This first person narrative by Henook-Makhewe-Kelenaka recalls the death of an infant girl despite the performance of a healing ritual by a medicine man. The narrator recalls being sent by a medicine woman to make an offering to a spirit on behalf of her sick sister and her fear, when her sister died, that she had not performed the ritual properly.

1273.   Deer, Ada and R. E. Simon, Jr. *Speaking Out*. Chicago: Children's Press, 1970.

         Autobiography of a contemporary Menominee woman of Wisconsin who was active in the restoration of Menominee tribal rights.

1274.   Defenbach, Byron. *Red Heroines of the Northwest*. Caldwell, ID: Caxton Printers, 1929.

         Stories of Sacajawea, the Dorian woman, and Jane Silcott. Indian women are categorized as heroines for saving whites from the "savages."

1275.   Dominguez, Chona. "Bygone Days." *Cahuilla Texts*. Bloomington: Indiana University Press, Language Science Monographs 6 (1970): 148-52.

         This is an extremely brief life history of a Cahuilla Indian woman, which is actually a case history used to illustrate an ethnographic and linguistic study of Cahuilla Indians.

1276.   Duncan, Kunigunde. *Blue Star, as Told From the Life of Corabelle Fellows*. Caldwell, ID: The Caxton Printers, Ltd., 1938.

         A pioneer teacher among the Sioux, Fellows learned Santee Sioux at her first school and earned the name Blue Star from her female pupils whom she evaluated as equal to Sioux men. She determined to study tribal customs and records observations on both men's and women's activities and roles. She also worked with the Cheyenne and collected lore, especially on women and child rearing.

1277.   Eaton, Terry. *Joy Before Night: The Last Years of Evelyn Eaton*. Wheaton, IL: Theosophical Publishing House, 1988.

         This book is a tribute by the daughter of Evelyn Eaton to her mother who descended from Nova Scotia Micmacs and wrote several books about Native American spirituality.

1278. Eckert, Edward K. and Nicholas J. Amato, eds. *Ten Years in the Saddle: The Memoir of William Woods Averell*. San Rafael: Presidio Press, 1978.

Examines the relationship of Averell and Ah-tlan-tiz-pa, a Navajo woman.

1279. Enos, Lizzie. *Ooti: A Maidu Legacy*. Richard Simpson, ed. Millbrae, CA: Celestial Arts, 1977.

This short book is a record of Maidu life as told by Lizzie Enos, an eighty-seven-year-old woman from northern California. Lizzie Enos's comments are interspersed with explanatory notes by the editor. She tells of the mythology of the people and of the importance of the ooti, the acorn, to Maidu culture. Photographs show the gathering, grinding, and preparation of the acorns.

1280. Evers, Lawrence and Dennis Carr. "A Conversation with Leslie Marmon Silko." *Sun Tracks* 3, 1 (Fall 1976): 28-33.

Evers and Carr interview the author of *Ceremony* as well as of several short stories. Silko discusses the place of the oral tradition in Laguna life.

1281. Farnsworth, Frances Joyce. *Winged Moccasins; the Story of Sacajawea*. New York: Julian Messner, 1954.

Archival research and interviews with Sacajawea's Shoshone descendants provide the framework for this biography. Author uses considerable latitude in reconstructing characters and events from fragmentary data.

1282. Filomena, Isidora [Princess Solano]. "My Years with Chief Solano." Nellie Van de Grift, trans. Hubert Howe Bancroft, ed. *Touring Topics* 22 (February 1930): 39, 52.

Brief but colorful memoir of a northern California Churcto woman who married an important chief of the Suisun Indians, took on Indian identity, interceded for peace and decent treatment of enemies, observed traditional life, and compares it to the harsh subjection of Indians by whites.

1283.   Finks, Theodore, ed. "The First Indian Woman Physician." *Home Mission Monthly* 38, 4 (February 1924): 86-87.

Autobiographical sketch of physician Susan LaFlesche.

1284.   Finney, Frank F., Sr. "Maria Tallchief in History: Oklahoma's Own Ballerina." *Chronicles of Oklahoma* 38 (Spring 1960): 8-11.

This is a brief biographical account of ballerina Maria Tallchief with historical references to her family.

1285.   Fisher, Dexter. "Stories and their Tellers: A Conversation with Leslie Marmon Silko." In *The Third Woman*. Boston: Houghton Mifflin, 1980, 18-23.

Silko discusses community, sense of place, humor, myth, storytelling, and the relationship of tradition, environment, culture, and contemporary writing. Comments on how these issues relate to her novel *Ceremony*.

1286.   Fitzgerald, James and John Hudak. "Leslie Silko 'Storyteller.'" *Persona* (1980): 21-38.

Interview with the Laguna author about her writing.

1287.   Folsom, Ken. "The Home and Its Outlook: The Careers of Three Indian Women." *The Congregationalist and Christian World* 89, 11 (March 12, 1904): 374-75.

Three Indian women, an Arikara, an Omaha and a Winnebago, are described as models of domestic skill and behavior, though one, Susan LaFlesche is historically much better known as a physician and author; Angel De Cora was an artist of considerable success.

1288.   Forbes, Jack D., ed. *Nevada Indians Speak*. Reno: University
          of Nevada, 1954.

          Among the narratives anthologized in this work are several
          by Indian women who represent a fairly broad spectrum of
          tribal experiences. None of the narratives is long enough to be
          considered a full autobiography. All are concerned with first
          encounters with whites and the struggle to retain traditional
          ways.

1289.   Foreman, Carolyn Thomas. "Aunt Eliza of Tahlequah."
          Chronicles of Oklahoma 9 (1931): 43-55.

          A tribute to Eliza Missouri Busyhead, the daughter of a
          half-blood Cherokee and a missionary.

1290.   Foreman, Carolyn Thomas. "A Creek Pioneer: Notes
          Concerning 'Aunt Sue' Rogers and Her Family." *Chronicles
          of Oklahoma* 21, 3 (1943): 271-79.

          Biographical account of a Creek woman, Mrs. Susannah
          Drew Rogers, who represents the changing life style of a
          woman born in Indian territory, and who, before she died, was
          a guest in the White House.

1291.   Foreman, Carolyn Thomas. "A Cherokee Pioneer, Ella Flora
          Coodey Robinson." *Chronicles of Oklahoma* 7 (1929):
          364-74.

          Biography of a Cherokee woman born in 1847.

1292.   Foreman, Carolyn Thomas. *Indian Women Chiefs*. 1954; Rpt.
          Washington, DC: Zenger Publishing, 1976.

          Foreman summarizes the role of women in several tribes:
          Iroquois, Navajo, Chumash, Cherokee, Winnebago, and others.
          She discusses in detail well-known Indian women such as
          Nancy Ward and Sarah Winnemucca as well as lesser-known
          figures.

1293.   Foreman, Carolyn Thomas. "Two Notable Women of the Creek Nation." *Chronicles of Oklahoma* 35 (Autumn 1957): 315-37.

This is a biographical sketch of Mary Lewis Herrod (born 1840s), who was a teacher of Indian children for fifty years, and of her niece Kate Shawahrens (born 1864), who was also a teacher among the Indians.

1294.   Foster, Mrs. W. Garland. *The Mohawk Princess: Being Some Account of the Life of Tekahion-Wake* [E. Pauline Johnson]. Vancouver: Lions' Gate Publishing, 1931.

This is a biography of the Canadian Mohawk poet and includes a bibliography.

1295.   Fowler, Carol. *Daisy Hoee Nampeyo*. Minneapolis: Dillon Press, 1977.

The daughter of Nampeyo was born on the Hopi reservation, but left there as a child for eye surgery in California. She returned to Hopi and married, and later moved to the Zuni Reservation where she perfected both Hopi and Zuni pottery styles and taught pottery to younger women.

1296.   Freeman, Minnie Avdla. *Life among the Qallunaat*. Edmonton: Hurtig Publishers, 1978.

The writer has worked as a translator for the Canadian government since 1957. She was born at Cape Horn in 1936 and tells of her life and childhood in the North and her exposure to whites (Qallunaat), schools, Christianity, and the world outside her close-knit Inuit family.

1297.   French, Alice. *My Name is Masak*. Winnipeg: Peguis Publishers, 1976.

Autobiography of Alice French who grew up in the Northwest territories prior to World War II. Masak (Alice French) was born in 1930 on Baille Island. In telling her life story, Masak provides information on the place of women in traditional Eskimo society. After her mother's death, Masak was sent to a boarding school. Later she lived with her grandmother, a Suptaki (Eskimo doctor), and was boarded with other families. The account ends when Masak is fourteen.

1298. Frisbie, Charlotte J. "Traditional Navajo Women: Ethnographic and Life History Portrayals." *American Indian Quarterly* 6, 1-2 (Spring-Summer 1982): 11-33.

Frisbie analyzes ten basic ethnographies and fourteen published life histories of Navajo men and women to reach conclusions about the lives of Navajo women prior to World War II.

1299. Garbarino, Merwyn S. "Seminole Girl." *Trans-Action* 7 (February 1970): 40-46.

This is the story of "Nellie Green," a Seminole woman who was raised in a chickee, graduated from college, went back to the reservation, and had to deal with the frustration of living in two different worlds.

1300. Garnett, David. *Pocahontas, or the Nonpareill of Virginia*. New York: Harcourt, 1933.

Fictional account of the life of Pocahontas based on documentary research. Author states his intent to "draw an accurate historical picture" in artistic form.

1301. Gehm, Katherine. *Sarah Winnemucca*. Phoenix: O'Sullivan, Woodside, 1975.

A biography of Sarah Winnemucca (1843-91) which focuses on her achievements and importance to Indian people.

1302. George, Jan. "Interview With Louise Erdrich." *North Dakota Quarterly* 53, 2 (Spring 1985): 240-46.

Erdrich discusses her years in North Dakota as a resource for characters and events in her poetry and novels and comments on how she began her writing career and on her *Jacklight* poems.

1303.   Gerson Noel B. *First Lady of America: A Romanticized Biography of Pocahontas*. Richmond, VA: Westover Publishers, 1973.

This is another view of the life of Pocahontas which emphasizes the legendary aspects of her story.

1304.   Giese, Paula. "Free Sarah Bad Heart Bull (and the Other Custer Defendants)." *North Country Anvil* 13 (October/November 1974): 64-71.

The story of Sarah Bad Heart Bull, who was arrested at a demonstration in Custer, South Dakota, protesting the light sentence given to the murderer of her son. Includes a transcription of a radio interview with Bad Heart Bull.

1305.   Glancy, Diane. "Two Dresses." In *I Tell You Now: Autobiographical Essays by Native American Writers*. Brian Swann and Arnold Krupat, eds. Lincoln: University of Nebraska Press, 1987, 167-83.

This Cherokee writer sees poetry as singing against the difficulties of life by promoting stability and hope and a stay against despair. She discusses her childhood, family and education.

1306.   Goldenweiser, Alexander A. "Hanging Flower, the Iroquois." In *American Indian Life*. Elsie Clews Parsons, ed. Lincoln: University of Nebraska Press, 1967.

Brief story of a young woman who rises to an important position in her tribe and comes to influence the selection and eventual deposition of her son as chief. She represents the strong moral force women held among the Iroquois.

1307.   Goncier, B. "Indian Princess of Florida." *Hobbies* 52 (February 1948): 124.

Ulehlah, the daughter of Uctica, chief of the Hirrihigua tribe in Florida, was a southern version of Pocahontas. She pleaded with her father to save the life of a Spaniard Juan Ortiz in 1535.

1308.   Gray, Lynn. "The Power of Words: An Interview with Poet/Artist/Teacher Wendy Rose." *Akwesasne Notes* 17, 6 (Early Winter 1985): 14-15.

Interview with Rose in which she discusses writing, traditions, Indian women and the power of words.

1309.   Green, Norma Kidd. "Four Sisters: Daughters of Joseph La Flesche." *Nebraska History* 45, 2 (June 1964): 165-76.

Based primarily on information from the LaFlesche Family Papers at the Nebraska State Historical Society, this article summarizes the lives of Suzette, Rosalie, Marguerite, and Susan LaFlesche, daughters of Joseph LaFlesche (Iron Eyes), an Omaha chief.

1310.   Green, Norma Kidd. *Iron Eyes' Family: The Children of Joseph LaFlesche*. Lincoln, NE: Johnson Publishing, 1969.

Study of the LaFlesche family traced in letters and historical documents. Several chapters focus on Suzette and Rosalie LaFlesche. The lives of the other daughters, Marguerite and Susan, are also examined.

1311.   Green, Rayna. "Diary of a Native American Feminist." *MS* 11 (July-August 1982): 170-72, 211-13.

Green, then director of the Native American Science Resources Center at Dartmouth College, shares a journal of her experiences with Native American women covering 1977 to 1981.

1312.   Greene, Alma [Gah-wonh-nos-doh]. *Forbidden Voice: Reflections of a Mohawk Indian*. Middlesex, England: Hamlyn Publishing, 1972.

A clan mother of the Mohawk nation, the author recalls traditional stories; ceremonies; political systems and events; gives a biography of the Seneca prophet Handsome Lake; discusses dreams, visions, charms, witchcraft and omens; and expresses her disillusionment with Christianity.

1313.   Gridley, Marion E. *American Indian Women*. New York: Hawthorn Books, 1974.

Eighteen American Indian women are featured. The introductory chapter provides information about the tribal status of Indian women. It attacks both princess and squaw stereotypes, addresses roles of women in clans and myth as well as traditional forms of government. Author uses fictional techniques of dialogue as well as historical data in biography chapters.

1314.   Griffin, Connie. "Relearning to Trust Our Selves: An Interview with Chief Wilma Mankiller, Tahlequah, Oklahoma." *Women of Power* 7 (Summer 1987): 38-40, 72-74.

In this interview Mankiller tells of her childhood which was influenced by the relocation policies of the 1950s and her return home to Oklahoma in the 1970s. She explains her leadership role in terms of her own view of feminism and Indian tradition.

1315.   Gundy, H. Pearson. "Molly Brant--Loyalist." *Ontario History* 14, 3 (1953): 97-108.

Brant is profiled as a Mohawk woman who commanded the respect of Natives, soldiers, ordinary citizens, aristocrats, generals, governors, and the British Secretary of State. She was a woman of high principle who would not renounce her British connection in order to return to the Mohawk Valley after the American Revolution.

1316. Harjo, Joy. "Ordinary Spirit." In *I Tell You Now: Autobiographical Essays by Native American Writers*. Brian Swann and Arnold Krupat, eds. Lincoln, University of Nebraska Press, 1987, 263-75.

Harjo discusses her poetry as an expression of unity in her mixed-blood identity and traces her growth as a poet from her early work to the more complex poems she now writes.

1317. Harner, Nellie Shaw. *Indians of Coo-yo-ee Pah (Pyramid Lake)*. Sparks, NV: Western Printing and Publishing, 1974.

Harner tells the history of the Pyramid Lake Paiutes from the point of view of a Paiute woman who was born there, served for 37 years as a BIA teacher and counselor, and retired to the reservation.

1318. Hauptman, Laurence M. "Alice Jemison: Seneca Political Activist." *Indian Historian* 12, 2 (Summer 1979): 15-22, 60-62.

Alice Jemison (1901-1964) was an activist against the BIA through her organization, the American Indian Federation. Hauptman has examined government records and congressional testimony to document the contributions of this Seneca woman to the struggle of her people.

1319. Hauptman, Laurence M. "Designing Woman: Minnie Kellogg, Iroquois Leader." In *Indian Lives: Essays on Nineteenth and Twentieth-Century Native American Leaders*. L. G. Moses and Raymond Wilson, eds. Albuquerque: University of New Mexico Press, 1985, 159-88.

Kellogg (1880-1949) was one of the founders of the American Indian Association and later the Society of American Indians.

1320. Hauptman, Laurence M. "Medicine Woman Susan La Flesche, 1865-1915." *New York State Journal of Medicine* 78 (1978): 1783-88.

LaFlesche is seen as a doubly exceptional woman for a time when women, let alone an Indian woman, rarely challenged the male domain of medical education and practice. Her background, educational experiences, and role as Omaha agency physician are discussed.

1321.   Hebard, Grace Raymond. *Sacajawea: Guide and Interpreter of the Lewis and Clark Expedition*. Glendale, CA: Arthur H. Clark, 1933.

This is a researched account of the life of Sacajawea with an extensive bibliography.

1322.   Heizer, Robert and Albert B. Elsasser. *Original Accounts of the Lone Woman of San Nichols Island*. Ramona, CA: Ballena, 1973.

Heizer and Elsasser collected accounts of Juana Maria (subject of Scott O'Dell's *Island of the Blue Dolphins*), who spent eighteen years alone on an island off the coast of southern California.

1323.   Herbert, Belle. *Shandaa: In My Lifetime*. Jane McGary, ed. Anchorage: University of Alaska, Alaska Native Language Center, 1982.

Belle Herbert (d. 1982) was a Gwich'in Athabascan woman from Chalkyitsik, Alaska. She recorded her experiences in her Native language, and both the originals and the translation are provided. She tells stories, relates her personal history, and provides historical accounts of life in the Yukon.

1324.   Hewett, Priscilla. "Thoroughly Modest Millie." *Canadian Woman Studies* 10, 2 & 3 (Summer/Fall 1989): 31-32.

Millie Redmond is a Pottawatami from Walpole Island who has been active with the YMCA and with improving conditions for Native women.

1325. Highwalking, Belle. *Belle Highwalking: The Narrative of a Northern Cheyenne Woman*. Edited by Katherine M. Weist. Billings: Montana Council for Indian Education, 1979.

This is an autobiography of a woman born in 1892 who was not involved in tribal politics and who did not have any special knowledge of ceremonies or medicines. She wanted to record her life for her grandchildren, and she spoke in Cheyenne into a tape recorder. Her daughter-in-law, Helen Hiwalker, translated the narrative, and Weist arranged the material and provided notes. She tells of childhood and marriage and includes prayers, ceremonies, and stories. John Stands-in-Timber is Highwalking's half-brother, making possible some comparison of male and female roles within the Cheyenne culture.

1326. Hilger, Sister Mary Inez. *The First Sioux Nun: Sister Marie-Josephine Nebraska, S.G.M., 1859-1884*. Milwaukee: Bruce Publishing Co., 1963.

In this partially fictionalized story, Anapo, Little Dawn, became a sister with the Grey Nuns in 1884. She had been brought up at the Catholic orphanage and joined the sisterhood at St. Boniface, Manitoba.

1327. Hogan, Linda. "The Two Lives." In *I Tell You Now: Autobiographical Essays by Native American Writers*. Brian Swann and Arnold Krupat, eds. Lincoln: University of Nebraska Press, 1987, 231-49.

Hogan sees telling lives as important for future generations and traces not only her own life but those of her ancestors who are the source of her white and Indian identity. She sees her writing as a means of giving life order, discusses the importance of being spiritually conscious, and the force of poetry to address issues of racial justice.

1328. Hommel, Martha Hill. "More than One Pocahontas." *Hobbies* 60 (July 1955): 111-12.

Story of Juan Ortiz and the daughter of Ucita who saved his life and Atala, another Indian woman who saved the life of her lover who was a prisoner.

1329.   Hopkins, Sarah Winnemucca. *Life Among the Paiutes: Their Wrongs and Claims*. Mrs. Horace Mann, ed. New York: G. P. Putnam's Sons, 1883.

Though the work is a sustained first-person narrative, it incorporates oratory, history, ethnography, legend, treaty information, and Indian agent commentary. The daughter of Chief Winnemucca, Sarah Winnemucca spent a good deal of her life fighting unsuccessfully to get better treatment for her people. Because of her status and her skill in English, she was privy to important tribal events, and she reports them with detailed description, including dramatic dialogue. Among the most detailed incidents reported by this woman, born about 1844, is the first encounter of her tribe with whites, when she was only a child. As an adult, she taught school and later married a white man and moved to the East. The inflated Victorian prose style of the text reveals no apparent mark of her first language.

1330.   Howard, Harold P. *Sacajawea*. Norman: University of Oklahoma Press, 1971.

Howard has researched Sacajawea's experiences with the Lewis and Clark expedition and presents what is known of her later life.

1331.   Howard, Helen. "The Mystery of Sacajawea's Death." *Pacific Northwest Quarterly* 58 (1967): 1-6.

Though Sacajawea is among the best known and most widely written about Indian women, very little is actually known about her life and many controversies among historians rage over the mystery of her death. Author cites sources from 1783 through 1865 to piece together evidence concerning her role in the Lewis and Clark expedition and reports of her life and death after the journey.

1332. Hudson, Travis. "An Additional Note on the 'Lone Woman' of San Nicolas." *Masterkey* 52, 4 (October-December 1978): 151-54.

This is a brief addition to Hudson's earlier "find" of material on the "Lone Woman" in John P. Harrington's field notes.

1333. Hudson, Travis. "Some J. P. Harrington Notes on the 'Lone Woman' of San Nicolas." *Masterkey* 52, 1 (January-March 1978): 23-28.

Hudson has edited some of Harrington's notes on his work with the Chumash of Southern California. The "Lone Woman" or "Lost Woman" reportedly lived about 1836 to 1853. Harrington discussed a bone knife and reported on a song the woman sang.

1334. Hungry Wolf, Beverly. *The Ways of My Grandmothers*. New York: William Morrow and Co, 1980.

A member of the Blood group of the Blackfoot tribe of Canada, Beverly Hungry Wolf records the myths, legends, household practices and customs handed down to her from her female relatives and elder women of her tribe. Although the emphasis in her work is on traditional ways, she also focuses on her own life as it was shaped and influenced by the women of her tribe. An educated contemporary woman, she deliberately fosters traditional ways in her daily life and advocates the preservation of traditions for the benefit of future generations. Incorporated into her narrative are the life stories of the women of past generations who have contributed to her vision of Blackfoot life. Not a sequential narrative, the work is centered on various aspects of the teachings of her grandmothers, with personal anecdotes and stories interwoven with thematic material.

1335. Hunter, Carol. "An Interview With Wendy Rose." In *Coyote Was Here: Essays on Contemporary Native American*

Literary and Political Mobilization. Bo Scholer, ed. Aarhus, Denmark: University of Aarhus, 1984, 40-56.

Rose discusses her dual role as anthropologist and writer and denies any intention of being a spokesperson for Native Americans. She comments on the future of Indian literature and her own writing and discusses her poetry in relation to her ethnic identity.

1336.   Hunter, Carol. "A *MELUS* Interview: Wendy Rose." *MELUS* 10, 3 (Fall 1983): 67-87.

Rose, born in 1948, talks about the effects of her urban upbringing, her Miwok/Hopi identity, feminism and her own writing. She explains her goal to complete a comprehensive annotated bibliography of all writing by American Indians in terms of her frustration at the mis-categorization of all works of Indian authors as anthropology, and her desire to make Indian writing available to readers.

1337.   Issuth-Gweks. "An Excerpt from My Memoirs." *The Peak* 5, 15 (April 5, 1967): 11.

A Skeena woman's brief comments about her life.

1338.   Jahner, Elaine. "The Novel and Oral Tradition: An Interview with Leslie Marmon Silko." *Book Forum* 5, 3 (1981): 383-88.

Written in essay form, Jahner incorporates Silko's views on oral tradition as a source for contemporary fiction, the expansiveness of English as a language for fiction, the importance of landscape in her novel *Ceremony*, and the impact of critical attention on Native writers. Silko talks about the use of film to communicate Indian experience and comments about her novel *Ceremony*.

1339.   Joe, Rita. "The Gentle War." *Canadian Woman Studies* 10, 2 & 3 (Summer/Fall 1989): 27-29.

Letter, personal statement, and poem by Native writer Rita Joe.

1340.   Johnson, Broderick H., ed. *The Navajo and World War II*. Tsaile, AZ: Navajo Community College Press, 1977, 47-50; 116-22; 129-33.

This collection includes eleven accounts of men and women on their participation in World War II. Agnes R. Begay worked for the Bellmont Corporation at the Navajo Ordnance Depot and tells of her work and her brothers' participation in the war. Peggy Jane Chee worked in California in the Women's Army Corps. She told her story in Navajo and an English transcription is published. Myrtle Waybenais attended boarding school and BIA schools before joining the Women's Army Corps and going overseas.

1341.   Johnson, Broderick H., ed. *Stories of Traditional Navajo Life and Culture by Twenty-two Navajo Men and Women*. Tsaile, Arizona: Navajo Community College Press, 1977.

Included in this collection of narratives by elderly Navajo people are four life histories by women: Myrtle Begay, Mrs. Bob Martin, Jeanette Blake, and Molly Richardson. Their accounts of traditional life on the reservation include legend, Navajo customs, and philosophy, with emphasis on childhood and boarding school recollections. All four subjects express concern about the modernization of the reservation and deterioration of family and traditional ways.

1342.   Johnson, David L. and Raymond Wilson. "Gertrude Simmons Bonnin, 1876-1938: 'Americanize the First Americans.'" *American Indian Quarterly* 12, 1 (Winter 1988): 27-40.

Born in 1876 at the Yankton Sioux Agency, Gertrude Simmons Bonnin left when she was eight years old to be educated in Wabash, Indiana. She later taught at the Carlisle Indian School and studied music at the Boston Conservatory. She was an active reformer and editor of *American Indian*

Magazine. She gained the support of the General Federation of Women's Clubs for her efforts on behalf of Indians.

1343. Johnson, Thomas H. "Maud Clairmont: Artist, Entrepreneur, Cultural Mediator." In *Being and Becoming Indian: Biographical Studies of North American Frontiers*. James A. Clifton, ed. Chicago: Dorsey Press, 1989, 249-75.

Clairmont's background was Euro-American and Indian, and she was most closely associated with the Wind River Reservation. She was a reformer and teacher during the 1930s and throughout her life had to cope with a dual identity. Her experiences are characteristic of many Indians who were socialized in two cultures. Maud Clairmont was born in 1902 and this study was based on field research between 1966 and 1987.

1344. Kaglik, David, trans. "Susie Tiktalik--From Her Life Story." *Inuvialuit* 6, 3 (Spring 1982): 15-17.

Susie Tiktalik died in 1980 when she was nearly 100 years old. She tape-recorded her memories of life in the North long before any whites were there. She tells of snowhouses, shamanism, and her family.

1345. Kegg, Maude. *Gabekanaansing/At the End of the Trail: Memories of Chippewa Childhood in Minnesota, with Text in Ojibwa and English*. John Nichols, ed. Occasional Publications in Anthropology, Linguistic Series, no. 4 (1978), University of Northern Colorado Museum of Anthropology.

This narration of childhood experiences is published bilingually in English and Ojibwa with a brief introduction and linguistic study by the editor. The first chapter is inter-linear translation, which establishes the translation methodology. The narrative itself focuses on the personal and family life of a woman born in 1904 whose childhood was dominated by traditional customs and food-gathering practices of her people in the lake country of Minnesota. The text is dramatized by extensive dialogue and often made immediate by the use of the present tense in describing particular experiences, such as rice gathering and sugar making. Kinship terms are clarified by the editor, and a glossary is provided. Though episodic, the narration is lively and clear.

1346. Kegg, Maude. *Gii-Ikwezensiwiyaan/When I Was a Little Girl*. John Nichols, ed. Onamia, MN: Private printing, 1976.

In booklet form, this brief childhood memoir (a private printing of seven of the tales from Gabekanaansing) is published in side-by-side Ojibwa and English. The author recalls such traditional tasks as snow-shoe crafting, sap collecting and sugar making, wild rice gathering and drying, and berry picking in Minnesota. Also included are moments of childhood mischief. Dialogue with her grandparents gives the text immediacy and vitality.

1347. Keller, Betty. *Pauline: A Biography of Pauline Johnson*. Vancouver: Douglas, 1981.

Keller develops a critical biography of this Canadian Mohawk poet and short story writer who gained considerable recognition across Canada and travelled widely to make personal appearances.

1348. Kelley, Jane Holden. *Yaqui Women: Contemporary Life Histories*. Lincoln: University of Nebraska Press, 1978.

Narratives of Dominga Tava, Chepa Moreno, Dominga Ramirez, and Antonia Valenzuela with an introduction focusing on the editor's methodology and the background of the Yaqui people. Kelley analyzes characteristics of all Yaqui women on the basis of these four life histories.

1349. Keys, Lucy L. "From the Narratives of Lucy Lowrey Hoyt Keys: The Wahnenauhi Manuscript: Historical Sketches of the Cherokees, Together With Some of Their Customs, Traditions and Superstitions." Jack Frederick Kilpatrick, ed.

Bureau of American Ethnology Bulletin 196. Anthropological Papers 77 (1966): 175-213.

Written in 1889 by a woman whose mother was a full-blood and father white, Lucy Keys's narrative is a fairly comprehensive, though brief, history of her people, beginning with myths and describing the forced move to Oklahoma and the major events in the Cherokee leader Sequoyah's life, as well as the life of her white grandfather, George Lowrey. As an early written text, it is of interest, particularly because of the Victorian language the author acquired while attending the Cherokee Female Seminary. As editor Kilpatrick points out, Wahnenauhi was of the mixed-blood planter class, wealthy and educated. She is surprisingly well informed about her tribal history and customs and fiercely loyal to them. Despite little personal content in the narrative, the style and topics selected give considerable insight into a highly acculturated nineteenth-century mixed-blood woman's psychological and social posture.

1350. Kingston, C. S. "Sacajawea the Guide: Evaluation of a Legend." *Pacific Northwest Quarterly* 35, 1 (January 1944): 3-18.

Despite evidence to the contrary, Sacajawea is popularly seen as the guide who led explorers from Mandan country to the Pacific Coast. Records show that the Lewis and Clark expedition hired several Native guides during the westward journey and relied on tribes for supplies and information on navigable and passable routes. The author argues that had Sacajawea not been a member of the expedition, the journey would have been unaffected. Her usefulness to the journey was as an interpreter and as a woman of industry, character and presence of mind in times of peril. Her fame should be based on these verifiable qualities rather than on fictional deeds.

1351. Knudtson, Peter M. "Flora, Shaman of the Wintu." *Natural History* 84 (May 1975): 6-17.

Biographical account of Flora Jones, a practicing shaman in Northern California. She tells of her helping spirits and doctoring.

1352. Kraus, Carol, ed. "A Shaman's World View: Notes from an Interview with Leslie Gray." *Women of Power* 5 (Winter 1987): 53-55.

Gray (Oneida, Powattan, and Seminole) is a spiritual person who uses her training in psychology and shamanism to counsel and teach. She provides two case studies and discusses her approach.

1353. Kroeber, A. L. *Ethnology of the Gros Ventre*. Washington, DC: American Museum of Natural History, 1908, 216-21. Rpt. New York: AMS Press, 1978.

Includes the narrative of Watches-All as she tells of the battle with the Piegans in 1867, her capture, and eventual escape back to Gros Ventre.

1354. La Duke, Winona. "Interview with Roberta Blackgoat, a Dine Elder." *Women of Power* 4 (Fall 1986): 29-31.

Roberta Blackgoat lives at Big Mountain in the Hopi-Navajo Joint Use Area. She provides information about the forced relocation of the Navajo, and in this interview tells why she refuses to move from her ancestral land.

1355. Landes, Ruth. *The Ojibwa Woman*. New York: Columbia University Press, 1938, 227-47. Rpt. New York: Norton, 1971.

This work contains three life histories of Ojibwa women, none of which are full length narratives, though they do give a fairly complete illustration of family relationships and marriage practices in Ojibwa culture. The narratives are appended to a comprehensive ethnographic study of the role of women in Ojibwa life that also includes briefer case studies related to youth, marriage, and occupations. All three narratives are rather flat in tone with emphasis on events and responses; information useful to ethnographers is included.

1356.   Lane, Sheryl. "'We Don't Make Baskets Any More.'" *Salt: Journal of Northeast Culture* 4 (1979): 4-16.

Interesting interview with Madasa Sapiel, a seventy-five-year-old woman who is half Penobscot and half Passamoquoddy and who lives on "Indian Island" in the midsection of Maine. She tells of the old days and how things have changed. She also tells of the power of Indian women: "As I said, the man walked ahead and the woman walked behind. But she was the law."

1357.   Lantis, Margaret. *Eskimo Childhood and Interpersonal Relationships, Nunivak Biographies with Genealogies.* Seattle: University of Washington Press, 1960.

Recorded in 1946 with sequels collected in 1955-56, these seventeen personal narratives of Bering Sea Island in conjunction with Rorschach tests assess the lives of key men and women in the community. Genealogies place central figures in the community. Analysis is provided in notes keyed to personal narrative texts. Six women are presented, including a shaman and her family. Focus is on adulthood, not childhood as claimed in the title.

1358.   Lee, Bobbie [Lee Maracle]. *Bobbie Lee: Indian Rebel.* Don Barnett and Rich Sterling, eds. Richmond, BC: LSM Information Center, 1975.

This narrative, first of a projected two-volume life story, covers the first twenty years of a quarter-blood Metis woman reared in the Vancouver, B.C., area. Growing up in a turbulent household, Bobbie Lee leaves school and home in her teens to work in California vineyards and later to take up a hippie life-style in Toronto in the 1960s. Upon her return to British Columbia, she becomes involved in the Red Power movement, and the narration traces her growing awareness and involvement in Indian political action, including the fishing rights disputes in the Pacific Northwest during the late 1960s. The tough facade she portrays in her account is countered by a sensitivity to the difficulties of urban Indian life and a growing need to articulate and act upon her sympathies.

1359. Leevier, Mrs. Annette. *Psychic Experiences of an Indian Princess*. Los Angeles: Austin Publishers, 1920.

This autobiography of the daughter of Chief Tommyhawk tells of Leevier's experiences as a medium and healer. Her father was Ojibwa and her mother French. The life story reflects a mixture of Catholicism and belief in traditional religion.

1360. Liberty, Margot, ed. *American Indian Intellectuals*. St. Paul: West Publishing, 1978.

Liberty includes chapters on Sarah Winnemucca and Flora Zuni.

1361. Linder, Jo. *Polingaysi*. Mesa, AZ: Discount Printing, 1985.

This is a self-published tribute to Polingaysi Qoyawaywa (Elizabeth White), author of *No Turning Back*. The collection of letters and photographs was first published when Polingaysi was in her nineties and included a statement written by her from her home in New Orabi on the Hopi Reservation.

1362. Lindsey, Lilah Denton. "Memories of the Indian Territory Mission Field." *Chronicles of Oklahoma* 36 (Summer 1958): 181-98.

Lindsey was one-quarter Creek. She wrote her memories in 1938 of life at the mission school and her experiences as a teacher in Indian Territory.

1363. Little Bear, Mary. *Dance Around the Sun*. Alice Marriott and Carol K. Rachlin, eds. New York: Crowell Publishing, 1977.

This work combines both autobiographical and biographical techniques in relating the life story of Mary Little Bear, a mixed-blood Cheyenne woman. Born in a tipi in the Oklahoma Indian Territory in 1875, Little Bear participated in traditional Sun Dance ceremonies and learned the traditional crafts, particularly beadwork. She was educated in a white boarding school where she met and married a Caddo Indian. Her narrative traces her marriage and the raising of six children during a period of drastic change from traditional life to acculturation. Little Bear is both representative of her tribal ways and highly individual. The latter part of the work concentrates on her craftsmanship and relationship to Alice Marriott and Carol Rachlin, who become her "daughters." Presented primarily in a third person, biographical manner, the narrative is based on recollections told to Marriott and Rachlin over a period of several years before her death in the mid-1960s.

1364.   Lone Dog, Louise. *Strange Journey: The Vision Life of a Psychic Indian Woman*. Vinson Brown, ed. Healdsburg, CA: Naturegraph Co., 1964.

Strange Journey is a book centered on naive spiritualism rather than a true personal narrative. The author is highly acculturated, frequently quoting from Tennyson, Kahlil Gilbran, Dryden, and the Psalms, proselytizing toward spiritual betterment through a very personalized version of vision seeking. Her pursuit of a written treatment of psychic experience is disconnected from her Mohawk or Delaware tribal traditions. The quality of the writing and editing is amateurish, and the work gives a romanticized and extremely narrow view of Indian life that would mislead uninformed readers.

1365.   Lossiah, Aggie Ross. "The Story of My Life as Far Back as I Can Remember." Joan Greene, ed. *Journal of Cherokee Studies* 9, 2 (Fall 1984): 89-98.

Story of Aggie Ross Lossiah who was born in 1880 and wrote her life story in 1960. The story is in Aggie's own words.

She was the great granddaughter of Cherokee Principal Chief John Ross and grew up in east Tennessee.

1366. Lowie, Robert H. "A Crow Woman's Tale." In *American Indian Life*. Elsie Clews Parsons, ed. Lincoln: University of Nebraska Press, 1967, 35-40.

Traditional story of the courtship, marriage and capture, and escape of a woman who is rejected by her Crow husband when she returns. Tale is narrated by an anonymous Crow grandmother.

1367. Lowry, Annie. *Karnee: A Paiute Narrative*. Lalla Scott, ed. Reno: University of Nevada Press, 1966.

The text is a composite of personal narrative supplemented by material from anthropological works, legends, and tales, but all sources are well integrated into the narrative. The focus is on the affinities toward two cultures and the decision to adapt, despite the narrator's realization she will always remain marginal. She says, "I am a half-breed. That means I live on the fringe of two races." The first half of the work begins with the mother's desertion by her white father and traces the subject's life up to her marriage, using dramatic technique and flashback. The second half is more detached and objective, different in both tone and technique, perhaps because it was collected seven years after the first. It voices the subject's regret at disintegration of tribal life and values.

1368. Lurie, Nancy Oestreich. *North American Indian Lives*. Milwaukee: Milwaukee Public Museum, 1985.

Lurie expresses dismay that most of the historical records were made by white men, resulting in a fragmented knowledge about Indian women.

1369. Manitowabi, Edna. *An Indian Girl in the City*. Buffalo, NY: Friends of Malatesta, c. 1971. [Reprinted from "An Ojibwa Girl in the City," *This Magazine Is about Schools* 4, 4 (1970): 8-24.]

The brief autobiography traces the events in the life of a young Ojibwa woman whose life is severely disrupted when she is uprooted from the reservation to attend boarding school. The experience cuts her off from her family and leads to destructive urban incidents that culminate in a suicide attempt and months spent in a mental hospital. In time she comes to terms with her Indian identity and becomes involved in Native language study and revitalization of traditions. The style is terse and self-analytical, more sociological than literary.

1370.   Maracle, Lee. *I Am Woman*. North Vancouver: Write-on Press, 1988.

In this book the author of *Bobbie Lee, Indian Rebel* writes from a greater maturity, examining through her own life the realities of Indian women's experiences in Canada. The series of first-person essays and stories is complemented by Maracle's poetry.

1371.   Marquis, Thomas B. *The Cheyennes of Montana*. Algonac, MI: Reference Publication, 1978.

Includes a brief biography of "Ironteeth, a Northern Cheyenne Woman."

1372.   Marriott, Alice. *Maria, the Potter of San Ildefonso*. Norman: University of Oklahoma Press, 1945.

This is the story of the famous Pueblo potter who revived the traditional black pottery of her tribe. Both her personal life and career as a potter are examined.

1373.   Mathes, Valerie Sherer. "Dr. Susan LaFlesche Picotte: The Reformed and the Reformers." In *Indian Lives: Essays on Nineteenth and Twentieth Century Native American Leaders*. L. G. Moses and Raymond Wilson, eds. Albuquerque: University of New Mexico Press, 1985, 61-90.

This comprehensive essay gives a biographical account of the life of Susan LaFlesche with focus on her achievements as the first Indian woman to practice medicine. The author sees her as typical of her time in her assimilationist attitudes and her middle class dress and behavior.

1374. Mathes, Valerie Sherer. "Susan LaFlesche Picotte: Nebraska's Indian Physician, 1865-1915." *Nebraska History* 63, 4 (Winter 1982): 502-30.

Susan LaFlesche (b. 1865) was the first Indian woman physician. She graduated from Hampton Institute and Women's Medical College of Pennsylvania, returning to her Nebraska reservation in 1889 where she remained to care for Indians until her death in 1915.

1375. McClary, Ben. "Nancy Ward, the Last Beloved Woman of the Cherokees." *Tennessee Historical Quarterly* 21 (December 1962): 352-64.

Life story of Nancy Ward, a mother image for Cherokees since 1755.

1376. McDowell, John E. "Therese Schindler of Mackinac: Upward Mobility in the Great Lakes Fur Trade." *Wisconsin Magazine of History* 61, 2 (Winter 77-78): 125-43.

Story of Therese Schindler and her sister Madeline La Framboise, Indian fur traders on the Mackinac.

1377. McElroy, Ann. "Oopeeleeka and Mina: Contrasting Responses to Modernization of Two Baffin Island Inuit Women." In *Being and Becoming Indian: Biographical Studies of North American Frontiers*. James A. Clifton, ed. Chicago: Dorsey Press, 1989, 290-318.

Two Inuit women born in the 1940s are the subjects of this study of the psychological adaptation of the Inuit to modernization. Oopeeleeka is an activist and teacher; Mina is less involved with her community and less well adjusted to modern life. McElroy explains that family stability enabled Oopeeleeka to adapt more readily.

1378.   McLester, Thelma Cornelius. "Oneida Women Leaders." In *The Oneida Indian Experience*. Jack Campisi and Laurence M. Hauptman, eds. Syracuse, NY: Syracuse University Press, 1988, 108-25.

McLester provides brief biographical sketches of nine women born on the Oneida Reservation in Wisconsin: Laura Minnie Cornelius Kellogg, Melissa Edith Cornelius, Lydia Doxtator Bennett, Josephine Hill Webster, Lydia Wheelock Powless, Evangeline Wheelcok Metoxen, Florence Cornelius Jones, Irene Metoxen Moore, and Pearl Archiquette House.

1379.   McRaye, Walter. *Pauline Johnson and her Friends*. Toronto: Ryerson Press, 1974.

McRaye provides a biography of Tekahionwake, Pauline Johnson, a Mohawk poet of Canada. Her mother was English and her father was Indian. She was born in 1862.

1380.   Meachum, A. B. *Wi-ne-ma (The Woman Chief) and Her People*. Hartford: American Publishing, 1876.

This story of the woman who sought to save the Peace Commission to the Modoc in 1873 was written to tell the Indian side of Modoc-white relations.

1381.   Medicine, Bea. "Ella C. Deloria: The Emic Voice." *MELUS* 7, 4 (Winter 1980): 23-30.

Discusses Deloria's role as a "cultural mediator." She was a Yankton Dakota woman who was linguistic informant for Boas and developed her own skills as an anthropologist.

1382.   Medicine Eagle, Brooke. "Singing Buffalo Woman's Song: Eulogy for an Activist." *Women of Power* 9 (Spring 1988): 58-59.

In this tribute to Nancy Swansow, Medicine Eagle also pays tribute to the natural world and to Lakota women.

1383.   Meekitjuk, Annie. "Miss Annie Meekitjuk." *Canadian Indians and Eskimos of Today* 4 (May 1966).

In this autobiographical account Meekitjuk tells of her early life at Baffin Island and later at Frobisher Bay. Writing this at age 20, she admonishes Indian students to stay in school and take advantage of educational opportunities.

1384.   Michelson, Truman. "The Autobiography of a Fox Indian Woman." *Bureau of American Ethnology Fortieth Annual Report* (1925): 291-349.

Recorded in 1918, this is primarily a nineteenth-century narrative that concentrates on the teller's role as a woman in traditional culture. There is a fairly complete description of her instruction in traditional skills, behavior and virtue, her participation in puberty ceremonies, and marriage, childbirth and child-rearing experiences. The text is heavily weighted to advice she received from her elders on all aspects of her life. The tone and prose style is somewhat bland, lacking in detail and emotional description necessary for vitality. Stiff dialogue is partly responsible for this, but the subject's obvious passivity and lack of independence is the major factor. Despite the lack of spirit, she narrates a wide variety of tribal and personal events with a tone of satisfaction with her life. Good ethnological and linguistic notes accompany the narrative.

1385.   Michelson, Truman. "Narrative of an Arapaho Woman." *American Anthropologist* 35 (October-December 1933): 595-610.

The narrator does not develop an intimate portrait of herself, but through random recollections, rather than straightforward chronology, records the events of, and her responses to, her four marriages, the final one to a chief. The lack of detail by the seventy-seven-year-old narrator is, she reports, a mark of respect for the male members of her family. Michelson's footnotes are useful and nonintrusive.

1386.   Michelson, Truman. "The Narrative of a Southern Cheyenne
          Woman." *Smithsonian Miscellaneous Collections* 87 (1932):
          1-13.

          This brief narrative develops a characterization of an
          independent, confident, yet innocent and dutiful daughter much
          loved by her family. The narration develops a strong sense of
          personality, but the focus on the narrator is lost in details of
          ceremony and ritual in the last few pages. Ethnological
          footnotes are helpful in comprehending rituals and tribal ways
          in this narrative collected in 1931.

1387.   Miller, Carol. "The Story is Brimming Around: An Interview
          with Linda Hogan." *Studies in American Indian Literatures*
          2, 4 (Winter 1990): 1-9.

          Hogan, a Chickasaw poet and novelist, talks about her
          composing processes and her book *Mean Spirit*. She also
          discusses her identity and connections with Oklahoma.

1388.   Miller, Jay. *Mourning Dove, A Salishan Autobiography*. Lincoln:
          University of Nebraska Press, 1990.

          A partial manuscript left at her death in 1936 has been
          organized and edited. Mourning Dove narrates her views of
          life on the Colville reservation in the late nineteenth century
          and early twentieth century. Includes detailed commentary on
          the traditional roles of women in respect to religious training,
          courtship, marriage, domestic life, child rearing, and
          widowhood. More focus on seasonal activities and tribal history
          than personal narration and revelation.

1389.   Minor, Nono. "The American Indian: Famous Indian Women
          in Early America." *Real West* (March 1971): 35, 78.

          Brief biographies of Indian women other than Pocahontas
          and Sacajawea are evidence of the important roles tribal
          women have played in the history of North America. Kateri
          Tekakwitha (Mohawk), "Queen Anne" (Paumunkey), Mary

Bosomworth/ a.k.a. Musgrove and Mathews (Creek), and Susan LaFlesche (Omaha) are discussed.

1390. Modesto, Ruby and Guy Mount. *Not for Innocent Ears*. Angelus Oaks, CA: Sweetlight Books, 1980.

This collection of materials on Cahuilla curing practices contains a brief autobiographical narrative from a medicine woman as well as her versions of several folktales; however, the work is heavily interpreted by Mount with the intention of advocating a "spiritual" understanding of holistic medicine and relies heavily on Mount's adherence to the tenets of Carlos Castaneda's books. What personal narrative exists is superficial because of the manipulation of the co-author and is more ethnographic than literary.

1391. Moran, Bridget and Mary John. *Stoney Creek Woman: The Story of Mary John*. Vancouver: Tillacum Library, 1988.

Mary John, a Carrier Indian in British Columbia, told the story of her life to Bridget Moran, a social worker who has spent over thirty years on reserves in Canada. Life on the Stoney Creek Reserve was harsh and the people there endured the racism of the Canadian government along with illness and poverty. She recollects the influence of other family members, the mission schools, and the Indian Act on her life and tells of her efforts to revive the Carrier language and teach traditional ways to young Indians. There is no information on the methodology Moran employed.

1392. Morris, Terry. "LaDonna Harris: A Woman Who Gives a Damn." *Redbook* 134, 4 (February 1970): 74, 115, 117-18.

Comanche LaDonna Harris is profiled for her work in founding Oklahomans for Indian Opportunity which promotes Indian leadership. The profile includes a brief biography and discussion of her work for off-reservation Indians over the past decade.

1393.   Morrison, Dorothy Nafus. *Chief Sarah: Sarah Winnemucca's Fight for Indian Rights*. New York: Athenaeum, 1980.

This Paiute woman served as interpreter for O. O. Howard and attempted to help others understand Indian rights and needs. Book is based on her autobiography and other records. Illustrated.

1394.   Morton, Henri Mann and James Prier Morton. "Doctor--Doctor." *Winds of Change* 5, 1 (Winter 1990): 54-58.

Biographical sketch of Henri Mann Morton, a Cheyenne woman from Oklahoma who is currently Director of Native American Studies at the University of Montana.

1395.   Moses, L. G. and Raymond Wilson. *Indian Lives: Essays on Nineteenth and Twentieth Century Native American Leaders*. Albuquerque: University of New Mexico Press, 1985.

This collection of essays on prominent American Indians contains analytical biographies of Minnie Kellogg, Nampeyo and Susan LaFlesche which interpret their lives in the context of their work, times, and influence within their tribes and nationally.

1396.   Mossiker, Frances. *Pocahontas: The Life and the Legend*. New York: Alfred A. Knopf, 1976.

A critical biography of Pocahontas is told in the context of historical and political events beginning in 1607. The author also traces the representation of Pocahontas in legend and literature and attempts to sort out fact from fiction based on historical materials and records of the Rolfe family. A useful bibliography and illustrations of Pocahontas as depicted in art from 1650-1956 are included.

1397.   Mountain Wolf Woman. *Mountain Wolf Woman, Sister of Crashing Thunder: The Autobiography of a Winnebago Indian*. Nancy Oestreich Lurie, ed. Ann Arbor: University of Michigan Press, 1961.

This narrative spans a period of traditional Winnebago life from thriving hunting and ceremonial practices to the period of dispersal and government dole, tracing the life of the narrator through childhood, marriages, and conversion to peyotism. The narrative style is rather flat, but detail is abundant and the variety of experiences broad. The work is especially valuable in relationship to her brother's autobiography edited by Paul Radin.

1398. Murray, William H. *Pocahontas and Pushmataba: Historical and Biographical Essays with Personal Sketches of Other Famous Indians and Notes on Oklahoma History.* Oklahoma City: Harlow Publishing, 1931.

Pocahontas is depicted as an "ambassadress" between Natives and colonists. Her conversion to Christianity, marriage to John Rolfe, and her trip to England where she died are described, and seven generations of descendants in public life are enumerated.

1399. Nelson, Mary Carroll. *Annie Wauneka.* Minneapolis: Dillon Press, 1972.

This is a biography of the first woman elected to the Navajo Tribal Council and winner of the Medal of Freedom in 1963. Wauneka has been a crusader for improved health care for the Navajo.

1400. Nelson, Mary Carroll. *Maria Martinez.* Minneapolis: Dillon Press, 1974.

Maria Martinez is famous among Southwest Indian potters as the woman who rediscovered the traditional black-on-black technique that had been lost for generations. The story, however, does more than trace the complex search for the exact process of the old technique. Martinez's narrative details the relationship of herself and her art to her family, personal loss and tragedy, and the passing on of her art to her family and tribe. Because the impact of her pottery raised the standard of life for the whole village, she was called the Mother of the Pueblo.

1401.   Nelson, Mary Carroll. *Pablita Velarde*. Minneapolis: Dillon Press, 1971.

This is a biography of the Tewa artist Pablita Velarde, born in 1918 at Santa Clara Pueblo. Velarde used the traditional art forms of her people; the book discusses the conflicts between the artist's Indian heritage and the Anglo world.

1402.   Nicholas, Ellen. *Images of Oregon Women*. Salem, OR: Madison Press, 1983.

This collection includes a brief biography and career profile on Faith Wright Mayhew (Klamath) who is an activist for tribal causes in the Northwest.

1403.   Nowik, Nan. "Interview with Louise Erdrich." *Belles Lettres* (November/December 1986): 9.

Erdrich's preference for first person narrative is illustrated with discussion of *The Beet Queen* and some comments on *Love Medicine*. Her fiction is described as "short story sequences that transcend themselves to become novels."

1404.   Nunez, Bonita Wa Wa Calachaw. *Spirit Woman*. Stan Steiner, ed. New York: Harper and Row, 1980.

Drawn from diaries and autobiographical fragments, this work is a loose series of episodes in the life of a Luiseno Indian woman born in 1888 who was raised by a prominent New York family. She was trained in art and sciences, considered a child prodigy, and later in life became an active spokeswoman for Indian causes. The tone of the material is rather obscurely psychic, in part because of the nonstandard English usage and syntax that makes the material difficult to comprehend. The author's rather mystical approach to her experiences casts some suspicion on the reliability of the work, but the text does record the distress caused by isolation from her natural heritage and the efforts of the author to create an Indian identity in an alien environment.

1405. O'Brien, Lynne W. *Plains Indians Autobiographies*. Boise: Boise State College, 1973.

Plains autobiography is related to traditional tribal pictography and analyzed as an outgrowth of oral narrative, O'Brien analyzes only one narrative by a woman, the Crow Pretty Shield.

1406. Ohoyo Resource Center. *Resource Guide of American Indian-Alaska Native Women*. Newton, MA: WEEA Publishing Center, 1980.

A biograhical listing of contemporary American Indian and Alaskan women who have served in a variety of occupations and services and who have improved the lives of Indian people.

1407. Ortiz, Bev. "Beyond the Stereotypes." *News From Native California* 5, 1 (November/January 1990-91): 32-33.

In a brief article, Ortiz profiles Vivian Hailstone and Genny Mitchell, two women active in presenting accurate information about Indian life to school children in California.

1408. Ortiz, Bev. "Laura Fish Somersal, 1892-1990." *News From Native California* 5, 1 (November/January 1990-91): 4-5.

Laura Fish Somersal was a Pomo basketmaker in Northern California, a museum consultant, and a carrier of tradition. Somersal received the Woman of Achievement Award in Sonoma County and was honored for her community work.

1409. Owens, Narcissa. *Memoirs of Narcissa Owens*. 1907; Rpt. Siloam Springs, AR: Siloam Springs Museum, 1980.

A written, nonsequential memoir, this narrative by a well-educated, genteel and scholarly Victorian woman whose grandfather was the last hereditary Cherokee war chief includes a brief history of her tribe, a family genealogy, descriptions of curing practices, vignettes of friends, family members, and important Cherokee leaders, as well as her experiences living in the South during the Civil War and later as a teacher at the Cherokee Female Seminary. The memoir is addressed to her family to preserve her knowledge of history and tribal ways and also fills her purpose to "show the world that the Cherokees were a cultured and civilized people."

1410.   Parrish, Otis and Paula Hammett. "Parrish: A Pomo Shaman." *Native Self-Sufficiency* 6 (1981): 8-9.

A spiritual leader of her tribe, Essie Parrish was a healer and visionary and a mediary with white culture. Before her death in 1979, she served as a role model in a tribe where the female role is dominant.

1411.   Parrott, Robert E. "One Day in August." *The Christian Century* 104, 23 (August 12-19, 1987): 679-80.

Parrott recollects an event in his family history. Only when his mother was ninety-three did she reveal that she was a Cherokee-Creek woman. Her reluctance was based on her own mother's deathbed advice never to tell anyone she was an Indian.

1412.   Pence, Mary Lou. "Ellen Hereford Washakie of the Shoshones." *Annals of Wyoming* 22 (1950): 3-11.

This is a biographical account of a woman of Fort Washakie, Wyoming.

1413.   Peter, Katherine. *NEETS' AII GWIINDAII: Living in the Chandalar Country*. Fairbanks: University of Alaska Press, 1981.

Peter's story from 1927 to 1947. Bilingual text in Gwwich'in and English. This is the first extended narrative in that language. Narrator was orphaned and raised by Esias and Katherine Loola of Ft. Yukon.

1414. Petrone, Penny, ed. *First People, First Voices*. Toronto: University of Toronto Press, 1983.

Writings and speeches from the 1630s to the 1980s. Includes a number of contemporary Indian women of Canada.

1415. Phillips, Leon. *First Lady of America: A Romanticized Biography of Pocahontas*. Richmond, VA: Westover Publishing, 1973.

Phillips attempts to tell, free from legend, the story of the historical Pocahontas.

1416. Pitseolak. *Pitseolak: Pictures Out of My Life*. Dorothy Eber, ed. Seattle: University of Washington Press, 1972.

This narrative with text in Eskimo as well as English relates the story of an Eskimo artist from Cape Dorset on Baffin Island. The narrative includes drawings that relate to her telling of childhood events, her marriage and childbearing experiences, and the effect of new ways on her life and traditions in her arctic society.

1417. Poelzer, Dolores T. and Irene A. Poelzer. *In Our Own Words: Northern Saskatchewan Metis Women Speak Out*. Saskatoon, Saskatchewan: Lindenblatt & Hamonie, 1986.

The life experiences and perceptions of several Metis women of northern Saskatchewan, organized and categorized according to topics and insights that surfaced in the interviews with the women.

1418. Potts, Marie. *The Northern Maidu*. Happy Camp, CA: Naturegraph, 1977.

An eighty-one-year-old Maidu traditionalist writes of her own experiences and the life and history of her people.

1419. Preston, Sarah C. "Why Did Alice Go Fishing: Narrative from the Life of a Cree Woman." In *Papers of the Eleventh*

Algonquian Conference. William Cowan, ed. Ottawa: Carleton University, 1980, 71-78.

Brief narrative from a twenty-year old Cree woman. Although the account focuses on adversity, Alice Jacob introduces humor into the account of her fishing trip.

1420.   Pretty-shield. *Pretty-shield, Medicine Woman of the Crows*. Frank B. Linderman, ed. Lincoln: University of Nebraska Press, 1972. (Originally published as *Red Mother*, 1932.)

Born in the 1850s, this Crow woman is reluctant to discuss reservation times, expressing confusion and regret over deterioration of old ways. Although there is no detailed discussion of her role as medicine woman, she is from an important Crow family and gives detailed attention to events in her childhood and early maturity, incorporating myth, legend, and historical event into her narrative. The story is roughly chronological, its order dictated by the format of a dialogue with editor-recorder Frank Linderman. This methodology leads to intrusion of the editor and excessive commentary by him.

1421.   Price, Anna [Her Eyes Grey]. "Personal Narrative of Anna Price." In *Western Apache Raiding and Warfare*. Keith H. Basso, ed. Tucson: University of Arizona Press, 1971, 29-39.

Limited to childhood observations, this narrative actually relates the war and raiding activities of Price's father, an influential chief of the White Mountain Apache tribe, during their conflicts with Mexican and Navajo enemies. Some details of the author's childhood are related.

1422.   Qoyawayma, Polingaysi [Elizabeth Q. White]. *No Turning Back: A True Account of a Hopi Girl's Struggle to Bridge the Gap between the World of Her People and the World of the White Man*. Vada F. Carlson, ed. Albuquerque: University of New Mexico Press, 1964.

This full-length personal narrative by a Hopi woman born at the end of the nineteenth century focuses on the conflicts and difficulties she faced on account of her choice in early youth to live in the white world. The narrative includes legend, ceremony, and ritual, but the emphasis is on the individual process of acculturation while still preserving effective ties to tribal traditions and values.

1423. Quam, Alvina, trans. *The Zunis: Self-Portrayals by the Zuni People*. New York: New American Library, 1974.

This collection of oral narratives was recorded in 1965 by Zuni storytellers. It includes legends, myths and history and marks one of the first attempts by a tribe to record its own materials. The book is divided into categories of narratives on society, religion, war and defense, and fables. Includes women narrators.

1424. Ray, Verne. *Primitive Pragmatists*. Seattle: University of Washington Press, 1963.

Includes a 1930s account by Jenny Clinton, born in 1858 at Tule Lake, who moved to Oklahoma and returned to the Klamath Reservation in 1903.

1425. Reed, T. B. and Elsie Clews Parsons. "Cries-for-Salmon, a Ten'a Woman." In *American Indian Life*. Elsie Clews Parsons, ed. Lincoln: University of Nebraska Press, 1967, 337-63.

The life of Cries-for-Salmon is a vehicle for narrating the elements of a girl's education, domestic roles, and coming to power as a central figure in her village in her old age and as a conservative force against the intrusion of white values.

1426. Reichard, Gladys A. *Dezba, Woman of the Desert: Life among the Navajo Indians*. New York: J. J. Augustin, 1939. Rpt. Glorieta, NM: Rio Grande Press, 1971.

First published in 1939 to tell the story of an Indian woman over 60 years old, the incidents and details are true, but the relationships and specific episodes are fictionalized.

1427. Reid, Russell. "Sakakawea." *North Dakota History* 30 (January-October 1963): 101-10.

Reid discusses Sacajawea's identity based on the 1812 journal of John Luttig, a clerk for the Missouri Fur Company.

1428. Remley, David. "Sacajawea of Myth and History." In *Women in Western American Literature*. Helen Winter Stauffer and Susan J. Rosowski, eds. Troy, NY: Whitson Press, 1982, 70-89.

Acknowledging the disparate versions of the life of the "real" Sacajawea, Remley examines what is known about the guide to the Lewis and Clark Expedition from the journals of the voyage. He also traces the evolution of the myths of Sacajawea through popular literature.

1429. Richey, Elinor. "Sagebrush Princess with a Cause: Sarah Winnemucca." *American West* 12 (November 1975): 30-33, 57-63.

Discussion of the life of Paiute Sarah Winnemucca and her involvement with whites, her fondness for them, and her realization of the injustices her people had suffered since the white invasion. Her dream that the Indian hope of survival lay in emulating whites was shattered by indiscriminate killing of her people and the eventual relocation of her people in the Washington Territory.

1430. Richey, Elinor. *Eminent Women of the West*. Berkeley: Howell-North Books, 1975.

One chapter (pp. 125-151) focuses on Sarah Winnemucca, the Paiute woman who served her people by representing them to the government and acting as an interpreter.

1431. Robertson, Wyndam. *Pocahontas, Alias Matoaka, and Her Descendants*. Baltimore: 1887; reprinted Genealogical Publishing, 1968.

Genealogy of Pocahontas.

1432. Robinson, William G. "Sahakawea/Sacajawea--When and Where Did the Indian Bird Woman Die and Where Was She Buried?" *The Wiiyohi* (Pierre: South Dakota Historical Society) 10 (September 1956): 1-8.

Controversy about whether Sacajawea died at Wind River or at Fort Manuel is examined in light of journals and other documents and oral tradition. The author argues that she died at Fort Manuel, but makes no claim as to where she is buried.

1433. Rose, Wendy. "Neon Scars." In *I Tell You Now: Autobiographical Essays by Native American Writers*. Brian Swann and Arnold Krupat, eds. Lincoln: University of Nebraska Press, 1987, 251-61.

Rose discusses her biography in terse terms to emphasize her sense of isolation as a child and her emergence into a balanced, connected life in spite of the hardships of her past. She ends her essay on the promise of rebuilding herself on her Hopi roots.

1434. Ryan, Matthew. "Interview with Anna Lee Walters." *Wildfire* 4, 3 (Summer 1989): 16-21.

Matthew Ryan interviews Walters about her newest book, *Ghost Singer*, which deals with the "ownership of Indian artifacts and relics." The Smithsonian is used as the setting for her novel.

1435. Sanapia. *Sanapia, Comanche Medicine Woman*. David E. Jones, ed. New York: Holt, Rinehart and Winston, 1972.

A twentieth-century autobiography by a Comanche woman deeply affected by peyote culture and Christianity, this story is both a personal and cultural history with inclusion of detailed ethnographic material which she hopes to pass on to influential members of her tribe. The intention of the author to address information and personal narrative to her own tribal members sets this text apart from others, most of which are aimed at white audiences.

1436.   Sanford, M. C. "Sacajawea, The Birdwoman." *Women's Home Companion* 32 (June 1905): 5.

A brief history of Sacajawea's activities as a guide to the Lewis and Clark expedition depicts her as an American heroine and relates her trek to the Pacific to the 1905 Lewis and Clark Exposition in Portland, Oregon.

1437.   Sapir, Edward and Harry Hoijer. *Navajo Texts*. Iowa City: Linguistic Society of America, 1942.

A section on personal narrative includes "The Story of a Navajo Woman Captured by the Utes" who escapes and returns home to her hogan. Another kidnap story is entitled "The Near-Water Woman and the Utes" and develops a plot of a mother and daughter who escape abduction.

1438.   Sargeant, Daniel. *Catherine Tekakwitha*. New York: Longmans, Green, 1936.

Biography of Iroquois woman who lived the life of a nun. Her tomb was visited by Indians who followed her Christian example, and she was believed by some to have been a saint.

1439.   Sarris, Greg. "On the Road to Lolsel: Conversations with Mabel McKay." *News from Native California* 2, 4 (September/October 1988): 3-6.

Mabel McKay is a member of the Cache Creek band of Pomo in California. She is a basketweaver and one of the few Pomo left who remember the old ceremonies. She reminisces about the history of her people.

1440. Schaeffer, Claude E. "The Kutenai Female Berdache: Courier,
Guide, Prophetess, and Warrior." *Ethnohistory* 12, 3 (1965):
193-236.

Biography of a Kutenai woman whose unconventional
masculine roles, including warrior and peace mediator, led to
her prominence and records of her activities by traders and
American military men. Generally referred to in accounts as a
female berdache characterized by "bizarre behavior," she is
reported to have married a Canadian voyageur but returned
home a year later claiming to have been transformed into a
man and calling herself "Gone to the Spirits." She wore men's
clothing, pursued young girls, attempted to marry one but was
refused. She gambled with men, went about armed, raided
against the Colville, took several female companions and was
finally mortally wounded in a war expedition. Quotations from
many contemporary sources are included in the biography.
Schaeffer compares her to other Plains women who took on
warrior roles, cites many sources which characterize her as a
unique personality among the Kutenai, and notes that she is
still an important figure in Kutenai storytelling.

1441. Scholer, Bo. "Minerva Allen: 'A Few Good Words.'" *Wicazo Sa
Review* 3, 1 (Spring 1987): 1-7.

Minerva Allen is an Assiniboine active in educational
administration on the Fort Belknap reservation where she has
produced several volumes on bi-lingual education. She has also
written several unpublished collections of poetry which focus
on tribal life before contact with European cultures. An
interview with Allen reveals her feelings and intentions
regarding her creative writing.

1442. Schultz, James Willard. *Birdwoman (Sacajawea): The Guide of
Lewis and Clark*. Boston: Houghton Mifflin, 1918.

Schultz tells the story of Sacajawea through the tales he
received from older friends.

1443.   Schultz, James Willard. *My Life as an Indian: The Story of a Red Woman and a White Man in the Lodges of the Blackfeet.* New York: Beaufort Books, 1985.

Originally published in 1906, this narrative records the life of Nat-Ah'-Ki, the wife of the author and the center of the story. The text reads almost like a novel and Nat-Ah'-Ki is highly idealized, but the volume purports to be factual. Emphasis is on domestic life rare in narratives about Indian culture.

1444.   Schultz, Terri. "Indian Women Find Their Voice." *Playgirl* 2, 6 (November 1974): 49-50, 105, 111.

This article challenges negative stereotypes of Indian women by profiling three women: Ada Deer (Menominee), Lorraine Montour (Mohawk), and Leona Ear (Sioux) who have had effective lives in both traditional and contemporary roles.

1445.   Sekaquaptewa, Helen. *Me and Mine: The Life Story of Helen Sekaquaptewa.* Louise Udall, ed. Tucson: University of Arizona Press, 1969.

This narrative moves from the subject's childhood in a traditional tribal family, through her schooling and marriage, to an acceptance of white influence without hostility toward traditions or loss of Indian identity or attachment to the land. It covers all aspects of Hopi culture, both traditional and modern, but the personal and family narrative dominates. Though she is a Mormon, little emphasis is placed on Christianity other than details of her conversion. She dwells most on traditional ceremony, boarding school experiences, family life, farming and ranching. The narrative posits attitudes of adjustment and flexibility, a sense of control and contentment with life, despite hardships in raising a family and struggling for existence in a harsh landscape. Stylistically, the narrative is modestly related and well detailed.

1446. Seyerstad, Per. "Two Interviews with Leslie Marmon Silko." *American Studies in Scandinavia* 13 (1981): 17-33.

Silko discusses her childhood and youth at Laguna and her awareness that her gender imposed no limitations on her activities or future. She analyzes her writing as tied to a landscape that is particularly productive for storytelling and her community as a source of narrative, using "Tony's Story" and "A Man to Send Rain Clouds" as examples, and commenting on the Pueblo oral traditions as a means to knowledge and identity.

1447. Seymour, Flora Warren. *Women of Trail and Wigwam*. New York: Woman's Press, 1930.

After a general introduction, Seymour provides chapters on Sacajawea (Shoshone), Wih-munke Wakan (Sioux), Madame Montour (Seneca captive), Seneca Sisters (captors of Mary Jemison), Molly Brant (Mohawk), Daughters of the Wind Clan (Creek), Milly (Seminole), Margaret McLaughlin (Indian wife of a fur trader), Nellie Connolly (Oregon), Julia (Flathead), Owl Woman and Yellow Woman (Cheyenne), wives of mountain men, Appearing Day (Brule Sioux), Sarah Winnemucca (Paiute), Winema (Modoc), Cherry and Magpie Outside (Crow). The stories are interesting but are not documented.

1448. Shaw, Anna Moore. *A Pima Past*. Tucson: University of Arizona Press, 1974.

This personal narrative and cultural memoir is written in fictional third-person style when discussing family history and first person in telling her own story from youth through her education, marriage, move to Phoenix for employment, and eventual return to the reservation. The author places heavy emphasis on the effects of Christianity. Shaw expresses regret over lost traditions but desires to function effectively in the white world, returning to the reservation to regain contact with the land, but especially to engage in community service and church work. The narrative offers good detail, but it is somewhat simplistic.

1449.   Snyder, Gerald S. "The Girl of History who became a Woman of Fable." *Westways* 66, 3 (1974): 36-39, 71, 73.

This article reappraises the contribution of Shoshone woman Sacajawea to the Lewis and Clark expedition in light of the lore that surrounds her history.

1450.   Sootkis, Rubie. *The Cheyenne Journey*. Ashland, MT: Religion Research Center, 1976.

Sootkis discusses her personal view of the traditional Cheyenne way of life from birth to death, focusing on each of four stages: growth, Cheyenne values, kinship and the community.

1451.   Speare, Jean E., ed. *The Days of Augusta*. Vancouver: J. J. Douglas Ltd., 1973.

This Canadian Indian woman was born in 1888 at Soda Creek in British Columbia as Mary Augusta Tappage and lost her Indian status when she married a white. The book includes memories, poems, and pictures.

1452.   Stanley, Mrs. Andrew. "Personal Narrative of Mrs. Andrew Stanley." In *Western Apache Raiding and Warfare*. Keith H. Basso, ed. Tucson: University of Arizona Press, 1971, 205-19.

The author briefly records her daring escape from Fort Apache in the Arizona territory in the late nineteenth century and the hardships of her journey to rejoin her people in a renegade Apache band.

1453.   Starr, Michael L. "She Did Not Lead a Movement." *American History Illustrated* 15 (August 1980): 44-47.

Story of a woman chief, a Crow captive and warrior, who in 1834 rode against the Blackfeet at Fort Sarpy.

1454. Steber, Rick. *Women of the West*. Prineville, OR: Bonanza Publications, 1988.

Includes four brief, romanticized sketches of Indian women who figure in Oregon history.

1455. Stewart, Irene. *A Voice in Her Tribe: A Navaho Woman's Own Story*. Doris Ostrander Dawdy and Mary Shepardson, eds. Socorro, NM: Ballena Press Anthropological Papers No. 17, 1980.

More an oral memoir than a chronological autobiography, the work includes versions of traditional Navajo stories, discussion of tribal politics, Navajo social behavior, as well as incidents from the life of the author. Stewart was Christianized in her youth, but she still holds to belief in traditional healing practices and lifestyle with no apparent conflict. She describes the hardships of raising children from a brief early marriage and the satisfactions of a happy marriage in her later years when she became active in the Chinle Chapter of the Navajo Tribal Council as secretary and arbiter of disputes. Much of her knowledge of traditional ways comes from her father and from her second husband's stories, some of which are included in the text. The narrative style lacks vitality, but there is value in her assessment of Navajo life-ways and politics from her perspective of age and intense involvement.

1456. Stewart, Patricia. "Sarah Winnemucca." *Nevada Historical Society Quarterly* 14 (Winter 1971): 23-38.

Stewart summarizes the information available about the life of Sarah Winnemucca.

1457. Stowell, Cynthia D. *Faces of a Reservation: A Portrait of the Warm Springs Indian Reservation*. Portland: Oregon Historical Society Press, 1988.

Portraits of over twenty women ranging from housewives to poets and commentary on their recollections and concerns for present tribal life; includes some direct quotation, some interpretative text.

1458. Street, Douglas. "LaFlesche Sisters Write to St. Nicholas Magazine." *Nebraska History* 62, 24 (Winter 1981): 515-23.

In 1877 the four LaFlesche sisters, Suzette, Rosalie, Marguerite, and Susan, wrote to *St. Nicholas* magazine; the letters weren't published for three years. The editor Mary Mapes Dodge knew of the LaFlesche sisters. The letters are included in this illustrated article.

1459. Swann, Brian and Arnold Krupat, eds. *I Tell You Now: Autobiographical Essays by Native American Writers*. Lincoln: University of Nebraska Press, 1987.

A collection of eighteen short autobiographies focusing on the literary aspects of the lives of American Indian writers. Childhood, education, and relationship to the land, to language and to Native and Anglo cultures are recurring themes. The women writers included are: Mary TallMountain, Elizabeth Cook-Lynn, Paula Gunn Allen, Diane Glancy, Linda Hogan, Wendy Rose, and Joy Harjo. Each narrative is introduced with a brief summary of publications by the author.

1460. Swartz, Nelson A. "Princess Watahwaso." *Indian's Friend* 35, 5 (1923): 7-8.

A Penobscot woman from Old Town, Maine, is lauded for her recitals of tribal history, dances, and legends performed in Kalamazoo, Michigan, for educators. She is described as a soprano and as an effective speaker.

1461. Taber, Ronald W. "Sacajawea and the Suffragettes: An Interpretation of a Myth." *Pacific Northwest Quarterly* 58 (1967): 7-13.

Sacajawea was not proclaimed a national hero until she was rediscovered in 1902 by a woman who wrote historical fiction and was active in the suffrage movement. Eva Emery Dye promoted Sacajawea as an image of perfect womanhood through her novel *The Conquest* which led to the adoption of the Indian woman as a symbol of female strength and power and maternal virtue. Sacajawea became a rallying point in the battle for the right of women to vote, and legendary deeds and qualities were added to the historical records of her life.

1462. TallMountain, Mary. "You Can Go Home Again." In *I Tell You Now: Autobiographical Essays by Native American Writers*. Brian Swann and Arnold Krupat, eds. Lincoln: University of Nebraska Press, 1987, 1-13.

TallMountain narrates her response to her return to Alaska after a fifty year absence, recalling being ripped out of her family as a child and the crushing of her creativity until the 1960s when she began to write poetry and reestablished ties with her family.

1463. Tanner, Helen Hornbeck. "Coocoochee, Mohawk Medicine Woman." *American Indian Culture and Research Journal* 3, 3 (1979): 23-42.

Coocoochee, born about 1740, led a sheltered childhood but her adulthood as a specialist in herbal medicine and spiritual mediary was spent in a traumatic environment threatened almost perpetually by war and displacement which finally placed her among the Shawnee in her later years. She gained respect in the many tribes where she and her family took refuge. The events of her life are reconstructed from the narrative of a white captive who lived in her household for several months.

1464. Theisz, R. D. "The Critical Collaboration: Introductions as a Gateway to the Study of Native American Bi-Autobiography." *American Indian Culture and Research Journal* 5, 1 (1981): 65-80.

The author recommends close analysis of introductions to American Indian bi-autobiographies as a means of interpreting and assessing the reliability of composite authorship narratives. Among the examples discussed are four women's narratives.

1465.   Ticasuk [Emily Ivanoff Brown]. *The Roots of Ticasuk: Eskimo Woman's Family Story*. Anchorage: Alaska Northwest Publishing, 1981.

The narrator of this memoir is the surviving daughter in the line of an Eskimo leader of legendary fame. Taken from oral tradition and recollections of other people, the narrative is actually a dramatized genealogy, primarily anecdotal and episodic, including character vignettes, some ethnographic material, but little actual autobiographical information.

1466.   Tsianina. *Where Trails Have Led Me*. Burbank, CA: Tsianina Blackstone, 1968.

Cherokee-Creek woman born in 1892, toured Europe 1919-1918 with the American Expeditionary Forces, and participated in many Indian ceremonials. She founded the Foundation for American Indian Education.

1467.   Tucker, Norma. "Nancy Ward, Ghighau of the Cherokees." *Georgia Historical Quarterly* 53 (June 1969): 192-200.

This is a biography of Nancy Ward, "beloved woman" of the Cherokee.

1468.   Vanderburgh, Rosamund M. *I Am Nokomis Too: The Biography of Verna Patronella Johnston*. Don Mills, Ontario: General Publishing, 1977.

This is a popular account of the life of Verna Johnston (Ojibwa) based on her recollections and community memories of Cape Croker, Ontario. She is interested in Indian adaptation to urban life and had a boarding house in Toronto during part of her life. In 1976 she was named Indian Woman of the Year by the Native Women's Association of Canada. Includes an interview with Johnston.

1469. Velarde, Eleanor, ed. *Rough Stones Are Precious Too.* . . . Rough Rock, AZ: Navajo Curriculum Center, 1978, 70-93.

Includes brief narratives of three Navajo girls collected as part of a curriculum project.

1470. Velarde, Pablita. *Old Father, the Story Teller.* Globe, AZ: D. S. King, 1960.

A major painter of Pueblo life, whose murals can be seen in public buildings in New Mexico, Velarde relates stories and legends heard from her grandfather and great grandfather at the Santa Clara Pueblo, weaving them into the narrative of her family history and own personal narrative.

1471. Waheenee [Maxi'diwiac, Buffalo-Bird Woman]. *Waheenee: An Indian Girl's Story, Told by Herself.* Told to Gilbert L. Wilson. St. Paul, MN: Webb Publishing, 1921. Rpt. in *North Dakota History* 38 (Winter-Spring 1971): 7-176. Published as an Occasional Publication no. 4, Bismarck: State Historical Society of North Dakota, 1981. Rpt. Lincoln: University of Nebraska Press, 1981.

Although told in 1921, this is essentially a nineteenth-century narrative by Hidatsa Maxi'diwiac and is characterized by an attitude of regret at the passing of the old ways and the necessity for modern Indians to accommodate white ways. Little attention is paid to reservation times other than to lament the breakdown of traditional ways.

1472. Waldie, Jean H. "The Iroquois Poetess, Pauline Johnson." *Ontario History* 40 (1948): 65-75.

This biographical profile concentrates on Johnson's career and her contributions to Canadian literature and culture, though the major events of her life are also presented.

1473. Waldowski, Paula. "Alice Brown Davis: A Leader of Her People." *Chronicles of Oklahoma* 58, 4 (Winter 1980-1981): 455-63.

Alice Brown Davies, a Seminole born in 1852, served her tribe in Oklahoma throughout her life. Her father was a government physician who accompanied the Seminole on the Trail of Tears and married Lucy Redbird. Alice was well educated and later in life was superintendent of the Seminole girls' school, Emahaka. She was an assimilationist who, nonetheless, believed the Seminole should retain their heritage while taking advantage of the benefits of the dominant culture.

1474. Waldraven-Johnson, Margaret. *The White Comanche: The Story of Cynthia Ann Parker and Her Son Quanah*. New York: Comet Press Books, 1956.

A captive, Parker rises in status to become a central figure in the Comanche tribe and the matriarch of a family central to Comanche tribal history.

1475. Wallace, Michael. "Hail to the Chief: Wilma Mankiller is the First Woman to be Elected Cherokee Nation Chief." *Philip Morris Magazine* (October 1989): 37-39.

This forty-three-year-old grandmother and political activist is the first woman chief of the Cherokee tribe and the first woman to lead "a major Indian tribe." She sees herself as a model to young Indian women. A brief biography is included.

1476. Wallace, Michele. "Wilma Mankiller." *MS* 16, 7 (January 1988): 68-69.

Profile of Mankiller, chief of 78,000 Cherokee of Oklahoma.

1477. Waltrip, Lela and Rufus Waltrip. *Indian Women*. New York: David McKay, 1964.

Biographical sketches of thirteen Indian women from 1535 to the present are included: Big Eyes, Pocahontas, Sacajawea, Winema, Cynthia Ann Parker, Sarah Winnemucca, Indian Emily, Dat-So-La-Lee, Tomasse, Neosho, Maria Martinez, Annie Dodge Wauneka, Pablita Velarde.

1478. Wapiti, Marisa. *Ropes of Sand, Manuscript of Just a Little Half-Breed*. Smithers, BC: Tanglewood Press, 1972.

In this volume of the story of her life, Wapiti tells of her family and community in Canada. Wapiti writes in an afterword that she recorded the story of Marie Belanger, a miner's wife; in spite of the appearance of reality, a disclaimer says all the names are fictitious.

1479. Waseskuk, Bertha. "Mesquakie History--As We Know It." In *The Worlds Between Two Rivers: Perspectives on American Indians in Iowa*. Gretchen M. Bataille, David M. Gradwohl, and Charles L. P. Silet, eds. Ames: Iowa State University Press, 1978, 54-61.

Bertha Waseskuk writes history from the point of view of a Mesquakie woman who has lived on the Settlement near Tama, Iowa. It is based on accounts by Mesquakie historians.

1480. Watson, Virginia. *The Princess Pocahontas*. Philadelphia: The Penn Publishing Co, 1927.

This biography depicts Pocahontas as a pivotal figure in American history because of her mediating with whites and ensuing influence over the future of the nation. The biography is based on early historical chronicles but written in a fiction style and illustrated with romanticized color plates.

1481. Whyard, Flo. "The Yukon's Edith Josie." *Alaska* 39, 1 (January 1973): 12-13, 53-54.

A short biography of Edith Josie, a Loucheux woman, who wrote a column for the *Whitehouse Star*. Includes excerpts from her column and personal recollections from the author.

1482.   Willard, William. "Zitkala-Sa: A Woman Who Would Be
         Heard." *Wicazo Sa Review* 1, (Spring 1985): 11-16.

         A brief biographical essay of Yankton Sioux political
         activist and writer Gertrude Bonnin who died in 1938 after
         battling government agencies over the consistent mistreatment
         and exploitation of Native peoples. She left a legacy of activism
         to future generations and significantly influenced Indian policy-
         making during her career.

1483.   Williams, Alice. "Gladys Taylor: A Portrait." *Canadian Woman
         Studies* 10, 2&3 (Summer/Fall 1989): 21-23.

         Excerpts from the diaries and other writings of a seventy-
         five-year-old elder from the Curve Lake reserve in Ontario.

1484.   Williams, Walter L. "Twentieth Century Indian Leaders:
         Brokers and Providers." *Journal of the West* 23, 3 (July
         1984): 3-6.

         The impact of Native American women in national
         leadership is largely overlooked. Gertrude Bonnin is cited as
         an important figure influencing modern struggles for power
         because of her part in conceiving pan-Indian identity. Current
         studies of Indian women's roles are seen as beginning to rectify
         the dearth of information on Indian women.

1485.   Willis, Jane. *Genieish: An Indian Girlhood*. Toronto: New
         Press, 1973.

         Story of mixed-blood Cree girl in Canada. She was born in
         1940 and raised by her Indian grandparents. She tells of her
         involvement with the Indian agency.

1486.   Wilson, Dorothy Clarke. *Bright Eyes: The Story of Suzette
         LaFlesche, an Omaha Indian*. New York: McGraw-Hill,
         1974.

This is a fictionalized biography of LaFlesche, who in the 1870s was a spokeswoman for her tribe as well as for the Poncas.

1487.   Wilson, Gilbert Livingston. *Agriculture of the Hidatsa Indians: An Indian Interpretation*. Minneapolis: University of Minnesota Studies in the Social Sciences no. 9, 1917.

Maxi'diwiac (Buffalo-Bird Woman or Waheenee) is the principal informant. The interpreter is her son Edward Goodbird. The account is described as an Indian woman's interpretation of economics. Focusing on Maxi'diwiac's sense of her people's relationship to the land and practices of raising crops, this collection of material includes creation stories, legends, and day-to-day agriculture practices, but it is autobiographical in nature because it is based on her recollections of family attitudes, customs, and practices and develops a clear personality and narrative style and relates personal information in a discernible chronology. The nurturing of growing things and the narrator's sense of the sacredness of the earth create a unifying thread.

1488.   Winnie, Lucille. *Sah-Gan-De-Oh: The Chief's Daughter*. New York: Vantage Press, 1969.

A twentieth-century Seneca/Cayuga woman who has lived on reservations in Oklahoma, Montana, and Kansas, Winnie is representative of modern acculturation and its effect on Indian women. There is little attention or concern for traditional ways; rather, she accepts white domination and blames her own people, particularly tribal politics, for poverty and other reservation problems.

1489.   Witt, Shirley Hill. "An Interview with Dr. Annie Dodge Wauneka." *Frontiers* 6, 3 (Fall 1981): 64-67.

Wauneka, born in 1913, is the daughter of Henry Chee Dodge, the last Navajo tribal chief. She was active in the 1930s and 1940s when the BIA forced the reduction of grazing animals, was the first woman on the Navajo Tribal Council, and received an honorary doctorate degree in 1976. She urges Indian women to be active in decision making to protect their Indian identity.

1490.   Wood, Beth and Tom Barry. "The Story of Three Navajo Women." *Integrateducation* 16, 2 (March-April 1978): 33-35.

Short biographies of Emma Yazzie, Claudeen Bates Arthur, and Elva Benson. They discuss their lives, poverty among the Navajo, and the future they envision.

1491.   Woodward, Arthur, ed. *Journal of Lieutenant Thomas W. Sweeny 1849-1853*. Los Angeles: Westernlore Press, 1956.

Sweeny waxes poetic about a particularly beautiful Yuman woman to whom he was attracted and describes their friendship.

1492.   Woodward, Grace Steele. *Pocahontas*. Norman: University of Oklahoma Press, 1969.

Presented by the author as a new evaluation of the role of Pocahontas in history.

1493.   Work, James C. and Pattie Cowell. "Teller of Stories: An Interview With Leslie Marmon Silko." *Colorado State Review* 8, 2 (Spring/Summer 1981): 68-79.

This interview with Laguna writer Leslie Silko highlights her short story "Tony's Story" and her novel *Ceremony*. She describes her process of writing and the influences on her work.

1494.   Wright, Frank H. "Dorothy, the Cheyenne Maiden." *The Missionary Review of the World*. 17, 7 (1904): 494-97.

A brief biography of a girl who is converted to Christianity and dies of an illness three years after her baptism. She is seen by the missionary author as an inspiration to other Indians who are demonstrating interest in baptism in the Presbyterian church.

1495.   Yoimut. "Yoimut's Story, the Last Chunut." In *Handbook of the Yokut Indians*. F. F. Latta. Bakersfield, CA: Kern County Museum, 1949, 223-76.

This narrative by the last full-blood Chunut woman, who died in 1933, concentrates heavily on descriptions of childhood recollections, particularly ceremonies; however, discussion of family life, hunting and fishing, and relationship to white settlers in northern California is included. The subject, who is fluent in Spanish and English as well as in four dialects of her Native language, includes ceremonial songs and translations. Though she records the struggle for survival of her people who are without a reservation and continually forced to abandon their settlements as they are taken over by settlers, her tone is regretful rather than bitter.

1496.   Young, Lucy. "Out of the Past: A True Indian Story." Edith V. A. Murphey, ed. *California Historical Society Quarterly* 20 (December 1941): 349-64.

The narrative is a brief record of a Wailaki woman writing in her nineties about her first encounter with whites in her childhood in which her father was killed and about the subsequent persecutions and the survival of her family in the wilderness. The story is one of acculturation in her adulthood, through her marriages to two white men. The narrative is without substantial detail, includes no tribal context, and is too brief to be adequately developed; however, stylistically it is interesting because it is written in nonstandard English.

1497.   Zitkala-Sa [Gertrude Bonnin]. "An Indian Teacher among Indians." *Atlantic Monthly* 85 (March 1900): 381-86.

Autobiographical account of Bonnin's outrage at the poor reservation living conditions she finds her family in when she return to recruit Indian students for a BIA school. She also expresses disillusionment with the BIA school system and the incompetence and corruption she encounters within it.

1498.   Zitkala-Sa [Gertrude Bonnin]. "Impressions of an Indian Childhood." *Atlantic Monthly* 85 (January 1900): 37-47.

The author's memories of her first eight years on the Yankton Reservation in South Dakota where she was born in 1876. Her recollections touch upon Native crafts, folkways, and legends, and end with the author setting out for mission school in Indiana.

1499.   Zitkala-Sa [Gertrude Bonnin]. "The School Days of an Indian Girl." *Atlantic Monthly* 85 (February 1900): 185-94.

This autobiographical story deals with the author's trauma of adjusting, at age eight, to mission school. Bonnin was forced to give up her native dress, forbidden to speak her Native language, made to cut her hair, and expected to adhere to the regimentation of the mission school.

1500.   Zitkala-Sa [Gertrude Bonnin]. "Why I Am A Pagan." *Atlantic Monthly* 90 (December 1902): 802-3.

Bonnin explains why she rejects Christianity and white ways, and prefers to adhere to traditional beliefs and ways.

1501.   Zuni, Lina. "An Autobiography." In *Zuni Texts*. Ruth L. Bunzel, ed. New York: G. E. Stechert and Co., 1933, 74-96. Publications of the American Ethnological Society.

Lina Zuni was seventy years old when Ruth Bunzel recorded her autobiography as part of her fieldwork on Zuni culture and language in 1926-27. Lina's daughter Flora Zuni translated the material for Bunzel.

1502.   Zwinger, Susan. "Viewpoint: An Interview with Artist Jaune Quick-to-See Smith." *El Palacio* 92, 1 (Summer/Fall 1986): 51-54.

Jaune Quick-to-See Smith, a Cree/Shoshone artist, notes that contemporary art by Indians is a problem for anthropologists who tend to see all non-traditional art as indications of abandonment of culture. She also discusses her history as a painter.

Film and Video

FILM AND VIDEO

1503.   *A Season of Grandmothers.* George Burdeau, 1976. KSPS-TV, Spokane, Washington. 16mm, 1/2" and 3/4" videotape, 28 minutes.

Interviews several elder women from the Spokane, Coeur d'Alene, Nez Perce, Kootenai, Colville and Flathead tribes, as they discuss their heritage and the old ways.

1504.   *A Weave of Time.* Produced by Susan Fanshel with John Adair and Deborah Gordon, 1986. 16mm, 3/4" and 1/2" videotape, 60 minutes.

Follows the lives of four generations of the Burnside family, Navajos from Pine Springs, Arizona. Includes the lives of Isabel Burnside and her mother Mabel Burnside.

1505.   *Abnaki: The Native People of Maine.* Produced, directed and written by Jay Kent. Produced for the Maine Tribal Governors, Inc. 1982. 16mm, 3/4" videotape, 28 minutes. Distributor: Barr/Centre.

Includes vignettes of contemporary Indian life, and comments by Penobscot leader Eunice Nelson.

1506.   *Again, a Whole Person I Have Become.* Shenandoah Films. Produced by Vern Korb and Carol Korb, 1985, 20 minutes. 16mm, 3/4" and 1/2" videotape.

Features a Wintu medicine woman, a Karok spiritual leader, and a Tolowa headman who discuss their beliefs and traditions.

1507. *Alice Elliot*. Produced by Media Generalists, 1975. 16mm, 11 minutes.

A film portrait of one of the last Pomo basketmakers of Northern California.

1508. *American Indian Artists--Part I*. "No. 1, Medicine Flower and Lonewolf." Produced by Jack Peterson, KAET-TV, Phoenix, 1976. 3/4" videotape, 30 minutes.

Illustrates and examines the techniques of Santa Clara potters Grace Medicine Flower and Joseph Lonewolf.

1509. *American Indian Artists--Part I*. "No. 5, Helen Hardin--Santa Clara Painter." Produced by Jack Peterson at KAET-TV, Phoenix, 1976. 3/4" videotape, 30 minutes.

This portrait of Santa Clara painter Helen Hardin shows the artist at work in her Tesuque, New Mexico, studio, and explores the influences and inspirations for her work.

1510. *American Indian Artists--Part II*, "No. 2, Jaune Quick-to-See Smith." Narrated by N. Scott Momaday, poetry by Joy Harjo. Produced by Native American Public Broadcasting Consortium, 1982, 30 minutes.

About a Shoshone French Cree painter of abstract paintings, from the Flathead Reservation in Montana.

1511. *Annie and the Old One*. Produced by Greenhouse Films, 1976. 16mm, 15 minutes.

A film about the relationship between a ten-year-old Navajo girl and her grandmother.

1512. *Annie Mae--Brave Hearted Woman.* Produced by Len Brooke
Ritz. 1979. 16mm, 84 minutes

Examines the mysterious murder of Indian activist Annie
Mae Aquash, who was killed after the 1973 occupation of
Wounded Knee. Her family, friends, and co-workers
remember her and paint a picture of a courageous woman.

1513. *Augusta.* Produced by John Taylor (NFBC), 1978. 16mm, 17
minutes.

A film portrait of Shuswap Indian Augusta Evans of the
caribou country of British Columbia. She was sent to an
English-only boarding school, and when she married a white
man she lost her status as an Indian. She reminisces about her
past and her heritage.

1514. *Basketry of the Pomo.* University of California American
Indian Films, 1962. 16mm.

A series of films documenting the variety in Pomo basket
making. The series includes an "Introductory Film" (30
minutes), "Forms and Ornamentation" (21 minutes), and
"Techniques" (33 minutes).

1515. *Box of Treasures.* Directed by Chuck Olin, produced by the
U'mista Cultural Society and Chuck Olin Associates, 1983.
16mm, 3/4" and 1/2" videotape, 18 minutes.

Focuses on the recovery of Kwakiutl ceremonial objects
seized by the Canadian government in 1921 and the Kwakiutl
efforts to revive their culture. Gloria Cranmer Webster,
director of the U'mista Cultural Society, discusses these
efforts to continue her culture.

1516. *Broken Rainbow.* Produced, written and edited by Maria
Florio and Victoria Mudd, 1985. 16 mm, 1/2" and 3/4"
videotape, 70 minutes. Distributor: Direct Cinema.

This study of the Navajo-Hopi land dispute and the effect of that dispute on Navajo people won the Academy Award for Best Documentary film in 1985.

1517.   *Colliding Worlds*. Produced by Orie Sherman, 1980. 16mm and videotape, 30 minutes.

A documentary following a Mono mother, grandmother and daughter in their daily activities in Northern California, stressing the continuity between generations. Made by a Mono filmmaker.

1518.   *Colours of Pride*. Produced by Henning Jacobson, NFBC, 1974. 16mm, 24 minutes.

Interviews with Native Canadian artists include Daphne Odjig, a Cree collage artist.

1519.   *Come Forth Laughing: Voices of the Suquamish People*. Produced by the Suquamish Tribal Cultural Center, 1983. Slide tape transferred to 3/4" and 1/2" videotape, 15 minutes.

Personal narratives from members of the Suquamish tribe living in the Puget Sound Region of Washington State.

1520.   *Concerns of American Indian Women*. Produced by Sandra Elkin, WNET, 1977. 3/4" videotape, 30 minutes.

Includes interviews with Northern Cheyenne Maria Sanchez, a judge, and Dr. Connie Uri, a Choctaw-Cherokee physician and law student, as they discuss the concerns of American Indian women--health issues, placement of Indian children in non-Indian homes, exploitation of Indian lands.

1521.   *Corn is Life*. Produced by Therese Burson and Donald Coughlin, 1982. Produced for the Museum of Northern Arizona. 16 mm, 1/2" and 3/4" videotape, 19 minutes. In English or Hopi.

Shows the role of corn in Hopi life, focusing on its ceremonial and symbolic uses as well as for food purposes.

1522. *Dream Dances of the Pomo*. University of California American Indian Films, 1964. 16mm, 30 minutes.

Shows the various ceremonial dances done by Pomo women under the direction of the Pomo shaman.

1523. *Earth Mother: Voices of Native American Women*. Filmstrip. Jane Katz, ed. Multi-Media Productions, Inc.

Filmstrip adapted from Katz's book *I Am the Fire of Time*. Native women tell of their contributions to tribal life and their history.

1524. *Ella Mae BlackBear: Cherokee Basketmaker*. Produced, directed and edited by Scott Swearingen and Sheila Swearingen, 1982. 3/4" and 1/2" videotape, 25 minutes.

Documents the craft of Ella Mae Blackbear, a Cherokee basketmaker living in rural northeastern Oklahoma. She talks of her life and work as she demonstrates her basketmaking skills.

1525. *Eskimo Artist Kenojuak*. Produced by John Feeny, NFBC, 1963. 16mm, 20 minutes.

Profiles the life and work of Eskimo artist Kenojuak, as she makes prints from stone cuts and carries out the duties of wife and mother.

1526. *Eskimo Arts and Crafts*. Produced by NFBC, 1944. 16mm, 22 minutes.

An ethnographic look at the life and culture of Baffin Island Eskimos, with emphasis on the role of women in Eskimo life.

1527.   *Four Corners of the Earth.* Produced by the Bureau of Florida Folklife Programs and WFSU-TV, 1985, 30 minutes.

Roles and culture of Seminole women in South Florida are explored through interviews with women of all ages.

1528.   *From Hand to Hand: Bethel Native Artist Profiles.* Series produced by Gretchen McManus for KYUK-TV and the Yugtarvik Regional Museum, Bethel, AK, 1985. 3/4" and 1/2" videotape, approx. 10 minutes per segment.

"Storyknifing" shows the Yup'ik Eskimo storytelling tradition of cutting images in the mud or snow to illustrate the story being told. Martha Larson describes the tradition from her memories, and Esther Green illustrates it by telling a story to a group of girls. "Lucy Beaver, Skin Sewer," discusses her life and her craft of making and decorating skin garments.

1529.   *Great Spirit Within the Hole.* Produced and directed by Chris Spotted Eagle for KTCA-TV, St. Paul, MN, 1983. 16 mm, 3/4" videotape, 60 minutes.

Interviews American Indian men and women held in prison who have become involved with Native American spiritual practices and discusses how this has altered their lives.

1530.   *Green Corn Festival.* Produced by Gary Robinson for the Muscogee Creek Nation Communications Center, 1982. 3/4" and 1/2" videotape, 20 minutes.

Documents the Green Corn Festival as practiced today in Oklahoma. Uses present day and archival footage from the 1940s to illustrate the festival. Includes a ribbon dance that honors the tribal women.

1531.   *Hopi: Songs of the Fourth World.* Produced and directed by Pat Ferrero, 1983. 16mm, 3/4" videotape, 58 minutes.

This film presents many facets of present-day Hopi life, profiling various members of the tribe, including Helen

Sekaquaptewa. It focuses on the role of women in Hopi society.

1532.   *I Know Who I Am*. Produced by Sandra Sunrising Osawa for KSTW-TV, Seattle, 1979. 3/4" videotape, 29 minutes.

This film, made by a Makah independent filmmaker, focuses on the cultural values important to Indian tribes of the Pacific Coast, and the importance of gaining a sense of Indian identity found in family and tribal traditions, and how these values and traditions are passed on by the women of the tribe.

1533.   *Images of Indians: Heathen Injuns and the Hollywood Gospel*. Produced by Robert Hagopian and Phil Lucas for KCTS/9 Seattle, 1980. 30 minutes.

Shows the distortions and misrepresentations of American Indian women, religion and values in Hollywood movies. Janet McCloud and other Native women explain the stereotypes often portrayed in movies.

1534.   *In the Best Interest of the Child: Indian Child Welfare Act*. Shenandoah Films. Produced by Vern Korb and Carol Korb. 1984, 20 minutes. 16mm, 3/4" and 1/2" videotape.

Sponsored by a California law firm to familiarize its audience with the problems of non-Indian foster care for Indian children, encourages Native Americans to take a more active part in the foster care process.

1535.   *Indian Art of the Pueblos*. Bert Van Bork, 1976. 16mm, 13 minutes.

A brief survey of the traditional art forms being produced by contemporary Pueblo artists of the American southwest, including pottery, baskets, jewelry. Stresses the work made with traditional materials and methods.

1536.   *Indian Experience: Urban and Rural*. People of First Light Series, 1979. 3/4" and 1/2" videotape, 28 minutes.

Contrasts the ways in which American Indian tribal heritage is preserved both on and off the reservation. Includes the experiences of Jo-Anne Rogers, a Pequot woman from Connecticut who left the city to live on the reservation with her children.

1537.   *Indian Hide Tanning.* Produced by Todd Crocker for the Trust for Native American Cultures and Crafts Video, 1981. 3/4" and 1/2" videotape, 35 minutes.

Shows the process of hide tanning as employed by the Cree of Northern Quebec. Individuals filmed include Sarah Bosum, Sophie Coon and Anna Trapper.

1538.   *Indian Pottery of San Ildefonso.* Rick Krepela. Produced by the National Park Service, U.S. Department of Interior, 1972. 16mm, 1/2" and 3/4" videotape, 27 minutes.

A comprehensive documentary showing step-by-step the process used by Maria Martinez to make her famous black on black pottery.

1539.   *Jaune Quick-to-See Smith.* Produced by Jack Peterson for the Native American Public Broadcasting Consortium, 1983. 16mm, all video formats, 29 minutes.

A profile of the painter Jaune Quick-to-See Smith, focusing on her life and career, including interviews and a discussion with artist Emmi Lou Whitehorse.

1540.   *Lakota Quillwork: Art and Legend.* Produced, directed and edited by H. Jane Nuaman, 1985. 16 mm, 3/4" and 1/2" videotape, 27 minutes. In English and Lakota.

An account of the origins of the traditional Lakota art of quillwork to its practice today by tribal members in South Dakota.

1541.   *Lenape: The Original People*. Produced, directed and edited
        by Thomas Agnello, 1986. 16mm, 3/4" and 1/2" videotape,
        22 minutes.

        Focuses briefly on the history of the Delaware, or Lenape
        people, but deals mainly with two elders living in Dewey,
        Oklahoma, who retain their Native language, customs and
        beliefs. Nora Thompson Dean, known as Touching Leaves
        Woman, was filmed shortly before her death. She shares
        memories of her mother and discusses her own efforts to
        preserve her heritage.

1542.   *Living Traditions: Five Indian Women Artists*. Produced,
        directed and edited by Fran Belvin, Denise Mayotte and
        Kathee Prokop for Womanswork and Iris Video, 1984. 3/4"
        and 1/2" videotape, 27 minutes.

        Shows how the different work of five American Indian
        women artists reflects their cultures, traditions and identities.
        Included are seamstress Elizabeth Kingbird, quilt maker Terry
        Brightnose, basketmaker Josie Ryan, quilt maker Edith
        Sigana, and fashion designer Cynthia Holmes.

1543.   *Lucy Covington: Native American Indian*. Produced by
        Odyssey Productions, 1978. 16mm, 16 minutes.

        Lucy Covington, leader of the Colville tribe of eastern
        Washington, gives her account of her efforts to prevent the
        federal government from disbanding the tribe.

1544.   *Mainstream*. Directed by Larry Littlebird and George
        Burdeau for The Real People Series, PBS, 1974. 16mm,
        1/2" and 3/4" videotape, 24 minutes.

        Based on an essay by Coeur d'Alene writer Janet
        Campbell, a young urban Indian woman rediscovers her ties
        with her family, land and tribe.

1545.   *Make My People Live: The Crisis in Indian Health Care*.
        Produced, directed and written by Linda Harrar for

WGBH-TV, Boston for the series NOVA, 1984. 16mm, 3/4" videotape, 60 minutes.

Discusses the Indian Health Care Improvement Act, which was before Congress in spring 1984. Examines the various types of aid given to different tribes and the quality of care received by Native Americans in urban areas. Shows Native doctors working in their own communities, including Lakota doctor Lucy Reifel.

1546.   *Maria and Julian's Black Pottery.* Arthur Baggs, 1938/1977. 16 mm, 11 minutes.

Originally shot in 1938 by Arthur Baggs, this film shows Maria and Julian Martinez, Pueblo potters, in the step by step process of making their famous black on black pottery.

1547.   *Mohawk Basketmaking: A Cultural Profile.* Frank Semmens, 1979. 3/4" videotape, 28 minutes.

Focuses on Mohawk weaver Mary Adams, her life and craft as it reflects Mohawk culture and survival.

1548.   *Mosori Monika.* Los Angeles Film Co-op, 1970. 16 mm, color, 20 minutes.

Deals with the acculturation of the Warao Indians, told by a nun who has worked with the Warao Indians, and by an old Warao Indian woman who discusses her life experiences.

1549.   *Mother of Manychildren.* Alanis Obomsawin, 1978. 16mm, 50 minutes.

The life cycle of American Indian women is the subject of this film, which features interviews with women from Canadian Cree, Ojibwa, Mohawk and Inuit communities.

1550.   *Native Land.* Thousand Oaks, CA: Atlantis Productions, 1976. 16 mm, color, 17 minutes.

Discusses Indian views of land and heritage, narrated by an Indian mother.

1551.   *Navajo Film Themselves*. 1966. 16mm, B&W.

A Navajo Weaver by Susie Benally. 22 minutes. Navajo Benally's mother is shown weaving a rug and carrying out other day-to-day activities.

Second Weaver by Alta Kahn. 9 minutes. Kahn shows her daughter Susie Benally weaving a belt.

1552.   *Navajo Girl*. Middletown, CT: Xerox Films. 16 mm, color, 20 minutes, 1973.

A Navajo girl narrates this film about her life on the Navajo reservation in Arizona. For junior and senior high schools.

1553.   *Navajo Talking Picture*. Produced and directed by Arlene Bowman. 40 minutes, 1986.

Bowman, a Navajo who has lived off the reservation, returns to film the traditional life of her grandmother. The film captures the conflicts and frustrations as two generations of women attempt to communicate.

1554.   *Navajo Way*. Produced by NBC, 1975. 16mm, 52 minutes.

The story of Mary Grey Mountain and her family, as they try to adapt to white society and still maintain their traditions--the Navajo Way.

1555.   *North American Arts and Crafts Series*. Geoff Voyce. Produced by North American Indian Films, 1977-1979.

Beads and Leather of Manitoba (10 minutes) shows Cecilia Ross, as Swampy Cree Indian, make a decorated buckskin jacket.

Birch Bark Biting (6 minutes) focuses on the Cree craft of biting unique designs and patterns into birch bark as practiced by Cree Angelique Mirasty.

A Corn Husk Doll (11 minutes) documents Cayuga woman Deanna Skye making a corn husk doll for her child.

A Malecite Fancy Basket (12 minutes) of black ash and sweet grass is made by Veronica and Jim Atwin of the Kingsclear Reserve.

A Micmac Scale Basket (12 Minutes) shows Rita and Noel Michael from Shubenacadie Reserve, making a splint basket from black ash.

A Moon Mask (10 minutes) is carved from alder wood by Freda Deising, a Haida Indian.

A Pair of Moccasins (15 minutes) shows Mary Thomas, a Salish Indian from British Columbia prepare and tan hides and make them into moccasins.

Porcupine Quill Work (10 minutes) decoration is demonstrated by Bernadette Pangawish, an Odawa Indian from Ontario.

Sara Smith, Mohawk Potter (18 minutes) is shown making contemporary pottery using traditional Mohawk design elements.

A Willow Basket (11 minutes). Florine Hotomani, an Assiniboine woman, makes a willow basket from both green and mature willow.

Wooden Flowers of Nova Scotia (14 minutes) are made by Matilda Paul, Micmac woman, from poplar shavings.

1556. *Omaha Tribe Films: The People.* Produced by Darrell Wheaton and David Conyer, 1978. 16mm and videotape, 30 minutes,

Deals with contemporary reservation issues, including alcoholism, housing problems, unemployment and education. Shows the conflict caused by education in the story of Denise Sansouci, who studies at a boarding school, and states that she will not return to the reservation.

1557. *On Common Ground,* and *In Her Own Write.* Geri Lange, hostess. Video series. San Francisco: KQED, 1978, 1979.

Readings by Carol Lee Sanchez. Fifteen- and six-minute segments aired in 1978 and 1979.

1558. *Onenhakenra: White Seed*. Produced and directed by Frank Semmens for the Akwesasne Museum, 1984. 16mm, 3/4" and 1/2" videotape, 20 minutes.

Discusses the place of corn in Mohawk culture, focusing on people's reflections of corn as a way of presenting the audience with a view of Mohawk traditions.

1559. *Our Dear Sisters*. National Film Board of Canada, 1975. 16mm, 3/4" videotape, 15 minutes.

A North American Native woman discusses her life on the reservation and what she faces as a single parent and working mother.

1560. *Our Lives in Our Hands*. Produced by Karen Carter and Harold Prins. Sponsored by the Aroostook Micmac Council, 1986. 16mm, 3/4" and 1/2" videotape, 44 minutes.

Tells the story of the Micmac basketmakers of Aroostook County, Maine, concentrating on their craft and culture.

1561. *Paula Gunn Allen: Interview, Paper, and Discussion*. Video production, Elouise Healie, producer. Los Angeles: KPFA, 1982.

Interview with Laguna poet, novelist, and critic.

1562. *Piki: The Hopi Way*. Produced by Pat Ferrero, 1980. 3/4" videotape, 7 minutes.

Concentrates on Hopi women and the flat bread made from blue corn, and the role the blue corn plays in everyday and ceremonial life.

1563. *Poetry of the American Indian Series: Wendy Rose*. Video series. American Visual Communication Bank, 1978.

Rose, a Hopi poet, reads from her work.

1564.   *Pomo Shaman*. By William R. Heick and Gordon Mueller. Produced by UCEMC, 1963. 16mm, 20 minutes.

A shortened version of *Sucking Doctor*, a film documenting the curing ceremony of Pomo shaman Essie Parrish.

1565.   *Running at the Edge of the Rainbow: Laguna Stories and Poems. Words and Place: Native Literature from the American Southwest*. Produced by Larry Evers, in cooperation with the Arizona Film and Television Bureau, 1978. 3/4" videotape, 27 minutes.

Laguna poet Leslie Marmon Silko reads and discusses her poetry and its relation to Laguna oral tradition.

1566.   *Songs in Minto Life*. Produced and directed by Curt Madison in cooperation with the Minto Village Council, 1985. 3/4" and 1/2" videotape, 30 minutes. In English and Tanana Athabascan.

A documentary focusing on the traditions and creativity of Tanana Indians living near Minto Flats, Alaska.

1567.   *Sucking Doctor*. William R. Heick and Gordon Mueller, produced by UCEMC, 1963. 16 mm, 50 minutes.

An unnarrated documentary film of a Pomo Shaman, Essie Parrish, practicing at a curing ceremony in Northern California.

1568.   *Summer of the Loucheux*. Produced and directed by Gordon McCrae, 1983. 16 mm, 3/4" and 1/2" videotape, 27 minutes.

Focuses on Alestine Andre, a Loucheux, or Kutchin, woman who works with her father to catch and preserve fish, and shows her day to day life and the traditions of these people who live above the Arctic Circle in Canada's Northwest Territories.

1569. *The Earth is Our Home.* Produced and written by Elizabeth Patpoff for Oregon Public Broadcasting, 1979. 16mm, 3/4" and 1/2" videotape, 29 minutes.

A documentary showing the traditional way of life for Northern Paiutes. Northern Paiute women share their memories of old ways of making baskets, clothing and other crafts, as well as food gathering and preparation.

1570. *The Enchanted Arts: Pablita Velarde.* Produced and directed by Irene-Aimee Depke for KRWT-TV, Las Cruces, NM, 1977. 3/4" videotape, 28 minutes.

Presents a portrait of the life and career of Pablita Velarde, one of the first American Indian women to paint professionally.

1571. *Through This Darkest Night.* Produced by Susan Malins, for the Denver Art Museum, 1986. 3/4" and 1/2" videotape, 12 minutes.

Documents the experiences of Native Americans during the early reservation period.

1572. *Turtle Shells.* Produced by Gary Robinson for the Muscogee Creek Nation Communication Center, 1986. 1/2" and 3/4" videotape, 28 minutes.

Documents Christine Henneha, a Creek woman, making a set of rattles for the traditional dance costume. Shows the process from catching turtles, preparing their shells, and preparing them to be worn.

1573. *Washoe.* Veronika Pataky, 1969. 16 mm, B&W, 56 minutes.

In Washoe with English narration. This film attempts to capture the day-to-day life of the Washoe people, and includes the girl's puberty ceremony and ritual.

Index

INDEX